God Gave Rock and Roll to You

God Gave Rock and Roll to You

A History of Contemporary Christian Music

Leah Payne

OXFORD
UNIVERSITY PRESS

Oxford University Press is a department of the University of Oxford. It furthers the University's objective of excellence in research, scholarship, and education by publishing worldwide. Oxford is a registered trade mark of Oxford University Press in the UK and certain other countries.

Published in the United States of America by Oxford University Press
198 Madison Avenue, New York, NY 10016, United States of America.

Library of Congress Cataloging-in-Publication Data
Names: Payne, Leah, author.
Title: God gave rock and roll to you : a history of contemporary Christian music / Leah Payne.
Description: [1.] | New York : Oxford University Press, 2024. | Includes index.
Identifiers: LCCN 2023051104 (print) | LCCN 2023051105 (ebook) |
ISBN 9780197555248 (hardback) | ISBN 9780197555262 (epub) |
ISBN 9780197555255 | ISBN 9780197555279
Subjects: LCSH: Contemporary Christian music—History and criticism.
Classification: LCC ML3187.5 .P28 2024 (print) | LCC ML3187.5 (ebook) |
DDC 782.25/16408827—dc23/eng/20231101
LC record available at https://lccn.loc.gov/2023051104
LC ebook record available at https://lccn.loc.gov/2023051105

DOI: 10.1093/oso/9780197555248.001.0001

Printed by Sheridan Books, Inc., United States of America

For Harmon and Theodore

Contents

Contents

Acknowledgments

This book is the biggest group project I've ever done, and it's hard to know where to start (or how to end) saying "thank you." My research has benefited from support from the Public Religion Research Institute (PRRI), the Wabash Center for Teaching and Learning in Theology and Religion, faculty research grants, and a generous sabbatical from my home institution.

Thank you to my editor, Theo Calderara, for thinking with me, from start to finish. I am grateful for colleagues who read drafts, offered critique, or conversed with me along the way, especially: Sammy Alfaro, Beth Allison Barr, Jennifer Axsom-Adler, Lloyd Barba, Will Bishop, Ryan Burge, James Byrd, Jonathan Calvillo, João Chaves, Dale Coulter, Don Cusic, David Dark, David Dault, Caroline Davis, Dara Delgado, Tim Dillinger, Chason Disheroon, Brian Doak, Kristin Kobes Du Mez, Christina Edmondson, Mika Edmondson, Kathleen Flake, Burke Gerstenschlager, Matthew Cooper Harriss, Jane Hong, Andrew Hudson, Daniel Isgrigg, Andrea Johnson, Marc Jolicoeur, Sam Kestenbaum, John Maiden, Andrew Mall, Gerardo Martí, Caleb Maskell, Mandy McMichael, Roger Nam, Bradley Onishi, Thomas Payne, Adam Perez, Daniel Prieto, Paul Putz, Daniel Ramírez, Erica Ramirez, Tanya Riches, Lester Ruth, Phillip Luke Sinitiere, Ted Smith, Devan Stahl, Randall Stephens, Matthew Taylor, Ekaputra Tupamahu, Doug Weaver, Trisha Welstad, Natalie Wigg-Stevenson, Lydia Willsky-Ciollo, and the faculty and staff of Portland Seminary.

I am grateful to the Billy Graham Center Archives, the Billy Graham Evangelistic Association, Salem Publishing, the Gospel Music Association, the Black Gospel Music Preservation Program and the Dunn Center for Christian Music Studies at Baylor University, the Holy Spirit Research Center at Oral Roberts University, the Southern Baptist Historical Library, and the Consortium of Pentecostal Archives. Thank you to Grace Babayan, Jessica Cox, Austin Day, Brianna Martin-Ortega, Christopher Symms, and Cara Vincent, student researchers who assisted me over the years.

This book benefited immeasurably from the insights of Steph Andry-Wilkinson, Grace Semler Baldridge, David Bazan, Matthew Blake, Daniel Burnham, Mark Chironna, Robert Cornwall, Frank Couch, Jake Dockter, Joey Elwood, Patti Gibbons, Thom Granger, Sara Groves, Joshua Harris, Dan Haseltine, Chris Hauser, April Hefner, Heather Hellman, Mike Hogan, Tyler

Huckabee, Rebecca Irwin, Laura Jenkins, Jennifer Knapp, Stephen Knight, Nikki Leonti, Alex MacDougall, Phil Madeira, Dan Mann, Mike Norman, Mike O'Brien, Mark Oestreicher, Jackie Patillo, Frank Peretti, Steve Potratz, Mark Rodgers, David Ruis, Gregory Rumburg, Adam Russell, Melissa Scruggs Gales, John Styll, Michael Sweet, Frank Tate, John J. Thompson, Leanor Ortega Till, Danielle Kimmey Torrez, Matthew Paul Turner, Nancy VanReece, Derek Webb, Troy Welstad, Chris White, and Becky Rice Yates. I'm also grateful for Andrew Gill and the PRX Big Questions Project team. For those who spoke off-the-record, I appreciate your contributions.

Thank you to Derric and Debbie Johnson, who taught me about the revivalist songbook tradition (among many other things). And, a special note of gratitude to Andi Ashworth and Charlie Peacock, for creating and curating the Art House world; to Molly Nicholas and Mark Nicholas, treasured first readers; and to the late Jay Swartzendruber, who believed in the work from the get-go.

To the 1,263 CCM Survey respondents (as of 2023)—what a gift to receive your stories and reflections; I hope you feel I did them justice in this book.

This book contains within it many decades of life and longing, and to my family—Aunt Connie and Aunt Teri, Mike, Amber, Annie, Aaron, April, Lowell, Tom, Tammy, Harmon, Theodore, and most of all Thomas—I can only say "thank you," and "I love you."

Introduction

CCM and the Industry of American Evangelicalism

Fourteen-year-old David Shields was nervous. Really nervous. It was 2005, and his death-metal band Skull Crushers was about to play a big show in Lexington, Nebraska. Skull Crushers may not sound like an unusual name for a death-metal band, and perhaps it is not. But what made it somewhat unusual was that it was inspired by a passage in the Bible: Romans 16:20—"The God of peace will soon crush Satan under your feet." Skull Crushers aimed to crush the heck out of the Devil that night. Their tools were biblically based lyrics screamed over distorted guitars. The band, booked by David's cool, skater youth pastor, played in the youth building of a Southern Baptist Church pastored by David's dad. "We were absolutely horrible," David recalled years later, but the small crowd of teenaged evangelicals cheered for more.

Southern Baptist churches of the 2000s were not widely known for being death-metal taste makers, but David and his bandmates did not see their work as metal, per se. Through the power of music, they were spreading the gospel. In a performance that was part rock concert, part religious revival, Skull Crushers sought to entertain *and* to bring the audience to Christ. "Our yelling unintelligible lyrics was suddenly holy work," he remembered, "because the lyrics were 'Christian.'"

David and the Skull Crushers were not unique. They were among thousands of bands and artists who, in the second half of the twentieth century, performed on sanctuary stages, in youth rooms and church basements, and at music festivals, denominational meetings, colleges, coffee shops, and camps around the nation. These performers—along with record-company executives, publicists, booking agents, radio DJs, journalists, and many more—were part of the thriving industry of Contemporary Christian Music, commonly called CCM. CCM encompassed many genres and often sounded like mainstream music, but what made it distinctive is that it was created by and for, and sold almost exclusively to, white evangelicals. Consumed by millions, CCM was the soundtrack of evangelical conversions, worship, adolescence, marriage, child-rearing, and activism. Few church services, youth all-nighters, sporting events, holiday gatherings, or political protests were complete without CCM accompaniment.

By the time Skull Crushers took the stage, CCM was in a precarious position. Once an almost billion-dollar industry with culture-shaping power, by the early aughts the genre was in decline. This book analyzes Contemporary Christian Music as an industry born from early twentieth-century Southern white revivalist hymn-singing networks, stoked by 1960s and 1970s baby-boomer converts on the West Coast, and fueled in the late twentieth century by a vast network of evangelical media makers and marketers, booksellers, denominations, congregations, parachurch organizations, educational institutions, lobbying organizations, and advocacy groups. As Contemporary Christian Music grew, enterprising conservative white Protestants recognized that songs of revival were (and are) powerful, portable vehicles for ideology.[1] The following pages trace how CCM produced music that served as a sonic shorthand for white evangelical orthodoxy and social action, prized for its capacity to disseminate evangelical messages about what it means to be Christian and American.

CCM songs often reflected—and drove—evangelical conversations about pressing social and political concerns like abortion, prayer in public schools, or teen abstinence. At the turn of the twenty-first century, however, Contemporary Christian Music was undermined by many of the market forces and cultural norms that built it. Even though the industry declined precipitously in the 2000s, however, the theological visions and political ambitions of CCM's leading music makers, and the media networks that connect them, continue to shape evangelicalism in the United States and abroad.

Contemporary Christian Music served adults and young children, to be sure, but the industry's core customers were suburban, middle-class, white American adolescents. CCM marketers were certainly not alone in recognizing the buying power of American teens, but evangelicals became convinced that teens were in a particularly precarious spiritual state, which meant that CCM sales had cosmic importance. For evangelical caregivers, the teen years were a must-win battlefield in the war for the future of the Christian faith, the nation, and even the world. Mass media, they reckoned, was an effective weapon to be employed in that fight, and they set out to save young souls and shape the nation through music.[2]

The following pages trace how white evangelical caregivers in the United States came to see Christian spins on American popular music—even transgressive genres like death metal—as invaluable tools for molding their children socially, spiritually, and politically. As the industry grew, so did confidence in CCM's ability to encourage teenage citizens to conform to conservative evangelical norms and strengthen the nation.

It is hard to overstate the power of CCM, and its ubiquity in late twentieth-century evangelical life. As the ambient sound of white evangelicalism, it felt inescapable. It certainly was for me, growing up in the 1990s as a Pentecostal pastor's kid in a working-class town in rural Oregon. My father had no love for CCM; he thought the quality of the music was poor, and he did not play it in my childhood home. And, as a family, we did not have the means to participate in the middle-class, suburban consumption patterns of CCM—the concerts, festivals, albums, t-shirts, and other merchandise. But many young people around me were immersed in the world of youth groups and Christian music festivals, and almost everyone I knew had either heard an Amy Grant song or performed a live-action version of a Carman hit.

In college, I was introduced to revivalist hymnody by Derric Johnson, a conductor, vocal arranger, and creator of a vocal ensemble that laid the foundation of what would become CCM. Derric and his spouse, vocalist Debbie Johnson, expanded my understanding of sacred music beyond the boundaries of the Pentecostal praise-and-worship tunes of my upbringing. He taught me to appreciate and recognize West Coast pop and jazz harmonies, along with Black Gospel and Southern Gospel standards.

After I graduated, I married an aspiring CCM artist and moved to Nashville, Tennessee, in 2001, when CCM was at its pinnacle in terms of prosperity and cultural influence. As a new Nashvillian, I found myself doing what a lot of my peers with humanities degrees did: working at a coffee shop. Two of my favorite customers were Charlie Peacock and Andi Ashworth, whom I knew only as fellow West Coast transplants. I discovered eventually that Charlie was an award-winning singer-songwriter, jazz artist, pianist, producer, and record-label executive, who had also written a book about CCM. Charlie ended up offering me a job as his assistant, and I worked at Charlie and Andi's legendary Art House studio for several years.

I did not understand, as a twenty-one-year-old barista, the scope of Charlie's influence and work. Nor did I grasp in the early 2000s that I was bearing witness to a transformative moment in the music industry in general, and CCM in particular. Eventually, I went to graduate school at Vanderbilt Divinity School, became a religious historian, and thought that my short, youthful stint in CCM was over.

As I studied American religion, however, my perspective on CCM began to change. I began to regard Contemporary Christian Music performances as more than quirky evangelical entertainment. Instead, I came to see CCM concerts as sites where power is created and negotiated.[3] At CCM performances, entertainers exerted influence over attendees by soliciting public conversions, stoking political action, and seeking donations for social causes. In these performances, bestselling CCM stars and their audiences also performed and enforced strict evangelical ideals about gender, sexuality, race, ethnicity, and class. Women who could and would be "womanly" according to straight, white, middle-class evangelical ideals were adored. Men who could and would be "manly" according to straight, white middle-class evangelical norms were admired. Those who could not—or would not—adhere to such standards were often marginalized.

For many participants and observers, the trappings of CCM—the evangelical pop stars, interpretive dancers, puppeteers, mimes, and bodybuilders—are silly expressions of kitsch or an embarrassing remnant of an evangelical past. Silly things, however, can be deadly serious to devoted fans—just ask anyone who has angered online fans of Beyonce or Taylor Swift. CCM had the capacity to be both.

The question that guides this book is: What can one learn about the development of evangelicalism by looking at CCM, one of the largest, most profitable forms of mass media produced in the twentieth century? I treat CCM charts as representative of a conversation among (predominantly, but not exclusively white) evangelicals about what kind of people they wanted to be, what sort of world they wanted to create, what kind of actions they thought would honor God. To listen to that conversation, I analyzed the music of twentieth-century songbooks and early recordings and radio programs, tracked the top-selling CCM through the pages of *Contemporary Christian Music Magazine* and the *Billboard* Christian music charts, and listened carefully to the top twenty-five CCM albums from the late 1970s to 2023.

As the soundtrack of white evangelical culture, Contemporary Christian Music carried, in music and merchandise, decades of musical conversations about evangelical identity and ideology. Because it was produced mostly by white evangelical men, and marketed *en masse* to white evangelical mothers and youth pastors for consumption by white evangelical children, it is also a large-scale, multigenerational conversation about evangelical values in the United States. Conversations about what music ought to be made, who ought to make it, and what messages it should include reveal how white evangelicals aimed to raise their children to be ideal citizens of the kingdom of God, and of the United States.

Part business, part devotional activity, part religious instruction, the trajectory of CCM also shows how the marketplace and technological innovations shaped evangelical identity and ideology. The story of CCM is the story of how white evangelicals looked to the marketplace for signs of God's work in the world. While there were always notable dissenters, for the most part those within the industry regarded profits as a sign of God's blessing. The top-selling artists and entertainers, then, reflected a consensus among consumers about what constituted right Christian teaching about God, the people of God, and their place in public life. Certain ideas thrived in large part because they appealed to white evangelical consumers. Other ideas faltered because they could not easily be sold.

In this way, the history of the CCM charts is a history of how consumers voiced their theological and political opinions unofficially through their buying practices. Year after year, white evangelical denominations and churches published official treatises and position papers and public statements, and all the while, the people who constituted these organizations purchased music that they came to believe represented true Christian life. CCM charts represented rank-and-file white evangelical consensus about what sorts of people evangelicals believed could be credible messengers of the gospel. And the charts displayed what sorts of ideas about God, the world, and the people of God were bankable evangelical theologies. Sometimes these off-the-books ideas aligned with official denominational or congregational teaching; sometimes they did not. Through the market, consumers challenged—and in some cases overturned—the traditional, institutional authority of their pastors, congregations, or denominations.

Because many white evangelicals viewed CCM as a distillation of Christian orthodoxy, a purveyor of godly activism, and a form of Christian parenting, Contemporary Christian Music was and is a high-stakes industry. I interviewed dozens of CCM journalists, publishers, producers, and artists, as well as businesspeople, church leaders, politicians, and activists in and around the industry. Not all wanted to be quoted on the record, and many of those who were willing were no longer heavily involved in the business. Some were retired, others left of their own accord, and some were no longer welcome in the fold, because they had rejected some of the strict ideological boundaries around CCM.

Those who asked for their comments to remain off the record did so for understandable reasons. People who work in evangelical industries and then publicly disavow evangelical norms risk their livelihood, along with their social, religious, and sometimes familial networks. I am profoundly grateful to those who were willing to speak with me about the industry and the dense network of organizations that constitute the "commercial religion" that is evangelicalism in the United States.[4]

To capture the silliness and seriousness of CCM among its listenership, I created "Contemporary Christian Music: A Survey" in 2020. The survey invited respondents to reflect on how they first started listening to CCM, their favorite (and least favorite) artists and entertainers, how they participated in the industry, how CCM may or may not have shaped their identities, what people unfamiliar with CCM should know about it, and their formative memories that involved Contemporary Christian Music. Some wrote that CCM was a peripheral part of their young adulthood, but most claimed that CCM shaped their lives profoundly, for better and for worse.

I had hoped to collect somewhere between fifty and a hundred responses, but I was soon overwhelmed. As of 2023, more than 1,200 CCM listeners from more than a dozen countries have participated in the survey. They shared stories of nostalgia, humor, and joy, and also stories of alienation, anger, and despair. Throughout this book, I have included representative observations and comments from these listeners.

Indeed, if there is a main character in this book it is the CCM listener—real and imagined. The biographies of particular CCM figures are material insofar as they were used to sell music to consumers and to serve as models for Christian living.

Those models, and the people who sold them, have always been overwhelmingly white and male. Like mainstream popular music, CCM is a male-dominated business, both behind the scenes and on the charts, where women rarely occupied more than 20 percent of the spots.[5] The situation was even more stark when it came to race. Non-white artists and entertainers rarely represented more than 10 percent of the top twenty-five albums and singles. Even as CCM singers and musicians appropriated Black Gospel music, hip hop, and rap, and even as non-Christian charts diversified in the late twentieth century, the demographics of CCM artists remained remarkably consistent. Like American Christianity as a whole, the CCM world was segregated.[6]

That segregation goes back to the industry's earliest days. CCM grew out of early twentieth-century white revivalism. The network of predominantly, if not exclusively, white churches, camp meetings, and Bible colleges served as the tracks upon which CCM would travel the nation. Many of these institutions resisted de-segregation well into the twentieth century. The tastes and buying habits of the consumers that were embedded in these networks, along with the racial hierarchies embedded within and expressed through these habits, allowed the industry to remain homogeneous for decades.

This book starts with these networks. Most books about CCM begin the story of bands like the Skull Crushers with the sounds of rock.[7] This book instead begins with CCM's roots in the business of early twentieth-century revival.

1

"The Magic Power of Song"

The Roots of Contemporary Christian Music (1897–1950)

Revival meetings were, in many ways, the rock concerts of the early twentieth century. They were spiritual events, to be sure, but they were also entertainment—outside observers sometimes compared them to traveling circuses. Under revival tents, preachers sought to breathe new life into supposedly dying forms of American Protestantism. They cajoled and extolled, sweated and sang, and urged Americans to turn from the fires of hell toward the hope of heaven. Attendees cried, laughed, shouted, wailed, fainted, danced, lifted their hands, and carried on with all manner of scandalous practices.

Piety and profits were often intertwined. Some revivalists sold lemonade and other refreshments. Many offered merchandise. Attendees purchased souvenirs to mark the occasion—like photographs of famous revival preachers, books that included popular sermons, and songbooks so they could keep the revival fervor going after the meeting ended.

Music swelled during the emotional peak of revival meetings, when attendees participated in a powerful ritual marking the conversion from sinner to saint.[1] Preachers invited converts to walk to the front of the gathering and be saved. When revival services were held in church sanctuaries, that moment usually took place in front of the altar. Revival meetings were quite portable, however, and as revivalists crisscrossed the nation, they created ad hoc altar spaces in grange halls, public parks, and campgrounds. Over time, that moment where attendees accepted Jesus Christ came to be known as an "altar call."

Some of the rowdiest revivals came out of the Holiness movement, a nineteenth-century Christian movement that grew mostly out of Methodism. Holiness people emphasized Christian perfection, the idea that a person could be entirely cleansed from sin or "sanctified," a moment often accomplished during an altar call, which meant that the moment was not just for the damned, but also for the cleansing of the saved. At the altar, Holiness people shouted, trembled, and wept under the transforming power of the Spirit.

When it came to creating music that encouraged revival, Pentecostals were, from their birth in the early twentieth century, overachievers. Pentecostalism is notoriously difficult to pin down, but in the United States it can be defined as a form of revivalism born out of late nineteenth-century Wesleyan-Holiness revivals, religious practices of the enslaved, and a host of other influences.[2] Early, interracial Pentecostal meetings transgressed social and legal boundaries. Black and white Pentecostals laid hands on one another, prayed for divine healing, prophesied, and spoke in tongues, although the movement re-segregated quickly in the early twentieth century. At many Holiness and Pentecostal revivals, they "tarried," which involved waiting for power and inspiration from the Holy Spirit.[3] At every meeting, they sang.

Until the nineteenth century, a lot of the music of Southern Holiness and Pentecostal revival meetings—folk tunes, spirituals, and hymns—was handed down across generations with little to no written record. Printing was labor intensive and expensive, and most hymnals were produced in historic Northeastern print publishing hubs like New York and Philadelphia.

In the 1800s, however, advances in print technology made publishing easier and less expensive than ever before.[4] This meant that songbook publishing was no longer restricted to established denominations or elite publishing houses. For middle-class white revivalists, who had a longstanding knack for publicity and promotion, and efficient distribution networks by way of their revival circuits, this development was a boon.

The Business of Salvation

One humid, Southern, summer evening in 1897, insurance broker John T. Benson and his piano-playing wife Eva Green Benson attended an outdoor tent revival in an abandoned lot in Nashville, Tennessee. That night, a preacher named J. O. McClurkan spoke about the imminent return and thousand-year reign of Jesus Christ. John and Eva felt compelled to join his "'emergency force,' and give the world its final warning, preparatory to the return of the Lord."[5] His teachings about sanctification at the end of time compelled the Bensons, and in 1901 John resigned from his day job in insurance and began working alongside McClurkan. In 1902, they started the Pentecostal Union Mission Publishing Company, to put the good news in print.

The Bensons were publishing novices who had no way of knowing they would create a foundation for what would become a billion-dollar industry with culture-shaping power. They probably thought the world would end before anything like that could occur. The Lord tarried, but the Bensons did not.

John and Eva became influential members of the Pentecostal Church of the Nazarene. Eva penned Holiness songs and wrote a column for McClurkan's Holiness periodical *Zion Outlook*. In 1904, they published their first songbook, *Living Water Sounds*. "When 'Tongues' people took over the name 'Pentecostal,'" recalled Benson's son, the publisher "half-heartedly, in semi-jest, changed the name of Pentecostal Mission Publishing Company to John T. Benson Publishing Company."[6]

At the dawn of the media age, printing pamphlets, newsletters, and songbooks about the Second Coming seemed like the fastest way to get the word out to sinners that the time to get right with God was at hand.[7] Southern Protestants had a long tradition of gathering for gospel singing conventions in Nashville, so the Bensons' hometown was an ideal location for a new music publishing business.

Songbooks eventually outsold pamphlets and newsletters at the Benson Company. "In every conference or convention, music has a large and vital place to fill," explained one Baptist revivalist. "We try to keep in stock the very best and latest song books published," wrote Pentecostal preacher G. F. Taylor, "all songbooks published by Benson."[8]

Benson was one of many white, middle-class businessmen, with get-up-and-go and a little bit of startup cash, who were promoting Christian ideas through the growing American market. Conservative white Protestants began to regard business as an ideal way to spread the good news and shape American public life. Influential "business-priests" like evangelical Henry P. Crowell, founder of Quaker Oats, went so far as to think of business itself as the altar where a businessman "serves the king."[9]

For many in the songbook business, the American marketplace was an altar to serve the returning Jesus, and a tangible way to measure the efficacy of the revivalist gospel. Each customer was a soul. Each sale was a bit of salvation.[10]

James D. Vaughn, a Nazarene and a Tennessean like the Bensons, believed fervently that singing and selling songbooks spread the "influence of the Holy Spirit." Vaughn founded the James D. Vaughn Publishing Company in the early 1900s and, eventually, "The Vaughn Conservatory of Music and Bible Institute." The conservatory taught music and educated "young men of the sunny South" to "build [their] manhood on Jesus Christ," and "win the love and admiration of a nation."[11]

Vaughn was a savvy salesman and born marketer. He quickly figured out that live events with professional musicians could drum up significant sheet-music sales. In 1910, he hired his brother Charles and three of his friends to tour churches, schools, and civic events in rural Tennessee. The four carefully coiffed, clean-cut, white Southern men with dazzling musical chops moved audiences and merchandise. After their first performance, attendees reportedly bought five thousand copies of Vaughn's songbooks.

Audiences fell in love with Vaughn's singers. As the vocal virtuosos toured the nation, they became part of the burgeoning American celebrity culture. Fans raced to buy the latest songbooks and eagerly purchased autographed photos of the handsome young men. Inspired by their glamor and their skill, other Holiness quartets sprang up throughout the South. Many came to study at Vaughn's conservatory.

With this profitable marketing strategy, Vaughn developed networks throughout the South, building ready audiences for acts like the Speer Family and Lee Roy Abernathy. Vaughn also inspired imitators like Virgil Oliver Stamps and Jesse Randall (J. R.) Baxter Jr., who founded the Stamps Baxter Music Company in Dallas, Texas, in 1924. Stamps got his start working for Vaughn, and, like the Vaughn Conservatory, the Stamps Baxter publishing company and school of music trained skilled musicians like the Blackwood Brothers, and eventually the Speer Family, who left Vaughn to work with Stamps Baxter.

Through the successful marketing of songbooks, Holiness people brought their sanctifying altar calls to churches around the country, along with imaginative renderings of premillennialism, the teaching that Jesus would physically return to earth and then establish a one-thousand-year reign.[12] Premillennialism was particularly popular among Holiness people, Southern Baptists, and Pentecostals, who pored over *The Scofield Reference Bible*, an innovative Bible created by businessman Cyrus Ingersol (C. I.) Scofield, which gave readers "absolutely scientific" biblical knowledge, approved by "all the evangelical bodies," that allowed them to understand biblical prophecy about the end times.[13] Premillennialists relished songs filled with hopes and warnings about the "millennial morn," when believers would greet the returning Christ.

Most premillennial believers were also dispensationalists, which meant that they believed that God worked in specific ways in specific times. Believing that they were living on the cusp of a new era—the Millennial Kingdom of Christ—early twentieth-century revivalists sang songs about how the true church would be taken from this world through an event called the rapture. No one could agree on the details of the rapture, but they believed that passages from the book of Revelation, the Gospel of Matthew, and other apocalyptic texts explained how the world would endure a time of God's wrath and suffering known as the "Great Tribulation." One of the agreed-upon signs of rapture was the "trumpet of the Lord," which became a popular motif for revivalists looking forward to "when the trumpet of the Lord shall be calling."

Anticipating the final trumpet and Great Tribulation, John T. Benson filled his newsletters with end-times analysis of global conflicts. One pamphlet, "The World War in Prophecy; the Downfall of the Kaiser, and the End of the Dispensation," explained how the Great War was a "ghastly cataclysm" that signaled the impending Great Tribulation.[14] Benson Company songbooks depicted the faithful as end-times soldiers and warriors in the divine army of the returning king Jesus. "Go forth," admonished Harriet E. Jones' "The King's Call," "go forth with armor on, and crimson flag unfurled, obey the call, the kingly call, go forth and win the world."[15]

Songs portraying Christians as warriors flourished alongside "muscular Christianity," a movement aimed at shoring up a supposedly feminized Christianity with robust American manliness. Motivated by a fear that the nation would falter if the faith of their Victorian forefathers could not stand up to the dangers of a rough, modern, scientific era, proponents of muscular Christianity got to work creating a strenuous, manly faith for the strenuous life. Their archetype was a "Christian soldier" prepared to fight for God—a virile, white, Protestant professional man of keen intellect and physical prowess who stood firm against the dangers facing the nation.[16]

That Old Time Religion

As Vaughn's songbook marketing scheme grew in popularity, his traveling quartets developed a full-fledged musical genre: Southern Gospel. If there was one definitive Southern Gospel song, it was "Old Time Religion." The song, originally an African American spiritual popularized by the legendary Fisk Jubilee Singers, was appropriated by white Southern audiences when music publisher Charlie D. Tillman created a popular arrangement in 1891. In the segregated South, few revival meetings were held with Black and white attendees worshiping together, and Tillman's tweaked version of "Old Time Religion" conformed specifically to white Southern tastes. Retooled for white audiences, the lyrics expressed, in a few simple lines, white Southern nostalgia, "'Tis the old-time religion/it's good enough for me."[17]

Through songs like "Old Time Religion," white Southern Gospel quartets expressed a desire for what they saw as a simpler (antebellum) era. An era in which religion was not tainted by the urbanizing, technology-driven modern world, or by the confusing new social order that Black citizenship might bring. Old time religion in the Jim Crow South was "elevating, inspiring, and worshipful" music for white consumers, who were, by and large, people who had the time and money to attend camp meetings, travel to see their favorite groups, and purchase their favorite compilations of songs.[18] The religion that white Southern revivalists yearned for was not old—it was, in the grand scheme of Christian traditions, quite new—but audiences overlooked this inconsistency, and "Old Time Religion" became a Southern Gospel staple.

Southern Gospel music's wistfulness for the past included a sense of deep sentimentality. In 1896, Tillman published his arrangement of M. B. Williams' "My Mother's Bible," in which the author looked back on a rose-colored childhood marked by an appreciation for the "blessed book, precious book" of the Bible and a family that upheld Victorian norms around womanliness and child-rearing.[19] By singing those lyrics, Southern Gospel audiences could bring Vaughn's vision of a "sunny South" admired by the nation from the past into the present.

One way to win the admiration of the nation was to glorify it, and Southern Gospel quartets sang patriotic standards like "America (My Country 'Tis of Thee)" and "The Star-Spangled Banner" as well as traditional church hymns. Because Southern Gospel seamlessly combined patriotism, traditional white Southern musical styles, cultural tastes, and political orientations, it was an ideal vehicle for promoting a form of American civil religion that was soaked in white Southern traditionalism. Reconstituting the antebellum world may be a lost cause, the songs seemed to say, but for one evening of revival, it was possible to re-create the chivalry and social order of those bygone days. Of course, the very notion that the antebellum era was one of chivalry and proper social order shows that whiteness was at the core of Southern Gospel—African Americans certainly did not experience it that way.[20]

By the 1910s, the influence of songbook publishers was on the rise, along with revivalist visions for a good and prosperous nation. Without question, the most critical earthly fight facing Holiness people like Benson or Vaughn in the early twentieth century was the fight against the "devil's brew" of alcohol. John T. Benson was on the board of trustees of the Tennessee Anti-Saloon League, and his passion for promoting social holiness through temperance permeated Benson songbooks.[21]

Temperance songs often connected the battle against alcohol to the coming apocalyptic battle. The evocative "The Great Judgment Morning" described the fate of those who drank and sold alcohol: "Together in hell they did sink."[22] The Temperance movement was composed of a broad coalition of American activists, but Holiness hymns were in heavy rotation at Prohibition rallies. There, rowdy "reformed inebriates" swayed and belted out songs of their sordid pasts. Frances Willard, leader of the Women's Christian Temperance Union, touted the "magic power of song to win the hearts of whom we may have supposed to be indifferent or opposed to Temperance work."[23]

Temperance hymns were especially valued for their appeal among American adolescents. The modern category of "adolescence"—the idea of a distinct transitional stage between childhood and adulthood—was created in the late nineteenth century, and in the United States it was tied directly to concerns about the future of the nation.[24] A strong, prosperous America, the logic went, depended upon the strength, purity, and *sobriety* of white Protestant adolescents.[25] Alcohol, with its propensity to lower inhibitions and cloud judgment, was seen as particularly dangerous to young people. At Prohibition rallies, young temperance activists sang about how the "Devil's drink" put the future of America at risk.[26]

The "flaming youth" of the 1920s bobbed their hair and guzzled booze, but Holiness youths sang songs of resistance against the devil's temptations. When the United States established Prohibition with the Eighteenth Amendment to the US Constitution, revivalists praised it as a major victory in the battle for the souls of the young and the soul of the nation.

By the 1920s, Southern white revivalists were using music as part of their efforts to shape American public life. When the Ku Klux Klan wanted to recruit new members, for example, they used songbooks to do it. Popular hymns like "Onward Christian Soldiers" were rewritten to promote the Klan's blend of white supremacy and patriotism ("Onward Ku Klux Klansmen").[27]

Texas-born Vernon Dalhart brought folksy so-called hillbilly ballads like "Wreck of the Old 97" to national audiences. He also sang a popular song about the 1925 Scopes trial in Dayton, Tennessee, in which high school teacher John T. Scopes was convicted of breaking the law by teaching students about the theory of human evolution. Dalhart's song, "The John T. Scopes Case," became a theme song for those conservative Protestants known as fundamentalists.

Fundamentalists, who sought to repudiate liberal "modernist" readings of the Bible, which they believed undermined the core components of Christian orthodoxy, were part of a national movement with roots in elite Northern theological institutions like Princeton Theological Seminary. But media coverage of the Scopes trial branded fundamentalism as back-woods, rural, Southern yokel ideology.[28] Dalhart's song sided firmly with the fundamentalists. The ballad painted Scopes, who was born in neighboring Kentucky, as a meddling outsider with "ideas new and grand." The song argued, with a classic Southern Gospel hook, that "the old religion's better after all."

Dalhart's hillbilly recordings sold well and attracted more investment in the genre. Ralph Peer, of the New Jersey–based Victor Talking Machine Company, recorded "The Bristol Sessions" in 1927, on the Tennessee-Virginia border. Known as the "big bang" event for hillbilly music, which would later become known as "country music," the recordings brought rural white revivalism to national audiences.[29]

As the songbook business grew, music and money made friends out of foes, bringing Pentecostals, Baptists, Holiness people, and Methodists together as consumers. Even when controversies surrounding the practice of speaking in tongues or the exuberant, interracial worship services of Pentecostals were at their height, J. T. Benson himself showed that he was willing to compromise and work with the tongue-speakers. Benson noted that while his denomination, the Nazarenes, forbade such indignities, Pentecostals were "contributing to the fellowship with money" and "furnishing songs for the Pentecostal mission."[30] As long as consumers kept buying media promoting Jesus' imminent return and white Southern political values, there was room for cooperation.

The Cathedral of the Air

Benson's pragmatic spirit of compromise carried on as revivalists began harnessing the new technology of radio. A few conservative Protestants rejected radio and said that church services broadcast over radio waves were "grotesque and irreverent." Some fundamentalists argued that radio waves were of the devil.[31] But, many more were entranced by the notion that radio could—miraculously, it seemed—spread the gospel in an instant. For most groups anticipating the rapture and return of Christ, radio seemed like the best thing that could have happened to the good news.

Out on the sunny California Coast, Pentecostal revivalist Aimee Semple McPherson was one of the first preachers to broadcast revivals over the airwaves. McPherson conceived of radio as a "Cathedral of the Air" with seemingly limitless potential.[32] "No barrier of steel, concrete, and iron is so strong that it can keep out the messenger of sound," she wrote, and from her home in Los Angeles, she sent "songs and messages" around the nation.[33]

McPherson was a part of a multi-denominational group of radio revivalists. In the early 1920s, the Bible Institute of Los Angeles created a radio station to broadcast fundamentalist church services.[34] Established American evangelical ministries, like Moody Radio, which carried the legacy of its media-savvy founder, D. L. Moody, into the radio age, brought preaching, teaching, and live music into the homes of Chicago-area listeners. Christian Missionary Alliance Paul Rader, fundamentalist preacher William Ward Ayer, Presbyterian Donald Grey Barnhouse, Lutheran Walter Maier, and Baptist Charles Fuller all created their own radio congregations. Soon, each preacher's radio audience far exceeded the number of people in the pews.

While many evangelical preachers purchased radio segments on the new National Broadcasting Company (NBC) and the Columbia Broadcasting System (CBS), those who owned their own stations found themselves having to fill programming hours. Round-the-clock church services were not feasible, so they needed new material. Aimee Semple McPherson's radio station filled the hours with music and entertainment segments like "the Kozy Hour" segments for children, Spanish-speaking services, Black Gospel quartets like the Silvertone Quartet and the Swanee Jubilee Singers, and Southern Gospel acts like the "Gospel Hillbillies."

Some religious stations, like McPherson's KFSG, ran on donations and advertisements. Others, like WLAC in Nashville, were sponsored by Life and Casualty Insurance, founded by Church of Christ booster Andrew Mizell (A. M.) Burton, and included news and other programming alongside church services. Radio ministries needed to show that advertisers could bet on their listeners as prospective customers. As a result, radio rewarded entertainment over theological nuance.

The most popular and profitable radio ministries were those that appealed to the buying habits of white, middle-class Americans.[35] Organ music flourished, as did operatic solos with western European orchestral accompaniment, and Southern Gospel music. In the 1920s, broadcasters featured gospel quartets and trios who upheld the traditional social order and contrasted with images of "bright young things" and flappers.[36] Teetotalling anthems enjoyed significant airtime in the 1930s. Radio revivals regularly included patriotic calls to support American troops during World Wars I and II.

By appealing to white, middle-class listeners, radio homogenized the sound of Christian entertainment. The church services that made it to the airwaves were usually largely white, middle class, and male led, though there were exceptions like Aimee Semple McPherson and Black radio pioneer Lightfoot Solomon Michaux, who had large radio audiences.[37] And, in 1939, NBC began broadcasting hillbilly and gospel music from the Grand Ole Opry, a weekly radio program held at Ryman Auditorium, a revivalist-sanctuary-turned-music venue.

As a rule, however, major broadcasters like NBC, CBS, and later the American Broadcasting Company (ABC) deferred to the stately sounds of traditional mainline Protestant music and preaching. The top productions were thoroughly urban (emanating from emerging media hubs like Los Angeles and Chicago), urbane, and "respectable." Some of the Southern Gospel music featured by evangelical broadcasters deliberately traded on stereotypes about poor, rural, white Americans (i.e., hillbillies), but slang, regional idioms, and Southern accents were kept to a minimum.

Radio also fused music and preaching with American celebrity culture.[38] For those revivalist celebrities who fit the respectable, middle-class bill, the new media platform was a kingmaker. Paul Rader, for example, enjoyed success on the American revival circuit, but radio was where he reached the nation and became a star. The musicians that graced revivalist radio stations, like the Texas Pals and the Silvertone Quartet, became celebrities too.

As more American households acquired radios, the format domesticated church entertainment. By 1940, 86 percent of American homes had radios and the average American listened to four hours of broadcasting per day.[39] Audiences listened at home or in their cars, which increased the amount of time and space church entertainment could occupy in people's daily lives. The preachers and song leaders who appeared on the radio could spend more time with the average listener than any other preachers or singers had done before them. The songs and sermons people heard, therefore, had potential to be far more formative than in-person church services.

Radio also seemed like an ideal medium for engaging youth. In 1931, fundamentalist Percy Crawford started the "Young People's Church of the Air" in Philadelphia. Crawford broadcast programming aimed at young people, and he sold hymnals that encouraged young listeners to sing along in their own congregational settings. Chicago Baptist minister Torrey Johnson was keenly interested in encouraging young people to convert to evangelical Christianity, and he got his start narrating *Songs in the Night*, a Chicago-based radio program, in 1943.[40] Johnson turned over emcee privileges to his friend, recent Wheaton College graduate William F. Graham, in 1944, in order to concentrate on his newly created organization for adolescents, Youth for Christ.

Songs in the Night became a key launchpad for the young Billy Graham, who understood very well the power of music to move the religious feelings of American youths. As a teenager, Graham had converted to Christianity at a Southern Baptist revival when he heard "Just As I Am," an altar-call hymn about an individual sinner pardoned and cleansed by the Lamb of God. On the radio, he delighted audiences with church choirs, soloists, and organ music, along with carefully crafted sermons. Known at the beginning mostly for his in-person revivalist "crusades," the airwaves made Graham a household name. Graham imitated radio evangelist Walter Maier and studied the cadence of news broadcaster Walter Winchell.[41] When Graham began touring as a paid Youth for Christ evangelist, his services were broadcast on radio stations around the United States.

Politics on the Air

Many Christian broadcasters sought to mobilize audiences for political action.[42] Reverend Sam Morris used his radio pulpit to recruit prohibitionists. Hellfire-and-brimstone preacher "Fighting Bob" Shuler preached in favor of prohibition and against the governor of his home state of Texas. Fundamentalist and antisemite Gerald Burton Winrod filled his church of the air with claims that God's chosen land, America, was threatened by "Jewish conspiracies" and the "devil," aka President Franklin Delano Roosevelt.[43]

In the 1930s and 1940s, the blurry line between broadcasters' theological claims and calls for political action elicited formal responses from major broadcasters. Corporations like CBS and NBC believed that "controversial" or "partisan" theological or political content would ultimately hurt profits.[44] Determining what constituted non-controversial, mainstream theological content was a matter of perspective, but in general, well-spoken, traditional mainline Protestant preachers like liberal Baptist Harry Emerson Fosdick were considered appropriate for mass audiences while enthusiastic, folksy evangelicals like Paul Rader were not. Broadcasters developed policies to ensure that the likes of Winrod and other extreme voices would be kept off their airwaves and away from their profits.

The federal government also intervened. The US government had been trying, and mostly failing, to regulate and professionalize radio broadcasting since the Radio Act of 1912.[45] Enterprising broadcasters in the underregulated early days often stole one another's broadcast frequencies, and revivalist broadcasters like Aimee Semple McPherson and Paul Rader were some of the worst offenders. McPherson and others argued that the imminent return of Jesus justified this action. She called efforts to keep revivalist services on the frequencies that they had purchased the work of "minions of Satan."[46] Undeterred by such ire, the US government passed the 1934 Communications Act and created the Federal Communications Commission (FCC), which established firmer broadcasting boundaries around what constituted free speech (and thus was exempt from regulation) and what constituted propaganda (and thus should be removed from American radio waves).

Regulated revivalists felt unfairly targeted by corporations and the US government. Ministers like Billy Graham and Torrey Johnson, who aimed to win the youth of America for Christ through radio, were especially keen to stay on American airwaves. In response, many white Protestants stepped up their efforts to collaborate in order to increase their power in the public sphere.

"Evangelical" grew into an umbrella term for conservative, activist white Protestantism in the 1930s and 1940s. Some of that activism was commercial, some of it missionary, and some of it explicitly political. Peter and Bernard Zondervan, nephews of publisher William B. Eerdmans, started their own evangelical press in 1931. The evangelical college ministry Intervarsity began stateside in 1939 and started publishing books in the 1940s. Conservative white Protestant groups led by luminaries like fundamentalists Bob Jones Sr. and Harry A. Ironside, Congregationalist Harold John Ockenga, Presbyterian Charles Woodbridge, and Free Methodist Leslie Roy Marston put theological differences aside and created the National Association of Evangelicals (NAE) in 1942.

Leaders in the largest white Pentecostal denomination, the Assemblies of God (AoG), were delighted to receive an invitation from the NAE. By joining the NAE, the AoG took a big step into the mainstream of American public life. The denomination's official periodical rejoiced that the NAE had done what "no other group of Fundamentalist believers had done before—they invited the brethren of the Holiness and the Pentecostal groups." This ecumenism among white fundamentalists, Holiness people, and Pentecostals was, indeed, a remarkable shift from the days when the Bensons changed their business's name to avoid association with Pentecostals.

This new evangelical coalition quickly expanded the scope of their work. Feeling threatened by liberal and mainline Protestants, Catholics, and Jews, who had created broadcast coalitions, they organized the National Religious Broadcasters (NRB) to represent evangelical broadcasting interests.[47] Together, top NRB broadcasters like Moody Radio, Charles Fuller, Paul Rader, and others spread conservative, white political views and premillennial dispensational theology.

They may have disagreed on the particulars of sin and salvation, but in 1950 a group of booksellers who shared the same conservative Protestant outlook and dedication to cultivating a "shared 'evangelical' identity" created the Christian Booksellers Association (CBA). Christian booksellers became key distribution hubs for the production of an evangelicalism that was not a timeless set of theological truths, but rather a timely "commercial religion" for the marketing age.[48] The founding of the CBA gave evangelicals a national distribution network for merchandise distribution for Bibles, Bible studies, songbooks, and recorded music.

With the power of radio, along with growing networks of magazines, newsletters, and book publishers at their disposal, the NAE aimed to exert influence over the American body politic in a way that no one denomination or publishing house could do alone. This alliance of politically minded revivalist preachers, singing celebrities, energetic businessmen, and market-savvy publishers became the backbone of white evangelical entertainment and activism in the mid-twentieth century.

Through popular music, the peculiarities of three white Protestant groups—Holiness people, Southern Baptists, and Pentecostals (as well as, eventually, their younger siblings, Charismatics)—became synonymous with the generic term "evangelicalism." West Coast media innovators and evangelical musicians created the soundscape of what would become known as the Religious Right.[49] The years of plenty for revival music, however, were yet to come. As the United States emerged victorious from World War II, the nation experienced the baby boom, and conservative white Protestants eagerly sought to use music to bring this new generation into the evangelical fold.

2

"The Game of Life"

The Cold War Origins of Contemporary Christian Music (1951–1970)

In 1951, twenty-one-year-old Jarrell McCracken, a sportscaster on KWTX radio in Waco, Texas, got a very Texan request: would he consider speaking to a local Baptist youth group on the subject of Christianity and football?[1] McCracken, a Southern Baptist minister's son and Baylor University graduate, did them one better. He recorded "The Game of Life," a sixteen-minute-long "thrilling play-by-play description of an imaginary football game."[2] On the mythical gridiron, Average Christian, coached by Jesus Christ and playing alongside his teammate Holy Spirit, won a barnburner over the Forces of Evil.

McCracken's innovative recording caused a sensation among Baptist youth pastors. Requests for copies of "The Game of Life" poured in, and, to meet the demand, McCracken and two others partners, Baylor business major Henry Sorelle and radio and television executive Ted Snider, created a new record label. Named after the call letters of the imaginary radio station from "The Game of Life," W.O.R.D., Word Records shared (and sold) the gospel through recorded sermons and music.

Word Records, along with the Benson Company and other evangelical popular music labels, brought to white evangelicals of the 1950s and 1960s musical antidotes to rock and roll, the rebellious form of popular music adored by adolescents. Rather than rebellion, recordings from those labels promoted patriotism and righteous living alongside end-times theology. Their efforts led to an expanding network of evangelical media businesses, attracted corporate sponsorships, and even gave evangelical pop singers access to the Oval Office. But their initial refusal to embrace rock severely limited their appeal among young Americans.

Word Records and the Sounds of Southern Baptists

Sound-recording technology has been around in the United States since 1877, but for many decades music recording was costly, and startup recording businesses were rare. In the postwar years, however, a confluence of circumstances—recording technology innovations like magnetic tape (which made recording less expensive and more portable), a musicians' strike that put major label recording on hold, and general postwar prosperity—created space in which small, independent labels could flourish.[3] Enterprising evangelicals around the nation took advantage and began creating entertaining recordings about the good news.

In Word's early days, McCracken captured the favorite sounds of Southern Baptist church services.[4] The label released hymns sung by the Baylor University Choir and the Bison Glee Club of Oklahoma Baptist University, as well as sermons by Baptist preachers of the mid-twentieth century like George Truett and W. W. Melton. Southern Gospel acts like Frank Boggs, the Matthew Brothers Quartet, and "Mr. Southern Gospel," Jack Holcomb, were Word artists. Frank Boggs' 1956 Southern Gospel album showcased popular revivalist hymns like "Amazing Grace," the 1934 Appalachian folk hymn "I Wonder As I Wander," and Dwight L. Moody's favorite, "Softly and Tenderly."[5]

Boggs' album also repeated the white Southern Gospel practice of appropriating Black Gospel spirituals like "Swing Low, Sweet Chariot," "Were You There?," and "Nobody Knows the Trouble I've Seen." The Baylor University Choir and artists like Boggs included a heavy dose of patriotic hymns like "Battle Hymn of the Republic," "America the Beautiful," and "God of Our Fathers," which was written in 1876 to celebrate the centennial of the United States. "God of Our Fathers," with its celebration of God's "love divine" leading a "free land," was particularly popular among postwar white evangelicals who were concerned that their democratic way of life was being threatened by communism.

Not to be outdone by the upstarts in Texas, Holiness songbook publishers also jumped into the recording business. John T. Benson Jr., the youngest son of John Sr. and Eva, took over the Nashville-based Benson Company in 1935 and expanded the reach of his father's ministry. By the time Waco-based Word Records was established in 1951, Benson Jr. had grown his company's revenue from $12,000 to $100,000 per year.[6] In 1962, Benson Jr. created Heart Warming Records and began recording Southern Gospel groups.

Heart Warming Records drew stars from the same Holiness and Pentecostal circles that were the backbone of the Benson publishing business. The Nazarene Speer Family, Pentecostal Dottie Rambo, and the Bill Gaither Trio (affiliated with the Church of God, Anderson) built the foundation of Benson's recording roster. In addition to nostalgia, appropriation of Black Gospel music, and patriotism, Heart Warming artists reveled in the apocalyptic anticipation of their Holiness and Pentecostal forebears. Songs like R. E. Winsett's 1942 "Jesus Is Coming Soon," which became a Southern Gospel standard and radio favorite by the 1960s, combined the longstanding Holiness appreciation for millennialism and the rapture with a World War II–era fear of waning American liberty. Especially popular among Baptists and Pentecostals, the song's vibrant spiritual world and dire predictions about the future were set to a deceptively peppy tune. "Troublesome times are here/ filling men's hearts with fear," they sang, "Freedom we all hold dear, now is at stake."[7]

Winsett's 1932 premillennial dispensationalist anthem "The Message of His Coming" also became a big hit for Southern Gospel artists in the 1960s and 1970s. The song portrayed believers "looking for His coming," anticipating the rapture, and listening for the "midnight cry" and the "final call." Dottie Rambo's 1965 "The Church Triumphant" echoed traditional Pentecostal appreciation for the Second Coming. "It's the old ship of Zion," she sang, "I'm talking about the church in the Book of Revelation."[8]

As was the case with other forms of Southern music like country and rhythm and blues, the sounds of Southern Gospel music—Dottie Rambo's growling alto and bouncy guitar rhythms, Jack Holcolmb's smooth tenor and organ accompaniment—appealed to listeners across the United States. It was no surprise, therefore, that as the recording industry of the mid-twentieth century grew, Holiness songbook publishers and fledgling labels built robust sales networks and put out catalogs aimed at national audiences.[9]

Southern Gospel groups like the Blackwood Brothers and the Statesmen Quartet signed to mainstream labels like RCA Victor, while many others joined newly formed church-based or parachurch-rooted record labels. A few were located in the Midwest like Billy Graham and Al Smith's Singspiration (1941), or on the West Coast like the Seventh-day Adventist Sabbath Music (1948), but Word and Benson were the two leading evangelical record labels of the 1950s. Word created its own Southern Gospel imprint, Canaan Records, in 1965 and signed Southern Gospel acts like the LeFevres and the Happy Goodman Family who, like the Rambos, recorded Holiness and Pentecostal songs filled with eschatological anticipation and upbeat, sometimes raucous, accompaniment.

In order to promote Southern Gospel music, several of the genre's biggest stars—including James Blackwood of the Blackwood Brothers and Vestal Goodman of the Happy Goodmans—created the Gospel Music Association (GMA) in 1964.[10] The GMA held an annual awards show called the Dove Awards, which recognized and promoted excellence in their genre. Winsett's 1942 "Jesus Is Coming Soon" won song of the year at the inaugural Dove Awards of 1969.

The GMA provided the Southern Gospel music industry with structure and organization, but in the 1950s the best way to get a wide audience was through radio. The sometimes rowdy, lowbrow aesthetic of many Southern Gospel acts (particularly those of the Pentecostal variety), combined with the fire-and-brimstone fundamentalist preaching that often accompanied such music, however, limited how, when, and where this music appeared on the airwaves. To take gospel music to the growing mainstream radio and record markets, the songbook establishment needed a mainstream ambassador.

Billy Graham and the Music of Radio Revivals

By the midcentury, the tall, well-spoken, impeccably dressed Rev. Billy Graham was a ubiquitous presence in American media. In 1950, he launched a weekly radio program called *The Hour of Decision*; it became a television program the next year. In 1951, Graham founded a film company called World Wide Pictures. Once a full-throated preacher of premillennial dispensationalism, as Graham's media presence grew and he became a leading figure in the National Association of Evangelicals (NAE), he developed a broadly appealing, pro-democracy message that seemed tailor-made for the scandal-averse commercial airwaves.[11]

According to Graham, the future of the United States depended on the resurrection of its past faithfulness and the preservation of the democracy that had sustained it. "You must decide," said Graham passionately, "whether you want to serve other gods or whether you will serve the true and the living God."[12] For Graham, the personal decision for salvation was of global import, especially as the predominantly Christian United States and the "godless" communist Soviet Union emerged as ideologically opposed forces in the Cold War. Many American evangelicals like Graham saw defending and expanding American democracy as central to defending the integrity of Christianity itself.[13] While the Cold War escalated, Graham billed himself as "A man with God's message for these crisis days" and framed his calls for conversion as part of the overall effort to strengthen the United States and the "free world." "For you," began his broadcasts, "for the nation, this is the hour of decision."

Music was a key medium for Graham's message. Graham understood the power of song to shape Christian thought and practice, and his closest colleagues included songleaders Cliff Barrows and George Beverly Shea. In keeping with Graham's desire to redeem the nation, promote democracy, and win the Cold War, Shea and Barrows made sure that patriotic music was a staple in Graham's many mass-media productions. Odes to America played a pivotal role in framing *The Hour of Decision*. Some broadcasts began with a choral version of "America the Beautiful." The official theme for the show was a "militant," rousing version of "The Battle Hymn of the Republic" sung by *The Hour of Decision* choir.[14]

Graham's television broadcasts were as patriotic as his radio shows. Broadcasts included "God Bless Our Boys," a World War I song extolling the American military as being on the side of God. In a 1950s context, the enemy was no longer Germany and the Kaiser, however, but the USSR. "God bless our boys who go to fight our country's foe," sang the choir, "Bless them tonight, Father of all, we pray, grant them to win the day, that o'er this world, for aye, shall reign the Right."[15] George Beverly Shea's 1957 album, "A Billy Graham Crusade in Song," included renditions of evangelical classics like "The Lord's Prayer" and "How Great Thou Art" as well as patriotic standards like "America the Beautiful," linking American democracy with American evangelicalism. The 1962 musical singalong film *One Nation Under God* featured Shea and Barrows along with the US Army Chorus and Jubilaires Choir singing "America the Beautiful," "My Country 'Tis of Thee," and the "Battle Hymn of the Republic."[16]

Graham's vision of American democracy had limits. He rejected the Rev. Martin Luther King Jr.'s request for public support and failed to offer full-throated support for Black enfranchisement or civil-rights protests. Instead, he focused on social and political problems that concerned his mostly white audience. And those problems all had the same solution. "The answer to divorce, ladies and gentlemen," argued Graham, "is the salvation of divorcees. The answer to teenage delinquency is the salvation of the teenager. The answer to corrupt business and labor leaders is the salvation of the leaders who are involved in corruption."[17] "All of our problems," he went on to say, "which stagger the experts who seem so concerned about the future of America, can be resolved at the foot of the cross. And in the conversions of the different people who are involved." If enough lawmakers experienced this conversion, he argued, the nation would benefit. "Thank God," he told his listeners, "for our few leaders in Washington who are beginning to pray: God show us the way."

Adolescents—"teenagers" as they were dubbed in the 1940s—were of particular concern to Graham.[18] He had a longtime interest in youth ministry and had been the first full-time evangelist for Youth for Christ in the 1940s. He partnered with the newly formed evangelical college outreach organization Campus Crusade for Christ in the 1960s.[19] But he did not just preach to young people. He gave them advice, including in "Billy Graham Answers Teenagers' Questions," a 1962 spoken-word recording wherein Graham discussed youth-culture topics like "hot rod cars," "going steady," and "clothes."[20] He even dramatized their struggles on film, in a World Wide Pictures production called *The Restless Ones* (1965). The film featured rebellious teenagers on the brink of extramarital sex and alcohol abuse who were out on their own in a wild and unforgiving teenage world. In the end, however, they returned to their parents and found salvation via a family altar call at a Billy Graham revival.

The Restless Ones featured a moving score written by Ralph Carmichael, a white Pentecostal pastor's son from California whom World Wide Pictures had hired to score its first film in 1951. Carmichael developed a wide-reaching, successful career in mainstream American media, working with artists like Nat King Cole and Roger Williams, but gospel music was his enduring love.[21] He longed to see church music that was as well-crafted—and as fun—as mainstream pop music. Carmichael founded Light Records, helping to launch the careers of artists like Black Pentecostal prodigy Andraé Crouch and the Disciples, and was always on the lookout for musicians who shared his dream of incorporating popular-music sensibilities into sacred spaces.[22]

As a media maker, Graham had many televangelist contemporaries—Pentecostal Rex Humbard, Southern Baptist Pat Robertson, fundamentalist Percy Crawford, Charismatic Oral Roberts, and Roman Catholic Bishop Fulton J. Sheen—but few peers, in part because he was a Southern Baptist. The 1940s and 1950s saw unprecedented growth in church attendance rising from 64.5 million in 1940 to 114.5 million, or 60 percent of the overall American population, in 1960. The Southern Baptists were the fastest-growing denomination during those decades.[23]

Graham was also a genius when it came to harnessing mass media. His disciplined public image, impeccable instincts for promotion, and top-notch music appealed broadly to white church-going audiences. The Billy Graham Evangelistic Association (BGEA) built its audience by amplifying each evangelistic project's reach and profitability through intricate marketing campaigns. World Wide Pictures' first film, *Mr. Texas*, typified BGEA's media savvy. The film's titular character found salvation by listening to a Billy Graham radio preaching moment on *The Hour of Decision*.[24] The BGEA also created an official soundtrack featuring Barrows and Shea and *The Hour of Decision* choir.[25] They arranged for a screening at the Hollywood Bowl, and *Billboard Magazine* covered the affair.

For all of the BGEA's success with music production and promotion, the work of Graham, Shea, Barrows, and Carmichael was decidedly *adult*, and Carmichael's embrace of American popular music in church settings was not widespread in the 1950s. No matter how much Graham and Youth for

Christ wanted to engage with the youth of the nation, and no matter how many questions Graham answered from teenagers or films he created about them, he could not get around the fact that the media young people were consuming seemed at odds with the patriotic, chaste, and sober values that evangelicals sought to impart. Thus, even though evangelicals successfully translated church services to radio, television, and film, many worried that they were losing the attention of the largest generation of white evangelicals the nation had ever seen. Young white American evangelicals of the mid-twentieth century (along with most other young Americans of the era) were embracing music that many believed would send them straight to hell. To rescue the youth of the nation, evangelicals faced the prospect of a deal with a musical devil.

The Rock-and-Roll Plague

In 1957, the Assemblies of God periodical *The Pentecostal Evangel* published a warning: the youth of America were stricken by a terrible disease that could destroy the United States. "Every church and religious body, every institution of higher learning, every family and decent American citizen," argued big-band leader Dorothy Parker, "should unite to put an end once and for all to this rock 'n' roll plague."[26] To the dismay of many of their parents and pastors, adolescents raised in white evangelical households had been infected with a terrible disease called rock and roll.[27] Once exposed, it seemed that no radio revival nor televangelist's plea could cure them.

Rock and roll, with its songs of teenage love, fast cars, and "social dancing," was almost universally condemned in evangelical circles as "a menace to Christendom."[28] Teetotalers of the early twentieth century had effectively deployed songbooks against the most energizing social and political concern of the day, alcohol and alcoholism, but rock music presented a trickier challenge for church people. For one thing, the music itself had actually been born in Southern churches.[29] Rock and roll's roots in the sounds and sensibilities of African American congregations and Black and white Pentecostal and Holiness churches are well documented.[30] Churchy rhythms, gospel chords, and Holiness theological language combined with the sounds of drums, electric guitars, blues, boogie woogie, and rhythm and blues came together in a heady musical mix that was hard to expunge completely from the communities that created them, even as churches quickly turned against rock and roll.[31]

Indeed, some of rock and roll's biggest stars, like Elvis Presley and Jerry Lee Lewis, came from rural Southern Pentecostal churches. Little Richard was a

Seventh-day Adventist who attended Pentecostal services. They exported to radio stations across the country the flamboyant aesthetic, undulating dance moves, rhythmic beat patterns, and passionate vocal performances from Black and white Pentecostal and Holiness congregations in Macon, Georgia; Tupelo, Mississippi; and Ferriday, Louisiana. Jerry Lee Lewis scandalously turned the Southern Pentecostal phrase for encountering the Holy Spirit, "Great Balls of Fire," into a very thinly veiled reference to sex.[32] Elvis "the Pelvis" Presley credited his dancing and his vocal inflections to the "spiritual quartets" and Pentecostal congregations that raised him.[33]

Among white revivalists, condemnations of rock music were often steeped in anti-Black racism. In 1957, "Musical evangelist" and rock-and-roll opponent Phil Kerr argued in *The Foursquare Magazine* that rock and roll was African in origin and as such, a form of foreign occultism. "The only difference between the leader of a modern orchestra, and a jungle medicine-man," he wrote, "is that the former is wearing a dress suit, instead of a grass skirt, and has a slim baton in his dainty hand instead of a ring through his nose!"[34] Kerr argued that this kind of "African" music would produce devilish results. "The effect of his music is the same as that of the medicine man," he continued, "Savage impulses stirred in the breast of a tuxedo garbed American are as vicious and dangerous as the appetites stirred in the breast of the half-naked African by the same Satanic music." For many concerned white parents of the midcentury, embracing this music was an unforgivable sin.

The fact that much of American rock and roll sounded like Southern Pentecostal and Holiness church music was a constant source of frustration for many Holiness and Pentecostal churchgoers, Black and white.[35] "The same music we worship by, pray by, weep by, believe and rejoice by," wrote Bennie Triplett, an exasperated youth pastor in 1957, "is being used by Dixieland jazz bands in the night clubs—used to get gain, entertain, deceive, defraud, and divide—to mock God. The actor on the stage mimics the Pentecostal and teases the audience."[36] This mimicry, Triplett argued, was the real spiritual danger of rock and roll. "The devil laughs," wrote Triplett, "for he has used the name of the church, the miracles of the church, and now the music of the church, for his purposes." For Triplett and others, rock and roll sounds co-opted the sacramental value of Pentecostal music and besmirched it with profits and celebrity. "To us," he wrote, "gospel music is sacred, and should be reverenced and respected. It is no wonder we are touchy when it is desecrated and profaned by spotlighted hypocrisy."

Pentecostals hated having their worship appropriated for "ungodly" profit, but it was the very Pentecostal nature of rock music that disgusted others. For white evangelicals, rock and roll's origins in "lowbrow" working-class Black and white culture, and indebtedness to African American music forms like jazz and boogie woogie, made the music especially distasteful.[37] Conversation about rock and roll was often inextricable from the national conversation about race, racism, and civil rights.[38] Debates about the sounds of church music became a kind of proxy conversation wherein whites (especially Southern whites) would argue that the sounds they produced (e.g., organ music) were holier and more moral than the sounds that African American–influenced music produced (e.g., drums).

Speaking to a concerned Woman's Missionary Union in 1961, A. Harold Cole, a forty-one-year-old secretary of the department of student work for the Baptist State Convention of North Carolina, diagnosed the problem of rock and roll in social and psychological terms. The problem was the very notion of adolescence itself. "Our society no longer wants or needs the labor of young people," he argued. "It simply says, 'Wait, we do not yet have a place for you.' "[39] "Music," said Cole, "reflects the ambiguities of his [the American teenager's] in-between-ness. Rock 'n Roll expresses his emerging power of sex, of aggression and submission, of moods and feelings unfulfilled and forbidden." In the dire imagination of the genre's church critics, rock and roll stoked the emerging powers of sex by creating tantalizing forms of "social dancing," which, in the minds of the fearful, led to extramarital sex and all manner of youth rebellion. For Cole and many others, there was almost no social problem among the young, whether it was alcoholism, "moral confusion," "rowdyism," or general disorder that could not be traced back to the "rock and roll craze."[40]

The attempt to stigmatize rock and roll as worldly, even satanic, and to distinguish it from sacred music was doomed from the start. For one thing, popular mainstream music with direct references to Christian spirituality undermined the effort to distinguish between "sacred" music and "secular/satanic" music. At no point did general market audiences in the United States, the vast majority of whom were Christian, show sustained hostility to Christian themes in popular music. In many cases, they welcomed implicit or explicit references to God. Frankie Laine's 1953 inspiring "I Believe," for example, assured listeners that their prayers did not go unheeded, because "someone in the great somewhere hears every word."[41]

In addition, the lines between rock and roll and the church communities who rejected the genre were regularly blurred by the rock and rollers themselves. Rock and rhythm and blues artists like Little Richard, Ray Charles, Elvis Presley, Sam Cooke, Johnny Cash; doo-wop groups like the Ravens and the Orioles; and country music stars like Jimmie Rogers, Hank Williams, the Carter Family, and Dolly Parton were raised as Pentecostals and Baptists, and they made no attempt to obscure their affection for church music.[42] Many included gospel songs, or samples of gospel tunes, in their recordings and live performances.[43] Elvis worked directly with artists like Heart Warming Records' Jake Hess, whose Southern Gospel supergroup the Imperials was a part of Elvis' backup group from 1966 to 1971.[44]

The fact of the matter was, satanic or not, rock and roll was pushing many radio revivalists off the prime-time airwaves.[45] As "old time" radio dramas, soap operas, and comedies migrated from radio to the visual medium of television in the 1950s, the gaps they left in radio programming were filled by popular music. Initially, the broadcasts were curated mostly by a slew of tastemaker broadcasters like Alan Freed and Dick Clark, known as "disc jockeys." But in the early 1950s, radio-station owners like Todd Storz created the Top 40 radio format. Radio stations played the Top 40 hits requested by listeners and indicated by record sales from stores like Sam Goody (established in 1951) and Tower Records (established in 1960).[46] By the 1960s, most radio-station playlists were remarkably focused and divided by genre.[47] Rock-and-roll stations quickly emerged as the uncontested favorite among the middle-class white American teenagers that advertisers wanted to reach.[48]

Radio revivalists began disappearing from Top 40 stations. In 1957, upon finding out that his Nazarene church services would be dropped by one local Kansas radio station because "Wichita is demanding a new concept in radio and that concept does not include religion," pastor G. A. Gough of First Church of the Nazarene in Wichita rallied his listeners to call in and save his airtime. "I just can't believe," he said incredulously, "that thousands of people in care homes, hospitals, and religious people who are unable to attend the church of their choice, would rather listen all day Sunday to Elvis Presley and 'Hound Dog,' . . . than have a chance to warm their hearts at the altar of God."[49] Gough's campaign won him back his time slot, but for younger listeners, the supposed spiritual dangers of rock music were not scary enough to keep them away from the exciting new sounds coming from their radios.

By the late 1960s, it was clear that there was no extinguishing the power of rock and roll in American youth culture. Rock and rollers successfully positioned themselves as proxies for teenagers who opposed the staid traditionalism of the past and looked toward a lively, prosperous postwar future. They also established themselves as the arbiters and marketers of "coolness." Coolness, which originated as a way of "negotiating a resistant mode of being in the world," by rebelling against mainstream culture's racism, sexism, and materialism, was a post–World War II–era concept that became a sought-after state of being for American teenagers. While church people wagged their fingers, rockers glamorized a cool posture of resistance and rebellion.[50]

The very rebellious qualities that made rockers cool were, of course, anathema to white Protestants. From the pulpit and in denominational literature, conservative white Protestants stubbornly celebrated the music of George Beverly Shea and Cliff Barrows and decried Jerry Lee Lewis and Little Richard. But many youth pastors and church musicians came to believe that that the standoff between the devil's music holdouts and cool teenage rock-and-roll fans had to end.[51] Church choir directors worried that if, given an ultimatum, the young would choose rock and roll over worship. To prevent an exodus, intrepid church musicians began experimenting with musical forms aimed at attracting American teenagers.

"Sacred Music for Young America"

The idea that this specific demographic—American youth—needed saving, and that they needed saving on their own cultural terms, was a part of a much larger theological project in midcentury American evangelical circles. In 1961, Dr. Donald McGavran revolutionized the way white evangelicals thought about evangelism by arguing that churches could grow quickly when church attenders share demographic similarities like race/ethnicity, class, language, and nationality. Rather than getting stuck doing the complex work of cross-cultural or cross-generational outreach, McGavran argued, every aspect of congregational life could (and should) grow first in what he called "homogeneous units."[52] Any other approach, according to McGavran, was "a self-defeating policy, and, with rare exceptions, contrary to the will of God."

For white middle-class audiences brimming with postwar wealth, this made sense. After all, the category of "homogeneous unit" bore a strong resemblance to a market niche, which was a familiar concept to Americans in the "golden age" of advertising culture.[53] It also made sense that the white American adolescent baby boomer was *the* prized demographic. Advertisers recognized that targeting young people could lead to a lifetime of consumer loyalty, and there had never been a bigger or more prosperous group of prospective consumers than white baby boomers.[54] Accordingly, denominations and congregations began emphasizing "youth ministry," and youth groups boomed in the 1960s, especially in white Protestant settings.[55] A growing conglomeration of parachurch organizations made up mostly of white evangelicals like Youth for Christ, Youth with a Mission (YWAM), and Campus Crusade for Christ worked to create forms of Christianity that appealed directly to teenage tastes.

Music was key to this effort. Youth for Christ minister and disc jockey Thurlow Spurr hosted a radio program aimed at saving the nation's youth called "Sacred Music for Young America." His selections included traditional "come one, come all" choral music that had sustained many evangelical congregations for decades. But he also featured recordings from young, small groups—male, female, and co-ed—that were modeled after Southern Gospel quartets, big-band jazz ensembles, pop groups like the Chordettes, doo wop groups like the Cadillacs, and barbershop quartets like the Confederates.[56] Many evangelical congregations began to add entertainment to worship services in the form of conservatively dressed singers performing tight West Coast jazz harmonies or Southern Gospel chords. Like Vaughn's touring Southern Gospel groups of an earlier era, talented acts, often from large and influential congregations or parachurch organizations like Youth for Christ, toured churches, denominational gatherings, and camp meetings to encourage believers and demonstrate the latest sacred songs and choral arrangements.

Rock and roll was certainly too risqué in the 1960s, but folk music seemed like a potential half-way point between the hipness of rock and roll and the squareness of church music. Folk musicians often used guitars, but usually not *electric* guitars, and the singing was often gentle. In addition, folk music of the 1950s and 1960s was almost exclusively white, which calmed the concerns of those white evangelicals who feared that rock and roll would lead to racial integration.[57] The performances of folk stars like the Kingston Trio, Bob Dylan, or Peter, Paul, and Mary had little of the flamboyance of Little Richard or blasphemy of Jerry Lee Lewis.

The lyrical content and political aims of many of the top artists in American folk, however, were another story. The value of "free thought" that emerged from the folk scene in places like Greenwich Village did not sit well with Southern churchgoers concerned with preserving the fundamentals of American Christianity. And the free-love practices of some folk stars contrasted sharply with the sentimental depictions of hearth and home in Southern Gospel songs.[58]

Folk music also included high-profile communists, which brought suspicion upon the genre, especially during the Cold War. Pete Seeger was called before the House Un-American Activities Committee in 1955. Seeger testified that he loved his country "very dearly," but he refused to cooperate with the committee's efforts to target performers who had supposedly supported communism through their art. Seeger's defiance led the singer to be convicted of contempt of Congress in 1961. The conviction was overturned a year later, but Seeger was blacklisted. The treatment of Seeger and others like him had a chilling effect on folk music, particularly among those with strong patriotic American sensibilities and conservative political views.

Folk musicians' anti-war messaging was also at odds with the God-and-country pop music produced by Billy Graham. The fact that folk songs like Barry McGuire's "Eve of Destruction" and Pete Seeger's "Where Have All the Flowers Gone?" were often used in protests against the Vietnam War made the genre even more suspect.[59] The shaggy-haired, casually dressed male folk artists and psychedelic-patterned-dress-wearing female singers were a visual rebuke of traditional Holiness codes. In addition, folk artists like Janis Ian, who critiqued racial segregation in the song "Society's Child (Baby, I've Been Thinking)," did not find favor among most middle-class conservative white Protestant listeners—particularly those in the segregated South.[60]

The popularity of American folk music on Top 40 radio, however, meant that the sonic benefits ultimately outweighed the ideological risks, and church-based music ministers in liturgical and revivalist congregations began incorporating folk into their liturgies. Father Geoffrey Beaumont's 1956 *20th Century Folk Mass* replaced organ or orchestral accompaniment with folk music. Folk became popular in congregations throughout the Anglican priest's home in the United Kingdom as well as in the United States.[61] In 1959, Thurlow Spurr, inspired by a meeting with Ralph Carmichael, created a touring thirty-person folk choir called the Spurrlows. In 1962, another Carmichael mentee, Portland, Oregon-based Youth for Christ director Cam Floria, became associate director for the Spurrlows and in 1963 created his own touring folk group. The Continentals, Floria's folk and pop music choir, released their first album on Word Records.[62] Roman Catholic singer-songwriter Ray Repp's *Mass for Young Americans* (1964) brought folk music into American Catholic churches.[63]

Rather than using folk to protest war or racial segregation, many of the conservative white Protestant groups formed in the 1960s used their music to counter what they thought of as the moral degradation of the mid-twentieth century. In 1965, Up with People, a group of enthusiastic young Americans singing folk songs about civic duty and personal purity, began traveling the nation and eventually the world for "love of God and love of country." An outgrowth of the parachurch Moral Rearmament (MRA) movement, Up with People embodied the postmillennial optimism of its founder, Frank Buchanan. Buchanan believed that God could and would create a perfect world, but unlike premillennial dispensationalists, he believed that God would bring about that millennial reign through the purity and good work of pious, honest, hardworking believers. Only after that came to pass would Jesus return.

Like many evangelical groups, MRA leaders were dismayed by what they perceived to be depravity in the form of the rebellious youth culture of the

1950s and the sex, drugs, and anti-war protests of the "hippies" of the 1960s. Beginning in the 1950s, Buchanan and the MRA began to disseminate their theological vision through popular music. They created "Sing-Outs," in which clean-cut, interracial youth choirs could perform catchy songs that were intended to be a visual and auditory "revolt against the cynicism and moral relativism which have diluted the country's traditions" and to signal that within the "moral American majority" there existed a "determination to take a responsible part in the task of society and nation building."[64]

Set up deliberately to counter the folk counterculture, Up with People placed rigorously "square" lyrics over folksy guitars and tambourines. They began performances with the national anthem before launching into a series of moral directives for creating a peaceful and prosperous society. The chorus of "You Can't Live Crooked (and Think Straight)" epitomized their message to America. "You can't live crooked and think straight, Whether you're a chauffeur or chief of state/Clean up the nation before it's too late."[65]

Like Billy Graham, Up with People preached that the solution to any social problem was personal spiritual transformation. Wherever the Up with People group went, they created local "Sing Outs," and by 1965, Sing Out South, created by a Virginian Moral Re-Armament devotee named Inez Thurston, was attracting youth from across the American South.[66] Up with People appealed directly to evangelical youth whose churches refused to incorporate pop sensibilities into their worship music, nowhere more so than in Nashville, Tennessee, the historic heart of choral-music publishing.

Three Southern Baptists noticed how the parachurch organization was siphoning youth-group members away from their congregations. Bob Oldenburg and Cecil McGee of the Church Recreation Department of the Southern Baptist Convention in Nashville, Tennessee, and Billy Ray Hearn, a Southern Baptist youth pastor in Thomasville, Georgia, decided to try to create a musical experience that would allow Southern Baptist youth to express themselves according to their generation's tastes and keep them from straying to the extra-denominational Sing Out South choirs.[67]

In order to bring young Southern Baptists back into the fold, Oldenburg, McGee, and Hearn gathered Baptist youth and workshopped a church-based musical event modeled after Up with People called *Good News: A Folk Musical.* "Do what Up with People does," said Hearn of their aim for *Good News*, "but only with more gospel in it."[68] *The Good News*, a musical revue written by eleven songwriters and arranged mostly by Oldenburg, was part church chorale, part Broadway musical, part folk and rock-and-roll revue. The folk and rock instruments and American slang in the lyrics were meant to connect with the "youth of today." "Music is your best aid" to communicate with kids, said Oldenburg, reflecting on the aims of the musical. "For teenagers, it's the way of saying 'it' " he noted, "Whatever 'it' may be."

The Good News portrayed the Southern Baptist gospel as a "fun" "way of living and giving" for a "moving generation" of baby boomers. "Why should we be smiling?" they asked, "Why should life be fun? Listen to our Good News, then come join along!"[69] The answer to these questions was: "the Christ-life," which would help participants "find sunshine when ev'ry where there's rain," maintain "excitement when ev'rything is plain," and be "at peace when ev'ry where there's war." The good news of *The Good News* exhorted America's youth to be moral, positive influencers in American society.

The opponents of the optimistic "Christ-life" were depicted in the song "I'm a Rebel." Sung by a small ensemble from the choir, the stage direction gave specific instructions for how to portray "rebels." "Dress four youths in 'hippie' attire," Oldenburg advised, "long hair, dark glasses, sweat shirts, dirty jeans; one with a guitar strapped to his back, two carrying picket signs reading, 'peace' and 'amen.' "[70] The hippie-attired rebels picketed their way to the stage and sang: "I'm a Rebel!"

According to *The Good News*, "rebels" were hippies who liked rebelling for rebellion's sake, and while they were willing to protest, they were not willing to fight, presumably a nod to the growing anti–Vietnam War student protests of the 1960s. "We want freedom," they sang, "we want rights! We will picket but we don't fight!" These rebels were made, not born. "You can sing your hymns, and pray," sang the former youth group kids, "I outgrew them yesterday!" The stage directions explained that: "The Rebels remain on the stage after the song ends as if waiting to see what reaction they get."[71] Soon after that, the rest of the choir entered to "visually and vocally present a retaliation to the Rebels," through song. Their rejoinder to the rebels, "We're Gonna Change This Land," celebrated America and sought to channel the rebels' discontent away from rebellion toward the embrace of "God's love."

The stage direction of *The Good News* encouraged "two or three Christian youths to give their testimonies" at the end of the production. These testimonies were to be crisp, well crafted, and brief ("approximately one and one-half minutes long"). "Plan to have the third testimony stress the importance of teen-age witness," recommended Oldenburg, "the idea of sharing with others the meaning of home, country, and God."[72]

The Good News was an immediate success. The Southern Baptist Convention's publishing house Broadman Press published it in 1967, and that year it outsold the denomination's hymnals.[73] *The Good News* launched a new genre of sacred-music publishing—the Christian Youth Musical—and its popularity and profitability inspired dozens of imitations by composers like Bob and Esther Burroughs, Ralph Carmichael, and Kurt Kaiser. Nazarene publisher Lillenas followed their Southern Baptist counterparts and published a series. Graham's Singspiration, which had been purchased by Zondervan Publishers, created several.

Jarrell McCracken began developing youth musicals at Word Records and hired Billy Ray Hearn to develop and promote them. The John T. Benson Company recorded and published several through their own label for "uptown" pop gospel music, Impact Records. Christian Youth Musicals were performed in many of the same places that hosted Southern Gospel quartets and promoted many of the same themes of conservatism, patriotism, and personal piety. By the mid-1970s, youth musicals had been performed in high school gymnasiums, city halls, parks, and parking lots throughout the United States.

Following in the footsteps of *The Good News*, Christian Youth Musicals were often a direct rebuke to some aspect of (often cartoonishly depicted) hippie counterculture. For example, Ralph Carmichael and Kurt Kaiser's 1971 *Natural High*, created in partnership with Word Records in Waco, argued that the "natural high" of life with God far outstripped the pleasures induced by marijuana or psychedelics. The lyrics featured warnings that used common catchphrases from counterculture icons like Timothy Leary, but reapplied to traditional conservative American Protestantism. "Open up your mind," they sang, "to some values that are true, before it's too late."[74]

Christian Youth Musicals were costly and labor intensive—licensed sheet music, orchestras, choirs, lighting, staging, and costuming was far more expensive than four singers and a piano—so they tended to be produced by large and wealthy congregations or coalitions of congregations. Their impressive sales indicated, however, that church leaders were sure that they engaged the young.[75] For participants, the power of Christian Youth Musicals was arguably in their theatricality. Their ability to re-engage straying young evangelicals hinged on inviting them to participate in ritualized productions of patriotism and revivalism. It was one thing to sing the national anthem in church; it was another to play the role of a rebel/drug dealer/anti-war protestor who is converted thanks to the positivity and enthusiasm of clean-cut young Christians. It was exciting and exhilarating to take back the nation from drug-addled hippies through song.

The Music of America's Young Majority

By the late 1960s, it was clear that the postwar era had been good to the evangelical music business. *Billboard Magazine* began to cover the "new look" of "religious-oriented" music and noted its increasingly "good economics."[76] Established sheet-music publishers like the Benson Company, denominational presses like Broadman and Lillenas, and record labels like Word Records, Heart Warming Records, and Impact Records had together amassed all the ingredients necessary to build a substantial, nation-wide industry. Songbook publishers like Benson expanded into the record- and book-publishing businesses.[77] Print publishers dipped their toes into the industry, with Zondervan purchasing the Stamps-Baxter Music Company and creating Zondervan Victory and Singchord records.

National Religious Broadcaster Radio stations proliferated.[78] Artists connected with evangelist Billy Graham performed and sold music to his television, radio, and stadium-filling in-person crowds. Christian youth musicals and choral folk groups like the Continentals, the Spurrlows, Roger Breland's Truth, and Derric Johnson's Re'Generation toured through churches, county fairs, and other civic centers as well as the well-worn "sawdust trail" of American revivalism such as Bible conferences and camp meetings.[79]

Revivalist fervor for spreading the gospel through popular music also burned brightly in the United Kingdom. British groups like Liverpool-based the Crossbeats (1963), a "beat group" with guitar-driven pop sounds, spread evangelical messages about God and heaven in churches and colleges. The Musical Gospel Outreach created *Buzz Magazine* in 1965, a periodical dedicated to covering musical efforts to use popular music to encourage young people to "Think About God's Love."

In the United States, the flourishing industry was well equipped to meet the longstanding revivalist aim of transmitting moral, theologically informed, nation-building ideas through entertainment. Record labels and publishers churned out music produced by musicians, choir directors, and arrangers like Ralph Carmichael, Thurlow Spurr, Kurt Kaiser, and Billy Ray Hearn, many of whom were alumni of Holiness, Baptist, or Pentecostal colleges like Baylor University, Southern California Bible College (now Vanguard University), Bob Jones University, or Wheaton College. Pastors' children or ministers of music in local Pentecostal, Baptist, or Holiness congregations, like Cam Floria and Hearn, became touring musicians or record-label executives and brought substantial denominational resources with them.

Evangelical entertainers in the United States promoted God and country, and corporations were eager to partner with them to sell much more. General Tire and Rubber Company–owned KHJ-TV in Los Angeles broadcast Ralph Carmichael's variety show "The Campus Christian Hour," for which Carmichael won an Emmy in 1949. Billy Graham's music enjoyed the support of the American Broadcasting Company in the 1950s. The Spurrlows had

Chrysler backing.[80] Top 40 radio stations seeking to sell listeners to advertisers eagerly sought this booming demographic. Gospel stations catering to white middle-class listeners with Southern Gospel and choral music expanded and multiplied.

Politicians also took note. In 1970, the Spurrlows were invited to perform for President Richard Nixon at the White House on Thanksgiving. The group presented the president with *In God We Trust*, an album commemorating their visit. The message of *In God We Trust* tracks like "I Am Thankful to Be an American" was clear: hippies may be discontented, but most American youth knew not to take their nation for granted. The back cover included a heartfelt letter to the president and to the American people: "We pledge to you our prayers and willing hearts to establish and secure the brightest future for our land," they wrote before signing off as "AMERICA'S YOUNG MAJORITY, The Spurrlows."[81]

The music of America's Young Majority benefitted from evangelical sales and marketing networks, corporate sponsorship, and even the ear of the president. But evangelical attempts to sanitize popular music lagged behind mainstream youth culture. Christian Youth Musicals and pop ensembles were created by adults for children, and it showed. Christian music was, in a word, uncool. Something crucial was missing, and it was the one thing that conscientious youth ministers worried that they could never provide: rock and roll.

3

"The Now Generation"

Creating Contemporary Christian Music (1970–1978)

Larry Norman could not sleep. The long-haired twenty-two-year-old Californian was at something of a crossroads in 1969: he wanted to be an end-times witness for Jesus, but he also felt compelled to create what his father had called "the devil's music."[1] As lead singer of the rock band People!, Norman had one of the biggest hits of 1968. But he became convinced that rock and roll and Christian ministry should not and could not mix, and he made up his mind to give up on music. On that restless evening in Los Angeles, however, Norman was awakened by the sound of his own voice singing in the darkness. He got up, sang into a tape recorder, and found he could finally rest.

The next day, Norman took stock of things. "I began wondering if perhaps God didn't want me to give up music," he recalled later, "the Bible says to 'test the spirits' to see if they are from God so I decided to write another song and see what it was like."[2] That song, "I Wish We'd All Been Ready," combined the end times Pentecostal fervor of his childhood with the rock and roll of his young adulthood. It became an anthem of Norman's generation.

Evangelical opposition to rock remained strong throughout the 1960s, but eventually, young musicians with stories of radical conversion proved that the much-feared "devil's music" could create new vistas for both prophecy and profit. The end-times-minded, evangelistic Jesus movement of the early 1970s used rock, folk, and West Coast countercultural aesthetics to preach the good news. As Jesus music and the music of America's young majority developed and converged in Christian bookstores, on Christian radio stations, and on music festival stages, their combined efforts, tensions, and contradictions came to be known as Contemporary Christian Music.

Jesus People and Jesus Music

A few intrepid youths of the 1960s produced albums that attempted to harmonize rock with evangelical messages.[3] Across the pond, the Crossbeats of Liverpool, England, backed by some three hundred "prayer partner" supporters, booked gigs in the UK and even toured the United States. *Buzz Magazine* continued to write about using popular music to reach a "crazy, mixed-up generation" that believed that "[t]he Beatles can do a much better job than the Archbishop of Canterbury."

Stateside, teenage Isabel Baker, who traveled with her evangelist father, wrote and recorded *I Like God's Style*. Baker's 1965 rockabilly album told listeners, "this world has never offered a teenager anything real, but the Bible teaches if we'll believe, then God's salvation we will feel." The Crusaders, a Southern California quintet signed to a subsidiary of Capitol Records, released *Make a Joyful Noise with Drums and Guitars* in 1966. The surf-music record included lyrics like, "we think of Him when we're playin / it's just as though we were prayin." They celebrated the album as a pioneering work. "Now, for the first time," the album liner notes claimed, "God is praised in song through the most contemporary music expression: The Beat."

Mind Garage, psychedelic rockers from West Virginia, were encouraged to create music to accompany West Virginia University's Episcopal campus ministry. The group began performing *The Electric Liturgy* in East Coast churches in the late 1960s, and they were welcomed at places like Princeton University. " 'The Mind Garage,' " wrote one appreciative attendee, helped "clear away the cobwebs of the traditional liturgy permitting some fresh light to shine on the real meaning of the Christian service."[4]

For most conservative white revivalists of the 1960s, however, rock and roll was still anathema. "Rock and roll living," according to Assemblies of God celebrity preacher David Wilkerson, threatened the nation by leading adolescents to gangs, drugs, alcohol, and sex. To address the problem, Wilkerson created Teen Challenge, a ministry aimed at rescuing "America's hopeless youth" from the urban "asphalt jungles of the cities."[5] Teen Challenge made Wilkerson a household name in Pentecostal circles; his 1963 memoir, *The Cross and the Switchblade*, which told readers of Wilkerson's adventures in urban evangelism, became a bestseller. In 1967, Wilkerson set his sights on the "goodniks," bored, suburban, mostly white, middle-class teens who should have been in Assemblies of God youth groups, but were instead being led astray by the "demonic pied pipers" of rock-and-roll living.[6]

Wilkerson warned parents of the particular dangers of the "Hippies of Haight Ashbury," who converged on that San Francisco neighborhood during the "Summer of Love" of 1967 and were leading the young "straight to hell."[7] Wilkerson was incensed by stories of hippie preachers like Lonnie Frisbee finding Jesus while tripping on hallucinogens. In a paternal huff, he traveled to the Bay Area in December of that year to confront Ted Wise and Steve

Heefner, two young "hippiezed Christians" who ran a small mission in San Francisco's Haight Ashbury district.[8] "I'm tired of these Bob Dylan preachers that tell people you can have LSD and Pot and Jesus too," said the short-haired, suit-and-tie-wearing Wilkerson. "What we need, is preachers in the Haight Ashbury telling these hippies they need to clean up."

Wise and Heefner's long-haired "hippieized Christianity" offended Wilkerson's sensibilities in large part because it was born amid the very folk and rock music culture that Teen Challenge and Christian Youth Musicals sought to cleanse from America.[9] Wise and Heefner's work began after the Summer of Love, wherein around 100,000 people descended on the Bay Area for folk and rock music, as well as enlightenment. Several of the young, mostly white Americans who arrived in California became disillusioned with their experiences.

Rather than drug-fueled spiritual insight, free love, peaceful protests, a rejection of materialism, and a rock-and-roll renaissance, they found spiritual emptiness, excess, addiction, sexually transmitted diseases, homelessness, and exploitation.[10] Some found love and hope in a radical, mystical experience with the person of Jesus. The Christian communities best-positioned to receive such spiritually attuned converts were often Pentecostal or Charismatic. Charismatics of the 1960s and 1970s embraced Pentecostal practices like speaking in tongues or healing, but did so outside established Pentecostal denominations or congregations. Young converts of the West Coast frequently found a home in these Spirit-infused outposts of evangelical Christianity.

Many who found Jesus in the midst of hippie culture saw no reason to give up on the sounds, styles, and anti-authoritarian ethos of their generation. Indeed, while *The Good News* depicted hippies as moral degenerates living in rebellion to God, hippie converts envisioned Jesus himself as a rebel revolutionary—the "ultimate hippie"—who disrupted the principalities and powers of the world with the good news that the Kingdom of God was near.[11] The youth who took this path—Jesus people, or Jesus freaks, as they were called—produced popular art that largely reflected their vivid conversion experiences. Ted Wise painted psychedelic interpretations of the Gospel of Matthew in the Bay Area. Greg Laurie, a teen who converted at a lunchtime Bible study run by Lonnie Frisbee in Newport Beach, California, created cartoon tracts depicting hippies preaching about sharing the good news with other hippies. The art form that became the hallmark of the Jesus movement, however, was Jesus music.

Origin stories for Jesus music abound. Larry Norman, Marsha Stevens, Andraé Crouch, Mylon LeFevre, and the bands Children of the Day, Agape, and Love Song are usually mentioned as founding parents of the musical movement that included 2nd Chapter of Acts, Daniel Amos, Randy Matthews, Resurrection Band, the Archers, Randy Stonehill, Keith and Melody Green, and many more. The music and the movement are arguably best understood as a collective of young voices responding to the foment of the times—the sex, drugs, rock and roll, and spiritual hunger of late 1960s popular culture—rather than as a specific musical genre with a particular progenitor. Some, like Larry Norman or Ralph Carmichael's mentee Andraé Crouch, had a background in Pentecostalism or Baptist Christianity. Others, Like Keith Green and Melody Green, had little familiarity with the forms of American Christianity that had created traditional gospel music.

What they all shared was that—unlike Jarrell McCracken's "The Game of Life" or the music of the Continentals or Truth, which were made up of youths but created and led by professional musicians with formal theological and musical training—early Jesus music had less "adult" supervision. Rather than coming from denominational publishing houses or youth ministers, most Jesus music was created in coffeehouses, on college campuses, and at beach-side church services up and down the West Coast. Songs sprang up from young adults sharing new religious and philosophical ideas through songs and poetry.[12]

In contrast to the Christian Youth Musicals, which told "rebels" to visually clean up their act for the Lord, many Jesus people kept the long-haired, psychedelic aesthetics of the hippie movement. The music that they made also matched the aesthetics of mainstream rock and folk. The tight harmonies of Jesus music rockers Daniel Amos were not dissimilar to the mainstream sounds of Crosby, Stills, and Nash. Annie Herring of 2nd Chapter of Acts would not have sounded out of place alongside Stevie Nicks or Karen Carpenter. Phil Keaggy sounded and looked quite a bit like Paul McCartney.

In terms of lyrical content, early Jesus music was largely testimonial and evangelistic and personal. In an effort to convert their listeners to a saving faith, Jesus people sang dramatic stories of drug trips and demonic apparitions giving way to God's love, the Holy Spirit, and clean living. In his 1970 "No More LSD for Me," Larry Norman poignantly explained how Jesus delivered believers from drug use and emotional and mental turmoil. "No more LSD for me," he wrote, "I met the man from Galilee."[13]

Many Jesus people were converted through ecstatic experiences, and Jesus music celebrated a believer's mystical connection with the spirit of God. This connection often had romantic overtones. "Since I opened up, opened up the door," Love Song lead singer Chuck Girard sang about his conversion to Christianity, "I can't think of anything else but You anymore."[14] "You touched me and You took away the darkness," wrote Randy Stonehill in his 1971 song

"Thank You," "And filled me with the rainbow of Your light."[15] Annie Herring of 2nd Chapter of Acts spoke about the act of creating her songs in mystical terms; she did not write them, but she "received" them from God as a prophetic act.[16]

The Jesus of Jesus music was a gentle, loving savior who above all desired intimacy with his people. Soon after her conversion, sixteen-year-old Marsha Stevens wrote of a tender encounter between a timid seeker and a compassionate Jesus who shared "all my sorrows." After opening her heart to God, she sang, "Jesus said 'Come to the water, stand by my side.' " This Jesus knew every detail of her suffering and angst, " 'I felt every teardrop / when in darkness you cried,' " he told her, " 'And I strove to remind you, that for those tears I died.' "[17]

This moment of conversion—wherein the believer experienced the power of the Spirit, and submitted to the gentle touch of the savior—was memorialized in many songs. "All my life I've been searching for that crazy missing part," sang Keith Green, "and with one touch, you just rolled away the stone that held my heart."[18] Jesus musicians often reveled in the notion that the savior of the universe was giving them personal attention. "Oh, just to think that He died thinking of you and me," sang the 2nd Chapter of Acts, "and the lives we would lead in the sin of our words and deeds."[19]

Because Jesus music served as a conduit to unify the singer with the savior and with the community of believers, the act of singing together took on a kind of sacramental function. Many felt that God was made present through the strumming guitars and sweet harmonies of Love Song and 2nd Chapter of Acts. Those who found such intimacy with Jesus were given spiritual power and ushered into a lively spiritual universe wherein Jesus was present and tangible—and Satan was too. Larry Norman asked, "why should the devil have all the good music?" in a tongue-in-cheek way, but the devil was not a metaphorical figure for most Jesus musicians.

In his 1977 album, *For Him Who Has Ears to Hear*, Keith Green's song "No One Believes in Me Anymore," a first-person narrative song written from the perspective of Satan, explained that a lack of belief in the devil allowed Satan to seek and destroy unsuspecting unbelievers. "You know, it's getting very simple now," sang Green, taking on the character of the devil, "'Cause no one believes in me anymore."[20] The work of Satan, according to the song, was widespread and could be found in gossip, magic spells, fortune tellers, newspapers, and magazines.

Pentecostal and Charismatic congregations on the West Coast did much to shape seminal bands and artists. Jack Hayford, the 1963 winner of the Billy Graham Evangelistic Association's national hymn-writing competition, mentored 2nd Chapter of Acts at Church on the Way, a Foursquare Church in Van Nuys, California. Chuck Smith, founder of Calvary Chapel Church in Costa Mesa (which broke away from the Foursquare Church in 1968), pastored Love Song and mentored many other singers and bands in the early 1970s. Kenn Gulliksen, co-founder of the Vineyard Church in West Los Angeles (which had broken away from the Calvary Chapel), and Vineyard co-founder (and professional musician) John Wimber in Yorba Linda, California, produced many influential musicians of the Jesus movement. The West Coast was the best-known center of the Jesus movement, but there were influential "hippiezed" congregations creating Jesus music in Chicago, Illinois; Fort Wayne, Indiana; Toronto, Canada; and London, England.

Like white Pentecostals of previous generations, Jesus musicians were largely premillennial dispensationalist in their orientation. They were convinced that at any point, the Great Tribulation would begin.[21] Larry Norman's iconic 1969 song "I Wish We'd All Been Ready," captured those visions of doom with surprisingly sweet vocals and gentle accompaniment. "There's no time to change your mind," he sang, "The son has come and you've been left behind."[22] In 1970, Southern Gospel legacy-turned-rocker Mylon Lefever recorded a rock arrangement of his Uncle Alphus' rapture hymn, "Old Gospel Ship," that celebrated the believer "going far beyond the sky," bidding "this old world goodbye," and joining Jesus "sailing through the air.[23] The aftermath of the Summer of Love, widespread social unrest related to the Vietnam War and the civil-rights movement, and rising Cold War tensions among the United States, China, and the USSR—all gave Jesus people reason to believe that the world was in its final days.

The Late Great Planet Earth

When former Campus Crusade preacher and Dallas Theological Seminary alumnus Hal Lindsey began teaching young adults in and around the University of California, Los Angeles, in the late 1960s, his theology of doom was welcomed by Jesus people convinced that the Second Coming was near. In 1970, Lindsey published his teachings in *The Late Great Planet Earth*, which updated and popularized many of the *Scofield Reference Bible*'s prophecies for a new generation. "This book is about prophecy," wrote Lindsey in the introduction, "Bible prophecy. If you have no interest in the future, this book isn't for you."[24]

Lindsey was convinced that there was something special about the current moment, and he encouraged his readers to embrace the notion that they were at the cusp of the Great Tribulation. "It is a mystic time," Lindsey wrote, referring to the spiritual openness of West Coast hippie culture. "Vibrations, spirits, stars, prophets—what an absorbing interest we have today in the unknown. The unseen. And the future."[25] Lindsey analyzed current events in order to forecast the end of the world, and he used virtually every tool at his disposal to do so: premillennial dispensational readings of prophetic texts like Daniel, Ezekiel, and the Book of Revelation; ancient figures like Cicero and Herodotus; modern philosophers like Hegel; American clairvoyants like Edgar Cayce and Jeane Dixon; pop culture references to spiritualism, astrology, magic, and mysticism; and a plethora of biblical scholars.

For Lindsey, the most mystic day in the twentieth century was May 14, 1948. On that day, the modern State of Israel was created, and for Lindsey, it was the day that set the end of the world in motion. "Since the restoration of Israel in 1948," he wrote, "we have lived in the most significant period of prophetic history. . . . We are living in the times which Ezekiel predicted in Chapters 38–39."[26] The final great war of "Armageddon," according to Lindsey, would be triggered by the establishment of Israel as a nation.

The bulk of *The Late Great Planet Earth* was dedicated to showing how vigilant, Bible-reading Christians could decode the prophecies of the past to understand the present. It was no small task. Like the *Scofield Reference Bible* before it, *The Late Great Planet Earth* purported to be a simple, commonsense reading of prophetic texts, but in reality, the book's examination of the end times was extraordinarily complex.

Analyzing monstrous, supernatural figures in Daniel, Ezekiel, and Revelation, Lindsey argued that (1) Russia was the "Bear," "King of the North," and "Gog and Magog" in Revelation that conquered the Middle East and threatened Israel, and would usher in the final battle of Armageddon; (2) China was the "Dragon" that would bring a "200 million militia" to the battle; (3) that "the Beast," "the Antichrist," the "diabolical Fuhrer," a handsome, charming "master of Satanic magic" would rise to political and religious power, unite all the nations of Europe, demand their worship and persecute dissenters, and create a one-world government and one-currency economy. He would, according to Lindsey, mark his followers with a tattoo on their foreheads with the mark of 666, create his own religion, persecute his enemies, and establish world peace. These great world powers would all converge at a final battle in Israel at Megiddo (Armageddon), at which point Jesus Christ would return.

Lindsey's vision reflected familiar Cold War concern with communist nations, but unlike Graham and others who saw the United States as the democratic hope of the world, the United States played a far less significant role in Lindsey's end-times cosmos. Lindsey believed that "according to the prophetic outlook" of the scriptures, the United States would either be greatly disempowered or become subsumed in the Beast's unified Europe. Lindsey argued that the United States had only instrumental value; if it could help Israel, it was important. Russia was a specific threat not because of its commitment to communism per se, but rather because "the Cossacks and other people of the Eastern part of Russia" threatened Israel.[27]

Lindsey may have believed that the United States would play no important role in the end of the world, but *Late Great Planet Earth* celebrated the special place that American baby boomers had in the divine plan. "It's happening," he wrote, "God is putting it all together. God may have His meaning for the 'now generation' which will have a greater effect on mankind than anything since Genesis 1." "Will you be ready," he asked his readers, "if we are to be a part of the prophetic 'now generation?' " The "now generation" was encouraged to keep a watchful eye on world events and consult with the prophetic texts that Lindsey identified as "filled with tingling vitality for the early twentieth century." Lindsey argued that the imminent rapture transported the "humdrum existence" of everyday Christians "into the worlds beyond."[28]

The Late Great Planet Earth struck a chord with the "now generation." "Rapture drills," or "rapture practice," in which watchful Christians prepared for their departure from the planet, became a kind of premillennial dispensationalist analogue to the "duck and cover" drills of the Cold War. While public school children prepared for atomic annihilation by ducking under their desks, Lindsey's readers hoped that they would escape the tribulation. *The Late Great Planet Earth* sold 7.5 million copies in its first decade, making it, according to *The New York Times*, the best-selling book of the 1970s.[29]

Zondervan was its first publishing home, but *The Late Great Planet Earth* crossed over into the general nonfiction bestseller world when it was republished in paperback by Bantam Books in 1973. Several eschatologically minded dispensationalist tomes soon followed. Tim LeHaye's 1972 *The Beginning of the End*, Jack Van Impe and Roger F. Campbell's *Israel's Final Holocaust* (1979), David Wilkerson's *The Vision* (1980), and Lindsey's own 1972 sequel, *Satan Is Alive and Well on Planet Earth*, all reveled in tales of the end of the world. In 1972, two Iowa-based filmmakers created *A Thief in the Night*, a low-budget horror movie that incorporated many of Lindsey's predictions and riffed on Norman's "I Wish We'd All Been Ready," verse—"A man and wife asleep in bed, she hears a noise and turns her head, he's gone, I wish we'd all been ready."[30] *A Thief in the Night* was a hit with evangelicals and led to multiple sequels. In 1978, *The Late Great Planet Earth* was made into a documentary-style film narrated by Orson Welles.

The apocalyptic themes swirling around Jesus people had a profound impact on Jesus music. "Are you watching?" asked 2nd Chapter of Acts, referring to an end-times parable about ten virgins (interpreted here as Christians) awaiting the arrival of their bridegroom (in this case, the Second Coming of Jesus), "Are you waiting? Are your lamps brightly burning for His returning?"[31] Randy Matthews' "Evacuation Day" emphasized the imminence of the rapture: "Got my bag packed, hope I leave this place tomorrow," he sang, "I'm gonna fly, fly, fly, Get on that ship and fly. With a ticket marked one way. Evacuation Day."[32] Love Song's "The Cossack Song" was a musical rendering of Lindsey's warning that Russia would, post-rapture, usher in Armageddon. "I wouldn't want to be a Cossack headed for that Palestine Road, thinking about what's written in the Word of God about the things that he's foretold," they sang.[33]

Lindsey's enthusiasm for Israel also found musical expression in Jesus music. Lamb, a messianic Jewish duo formed in 1972, celebrated the heavenly and the earthly Jerusalem. The song "Yahweh" by 2nd Chapter of Acts repeated Anglicized versions of Hebrew Bible names for God, including Yahweh, Eloi, and Emmanuel.[34]

An overt instance of this interest in Israel was Merla Watson's "Jehovah Jireh."[35] Merla and her spouse Merv led an influential Charismatic arts collective in Toronto, Canada, called "Toronto Catacombs." Like Lindsey, the Watsons fervently believed in Israel's importance in the last days and taught their thousands of Jesus people followers to do the same. The Watsons built on themes from the Latter Rain movement, a Canadian-born revival of the late 1940s. The movement was widespread in white Pentecostal circles, and influenced historically by British Israelism—the idea that people of British descent were the true people of Israel. Their services included enthusiastic "praise and worship" celebrations filled with biblical imagery, which linked the twentieth-century church to the nation of Israel.[36] "Send us the latter rain," sang the Watsons. They blew a shofar to signal their affinity with ancient Israel and borrowed sounds from Yiddish songs and klezmer music. "Jehovah Jireh," Merla Watson's best-known song, was a reference to the location where God relieved Abraham of his need to sacrifice Isaac.

While Christian Youth Musicals often framed "hippies" and "rebels" as a threat to American society, Jesus people saw the counterculture as, to borrow a biblical phrase, a field white unto harvest.[37] Many of their efforts at evangelism echoed the tried-and-true methods of the Pentecostal and Charismatic congregations that had welcomed them, which meant that music was key to making converts. Jesus musicians set up equipment wherever young people congregated—on beaches, in parks, on college campuses, even on abandoned lots. Chuck Smith's Calvary Chapel held their meetings in a circus-sized tent while they built a 2,500-seat auditorium to accommodate their Jesus-people-fueled growth. The Jesus people drew crowds in with music and then preached about the love of God and the imminent end of the world.

Calvary Chapel's old church building was bought by a businessman who turned it into Maranatha Village, a bookstore and artisan craft and gift shop, complete with an in-house audio studio and live-radio broadcasting capacity.[38] Following in the footsteps of D. L. Moody and Aimee Semple McPherson, Jesus musicians got the word out through flyers, West Coast Charismatic church networks, and radio spots on gospel stations. Singer-songwriter Keith Green self-consciously drew upon the legacy of nineteenth-century revivalist Charles Finney. In many ways, the evangelistic methods of Jesus people resembled the early twentieth-century tent revivals of J. O. McClurkan and the Bensons more than they did the respectable televangelism of the Billy Graham Evangelistic Association.[39]

Jesus people also put their own anti-authoritarian, hippie spin on the long-standing revivalist rejection of "cold religion" in favor of spiritual fervor. Like many in their generation, they prized "authenticity" and depicted their casual, expressive worship services as evidence of an authentic *relationship* with God as opposed to a superficial encounter with buttoned-down *religion*.[40]

"Little Country Church," by the group Love Song, expressed Jesus people's frustration with "stuffy" pastors. Their revival was about beauty and simplicity: "That little church has come alive, workin' with each other for the common good, puttin' all the past aside, long hair, short hair, some coats and ties."[41]

The idea that critics like Wilkerson were preoccupied with superficial things like haircuts and had lost sight of central Christian teachings was a common theme in Jesus music. Country Faith's "Ballad of the Lukewarm" by Chuck Butler lampooned those who invested in institutional "church and the state" but ignored the poor.[42] "Long hair" Jesus musicians had a lot of early detractors, like Wilkerson, but it did not take long for a few key "short hair" evangelicals to see in their beach-side baptisms the legitimate work of the Spirit of God.

Explo '72 and the "Silenced" Majority

Media-savvy evangelicals quickly recognized the power of Jesus music and sought to capitalize on its appeal among the young. In the spring of 1970, just a few months after Woodstock, United Methodist pastor and professor

Rev. Dr. Bob Lyon and a few of his seminary students at Asbury Theological Seminary created "Ichthus Festival."[43] Held at the Wilmore Campground in Kentucky, the site of turn-of-the-century Holiness revival meetings, Ichthus was meant to be an antidote to what Lyon and his students saw in the free-love, drug-infused debauchery in New York. At Ichthus, artists and their audience could worship, dance, and pray. Early Jesus musicians like Ron and Bill Moore, who were Methodist missionary kids, performed at the inaugural festival.

In 1971 it was clear that "hippie Jesus," his followers, and their music were having a moment in American pop culture. The Jesus movement had successfully "rebranded" Christianity, translating it into the language and aesthetics of 1960s counterculture.[44] Images of bearded, shaggy-haired young men baptizing young people on California beaches graced the pages of major news outlets. Andrew Lloyd Webber's rock opera *Jesus Christ Superstar*, which began as a chart-topping concept album in 1970, debuted, as did Stephen Schwartz's *Godspell*. Both productions depicted Jesus as a countercultural hero. On the cover of its Good Friday editions in 1966, *Time Magazine* had asked "Is God Dead?" Five years later, the cover depicted a psychedelic Jesus under the words "The Jesus Revolution."[45]

That year, Chuck Smith's Calvary Chapel Costa Mesa created the Maranatha! Music record label, which captured the music of the Saturday-night concerts at the church. Soon, conservative Bible-college students flocked to Jesus-music concerts in the Bay Area and Southern California. For many, the concerts were life changing. "I was at a Larry Norman concert where he taught that the opposition to Christian 'Rock' was based in racism," said Teri Sramek, a student at San Jose Bible College in the late 1970s, "and 2nd Chapter of Acts inspired me to dig deeper into the role of the Holy Spirit in my life."[46]

Televangelists took note. In 1971, Charismatic television preacher Kathryn Kuhlman invited Calvary Chapel's Chuck Smith and his mentee, the hippie evangelist Lonnie Frisbee, along with dozens of other long-haired Jesus people, to share the sights and sounds of the movement on her television program.[47] Both Kuhlman and *Time Magazine* saw the Jesus people as inheritors of the Pentecostal revivals of the past.[48] Billy Graham gave them a full-throated endorsement in the pages of *Christianity Today*, noting that the Jesus movement was largely responsible for the dramatic increase in the number of young people attending his crusades. "By and large," he wrote in the pages of the nation's most influential white evangelical outlet, "it is a genuine movement of the Spirit of God."[49]

From June 12 to June 17 of 1972, Graham helped welcome Jesus music into the heart of white evangelical activism. Graham was the main preacher for

"Explo '72," a Campus Crusade for Christ–sponsored "spiritual explosion" of a music festival in Dallas, Texas.[50] The event brought the Charismatic fervor of West Coast hippie evangelism together with the chief revivalist of the Baptist establishment. *The New York Times* gave the "religious Woodstock" front-page coverage and reported that 75,000 young people had attended (organizers argued that the crowd exceeded 100,000).[51]

Graham, ever the canny revivalist, saw in the enthusiastic response to Jesus music what he saw in radio and television specials: an opportunity to create converts in droves through mass media. Campus Crusade for Christ released a live recording of selections from the festival titled *Jesus Sound Explosion*. White Jesus-people acts like Larry Norman, Randy Mathews, and Love Song performed, as did Black Gospel artists like Willa Dorsey and crossover superstars Andraé Crouch & the Disciples. Country artists Connie Smith and the "Man in Black" Johnny Cash were also included. Southern Gospel legends the Speer Family closed the album with a rubato performance of Gloria Gaither's anthem to the Second Coming, "The King Is Coming." Armageddon, the Campus Crusade house band, gave a Billy Graham–esque invitation with their song "One Way." "Have you considered Jesus?" they asked, "Do you know what it means to know him? Has anyone told you, he loves you?" The album artwork featured pictures of sprawling crowds of festival attendees, as well as a photo of Billy Graham and Johnny Cash waving to the audience while standing before brightly colored staging meant to appeal to a psychedelic aesthetic.

In many ways, the preaching and musical lineup at Explo '72 also demonstrated that the efforts of the National Association of Evangelicals to create a coalition of the faithful under the category of "evangelical" were paying off. Fans of Southern Gospel, Black Gospel, and Jesus music may have occupied distinct demographic segments of society in the United States, but the fact that these diverse artists shared the stage at Explo '72 indicated that they could be brought together to encourage evangelical Christian conversion. Graham, Campus Crusade, and many others also recognized through Explo '72 that Jesus music had captured the ears and hearts of the youth group crowd. Graham was used to being the main event, but at Explo '72 he was not the primary draw. Graham's appeal in the 1970s rested on his status as a representation of middle-class white American values, his Southern Baptist ordination, his ability to draw crowds, and his proximity to the presidency. But there was nothing *cool* about Graham. That honor belonged to the jeans-wearing, sideburn-sporting Jesus rockers.

Billy Graham saw in Explo '72 a potential avenue for conservative political activism. Graham identified attendees as "not the silent majority—but the 'silenced' majority comprised of great, wonderful young people."[52] He tried to translate fervor for Jesus among the overwhelmingly white crowds of young people into political support for his friend Richard Nixon. Nixon had enfranchised eighteen- to twenty-one-year-old Americans when he signed the Voting Rights Act Amendment in 1970, and he was eager to connect with young conservatives. Bill Bright of Campus Crusade for Christ rejected Nixon's request to appear on stage, but Graham made sure to share his platform with the president. During the very week of the now-infamous Watergate break-in, he read a telegram from Nixon to a very receptive audience.[53]

On the surface, using Jesus music to drum up support for the Republican president seemed counterintuitive. After all, the imminent Second Coming made national elections pale in comparison. In addition, Nixon's "law and order" conservatism, while favored by mainstream white evangelicals, had limited appeal in the Jesus movement. Some Jesus people pointed to Jesus himself as the ultimate rebel as they protested the Vietnam War.[54]

Dallas, Texas, however, was a long way from the Bay Area. Explo '72 attendees reflected the Campus Crusade network more than they did the "Jesus freaks" of California. Graham rightly reckoned that Explo '72 attendees were by and large made mostly of "goodnik," Nixon-supporting, pro–Vietnam War conservatives.[55] The event took place between June 12 and June 17, which included Flag Day, and Campus Crusade organizers hosted a "5,000 Military for the Master" celebration of the United States armed forces. In an informal survey conducted by *The Dallas Morning News*, Explo '72 attendees supported President Nixon five to one over his Democratic challenger.[56]

As the 1970s wore on, there were signs that Graham's mainstream evangelical sensibilities were beginning to shape Jesus music. End-times fervor, for example, once core to the Jesus movement, became tempered by Graham's patriotic evangelical jeremiad.[57] After folk singer-songwriter Barry McGuire became a born-again Christian in 1971, he reframed his 1965 protest hit "Eve of Destruction." The original captured the fear of the geo-political unrest of the day and frustration with the United States' response to racism, hate, and war.[58]

To this gloomy take on the destruction of society, Barry added in 1974 a theologically minded addendum in the form of two songs on Myrrh Records. "Don't Blame God" absolved God of any blame for world crises, and "II Chronicles 7:14" invited the hearer to pray for the healing of their land.[59] For many of McGuire's listeners, this was a lament for the United States and a call for God to intercede on its behalf.

Myrrh Records artist David Meece encouraged the United States as a nation to respond to God in a manner similar to the prodigal son in his song commemorating the American bicentennial in 1976. Meece lamented that Americans had wandered away from God, who was pleading with them:

> Won't you come home America
> Won't you come home to me[60]

Contemporary Christian Music

Jesus people made a big splash in the early 1970s, but they were a relatively small subculture. The movement had largely faded from national headlines by the mid-1970s. Jesus music, however, left a lasting footprint in the wider American evangelical landscape. Pastors and congregants, especially on the West Coast, began to adopt the casual dress and slang of Jesus people. Lifting hands, crying, and dancing to worship music that included drums and electric guitars became commonplace in many Charismatic congregations.

"The Easter Song" by 2nd Chapter of Acts, Merla Watson's "Jehovah Jireh," and Children of the Day's "For Those Tears I Died" crossed over into the mainstream of white evangelicalism.[61] Love Song's eponymous album was *Billboard*'s top religious album of 1973.[62] A month after Explo '72, Word Records announced that it was launching an imprint called Myrrh Records, "a Jesus Rock label with a more modern sound than the company's flagship label."[63] Billy Ray Hearn ran Myrrh and signed influential Jesus-music artists like 2nd Chapter of Acts, Barry McGuire, Randy Matthews, Petra, and many others.[64]

Christian music festivals also became a go-to form of evangelical entertainment, education, and evangelism.[65] Festivals sprang up wherever there were fans of Jesus music: Salem, Oregon; Greenville, Illinois; Lansing, Michigan; St. Louis, Missouri; and many other cities and towns in the United States. Across the ocean, outside London, the Greenbelt festival began.

Like Ichthus, most Christian musical festivals were sponsored or hosted by churches and parachurch organizations with historic ties to Pentecostal, Holiness, and Baptist denominations. Many were held at venues that generations earlier had hosted camp meeting revivals.[66] The annual "Jesus" festivals—Jesus '73, Jesus '74, Jesus '76, and Jesus '78—began in Morgantown, Pennsylvania, but eventually moved near Disney World in Orlando when it partnered with Calvary Assembly of God.[67] Chuck Girard of Love Song, Phil Keaggy, Reba Rambo (daughter of Southern Gospel legend Dottie), the Imperials, and Andraé Crouch were certainly major festival draws.

Christian music festivals were just as indebted to big-tent revivalism as they were to rock concerts, and many artists gave evangelical altar calls, sermonettes, and exhortations for godly living. As Graham had done in Explo '72, Christian music festivals often featured fiery preaching about the need for America to turn back to God—from up-and-coming conservatives like C. J. Mahaney, Charismatic YWAM founder Loren Cunningham, "bapticostal" Pat Robertson—and, of course, end-times predictions from Hal Lindsey.[68]

In addition, Jesus music became a presence on revivalist radio airwaves. NRB-affiliated radio stations began to include rock and pop music hours (often late at night) aimed at younger listeners alongside their stable of radio preachers, church services, and operatic vocals with organ accompaniment.[69] Many radio revivalists of the "Electric Church" initially saw music as a side dish to the main course of Bible teaching and preaching, but as the 1970s progressed, the old-time listeners and young music fans began to share space on the evangelical airwaves.[70]

Christian bookstores arguably did more than any other institution to tie together the fates of old-school evangelical music and new-school rock and folk sounds. Label executives at Word and Benson and distributors like Gospelrama Productions wanted their music played on Top 40 radio and placed in mainstream music retail outlets like Tower Records, Sam Goody, or Wherehouse. But for the most part, the industry expanded in the 1970s by distributing music through CBA Christian bookstores.[71] While it was true that CBA bookstores did not have the distribution power of mainstream retailing giants, they had been growing steadily since the 1960s. Christian bookstores also had deep, longstanding ties to denominational bodies like the Southern Baptist Convention or the Assemblies of God, which were growing at unprecedented rates in the late twentieth century.[72]

Of course, even with Billy Graham's endorsement, there were holdouts when it came to Christian rock. Assemblies of God preacher (and cousin to Jerry Lee Lewis) Jimmy Swaggart refused to see anything but the devil in rock music. Conservative minister and media maker Bill Gothard taught that the "syncopated rhythms" of Christian rock were dangerous. The "rough sounds" of Jesus music were still a bit much for many evangelical churchgoers in the 1970s.

Figures like Word Records' Evie Tornquist, however, a teenaged Norwegian-American singer signed in the early 1970s, helped bridge the generation gap between gospel aficionados, inspirational music, and Jesus rock.[73] Known professionally in the United States as Evie, she recorded hymns like "Amazing Grace," Andraé Crouch's Black Gospel "The Blood Will Never Lose Its Power," and Holiness songbook legacy Bob Benson Sr. and Phil Johnson's "Give Them

All to Jesus." She also sang Kurt Kaiser tunes like "Pass It On," and Larry Norman's "I Wish We'd All Been Ready."

Evie's sweet vocals and smooth arrangements of Jesus rock softened some of the hard sonic edges of the genre. Her record label promoted the blonde singer's "pretty smile" and "enormous dimples" as much as they did her music, and many fans regarded her as the embodiment of the kind of femininity that figures like best-selling author Marabel Morgan were promoting in the 1970s: a beautiful Christian woman of virtue who was available and adventurous when it came to sex with her husband.[74] Evie's impressive sales and sold out arena tours demonstrated that blurring the boundaries between mainstay gospel sounds and innovative Jesus music could be profitable. Other pop hopefuls, like Kathie Lee Johnson (née Epstein) from Oral Roberts University, produced pop Christian albums in the late 1970s. Soon, even Southern Gospel mainstays like the Imperials began to experiment with newer, less nostalgic sounds.

For the most part, the core customers for most Christian bookstores in the late 1970s were parents—mothers in particular—who flocked to CBA stores to find music that would promote faith through popular music.[75] As many in the "now generation" settled into marriage and child-rearing, they voiced concerns about raising their children Christianly—just as their parents had. Albums like Word Records' 1974 *Agapeland* and Sparrow/Birdwing Records' 1977 *The Music Machine* and *Bullfrogs and Butterflies* (1978), as well as children's albums by Candle, a group that grew out of a Southern Californian Jesus movement group called Agape Force, were popular options for mothers of young children. *The Music Machine*, in particular, was a big seller for Sparrow and proved that there was a growing market for music created to teach Christian principles to kids.[76]

The varieties of music sold in Christian bookstores were indicative of how quickly the buying tastes of white American evangelicals were expanding. Once outlets for primarily Southern Gospel and choral arrangements, by the mid-1970s, CBA stores sold Southern Gospel music, Black Gospel music, "inspirational" music (formerly "sacred" music about God or Christianity that had pop-music sensibilities also sometimes referred to as middle of the road), and Jesus music.

Jesus music appealed to young people, but getting prominent placement in bookstores, which served a very conservative white Protestant consumer base, was another story. Larry Norman's frank musical depictions of LSD, STDs, and "the perfect lay," after all, were a far cry from the Bill Gaither Trio's wholesome rapture tunes or pop-princess Debby Boone's ballads.[77] By the late 1970s, however, business-savvy bookstores like Zondervan's Puente Hills Mall location in suburban Los Angeles, or Maranatha Village in Santa Ana, were each making around $500,000 a year—roughly a quarter of their total sales—from music, which proved that a Christian music industry was viable.[78]

One city symbolized the growing symbiosis among print publishers, record labels, and Jesus music: Nashville, Tennessee. John T. and Eva Green Benson's Holiness hometown and the Southern Baptist's publishing headquarters became home to a burgeoning Charismatic Jesus music scene in the 1970s, which further blurred the boundaries between traditional gospel and Jesus rock. The unexpected epicenter of Jesus music was Nashville's Belmont Avenue Church of Christ. As a Church of Christ congregation, Belmont followed the organization's strict prohibition of instrumental accompaniment. When Pastor Don Finto took over, however, the congregation experienced some of the Charismatic fires that had burned through Southern California a few years earlier. As in Costa Mesa, the revivals were accompanied by rock and folk music. Belmont Avenue Church of Christ opened Koinonia Coffeehouse in 1973 and aspiring artists, songwriters, and producers flooded the cafe to share music and see bands like Fireworks, 2nd Chapter of Acts, Honeytree, and Dogwood.[79]

The fact that Jesus music had made such inroads in the heart of the Southern Gospel scene demonstrated that Jesus people had—in the eyes of many evangelicals—successfully baptized rock and roll and incorporated it into the evangelical media marketplace. Graham's embrace was followed by a reluctant about-face by David Wilkerson, who acknowledged that *some* Jesus musicians were in it for the right reasons. Former critic Bob Larson had a similar conversion experience.

In 1974, *Billboard* reported that groups like Love Song were breaking religious music sales records, and that Myrrh Records' Jesus music roster was an "exciting" turn for parent company Word Records. It was clear that the grassroots Jesus music and traditional gospel music businesses were poised to grow together.[80] In the mid-1970s, Jarrell McCracken sold Word Records—with its gospel-, sacred-, and Jesus-music imprints—to media conglomerate ABC. In 1975, Continentals founder Cam Floria created the Christian Artists Seminar in the Rockies, an annual gathering that featured seminars, training, and talent showcases to highlight emerging talent. Attendance grew rapidly from year to year. In 1976 Billy Ray Hearn left Myrrh in Waco to found his own Southern California–based label, Sparrow Records, and signed Keith Green, who became one of the best-selling and best-known Jesus-music artists.

While Hearn was bringing Jesus musicians into the Word Records fold, one Sunday evening in 1976, a teen girl brought her guitar and a song from the Lord to Belmont Avenue Church of Christ in Nashville. Her earnest performance was welcomed heartily by people in the pews, even though as a Church of Christ church, instrumentation during worship was strictly prohibited. Belmont Church promptly left the Church of Christ and became a non-denominational Charismatic congregation.

That young woman, Amy Grant, and her youth leader from church, Brown Bannister, created a demo that got the attention of Word Records. Her debut album, *Amy Grant*, was released in 1977. Grant demonstrated how disparate strands of Christian-themed music could converge in one artist. Her great-grandfather A. M. Burton had helped establish revivalist radio in Nashville, which rooted her in the Holiness songbook tradition. Grant's presence at Belmont Church and in Koinonia Coffeehouse gave her music a sonic connection to the Jesus people.[81] Grant was also far more polished than Jesus rockers like Larry Norman, who scandalized listeners with songs about day drinking and gonorrhea, or Keith Green, who was known to sermonize as much or more than he sang. By contrast, Grant was poised, professional, and in many ways a pop-star version of the ideal evangelical young person that the Spurrlows and Up with People had sought to showcase.

This burgeoning evangelical music scene brought different (traditionally white) genres together through commerce and activism. Bill Gaither sounded a lot different than Randy Matthews, but they both performed at Explo '72, their music was sold at Christian bookstores, and their work was used by evangelical leaders like Graham to create coalitions. In addition, many Jesus musicians and Southern Gospelers shared a conviction that people were influenced by mass media, and that if Christians were going to influence their culture for the good, and create social change, the most efficient, common-sense way to do that was by creating media soaked in Christian ideas.[82] In previous eras that may have been accomplished through pamphlets or songbooks or radio; in the late twentieth century it was through recorded music.

The fact that there was no clear consensus about what constituted "Christian" thought when it came to the major moral and theological issues of the late 1970s, however, complicated the effort to unite different varieties of Christian music under one banner. The "short hair" versus "long hair" cultural and musical conflicts between rockers and traditionalists remained. The deepest point of contention was existential: what *were* the artists and record labels and music festivals at their core: ministry? art? entertainment? business?

No one could agree on a name for the music either—was it "sacred," or "inspirational," or "religious" music? Toward the end of the decade, a group of young journalists on the West Coast began to create what would become a record of those theological tensions and musical developments. In 1978, a local tabloid paper aimed at keeping the burgeoning Orange County Calvary Chapel community apprised of the goings-on in the area printed its first issue under the name of *Contemporary Christian Acts*. By far, the most popular content in the newsletter was music related.[83] In response to the growing demand, the newsletter morphed into a full-fledged music magazine. In its pages, readers found carefully researched sales charts, album reviews, industry news, and artists' profiles.

Born in the heart of the Jesus movement, the paper quickly became the *Billboard* of evangelical music. It covered the complex conglomeration of Southern Gospel, Black Gospel, Jesus rock, middle of the road/pop, and easy-listening music being sold in Christian bookstores and other venues. The name of the magazine, which would encapsulate the diverse theological, ethical, and political impulses of this growing group of media makers, would become synonymous with industry as a whole: *Contemporary Christian Music*.

4

"Hearts in Motion"

The Polish, Professionalism, and Political Activism of Contemporary Christian Music (1979–1991)

One chilly evening in November of 1979, two Assembly of God ministers from St. Paul, Minnesota, built a bonfire to ward off the devil. They were inspired by a story from the book of Acts, in which newly converted Christians burned magical books. The young people of the Twin Cities were asked to consign "demonic" music—AC/DC, Kiss, and Prince—to the flames. The ministers, brothers Steve and Dan Peters, had invited some local television reporters to cover the event, and soon, fiery images of such protests had spread around the nation. The Peters brothers and other self-taught evangelical "media experts" told parents and teens that popular music was a key battlefield in a cosmic war for the souls of the young and the future of the United States. Brandishing transgressive song lyrics and album covers, they offered workshops, published books, and created films urging watchful caregivers to avoid the dangers of popular music.

If music could be used by the devil to destroy American young adults, however, perhaps music—the right kind of music—could save them. Evangelical media experts reasoned that Contemporary Christian Music could be just what they needed. Their know-how shaped the buying practices of a growing group of suburban evangelical parents, youth pastors, and other caregivers. As the market niche of Contemporary Christian Music grew between 1979 and 1991, the top of the *CCM* charts were filled with figures who fulfilled these parental wishes. Pop stars like Amy Grant, rockers like Petra, theatrical showmen like Carman, and church-y virtuosos like Sandi Patty were deployed by parents, pastors, and other activists to preach the gospel, protect the young, strengthen the family, promote holiness, dramatize the Christian spiritual battle, bolster patriotism, and incite public action. While mass-media magnates like Jerry Falwell and Pat Robertson mobilized conservative white Protestants to lobby for conservative public policy as part of the "Reagan revolution," top-selling CCM created imaginative moral and spiritual visions that energized and shaped those efforts.

Building a Christian Legacy: Bookstores and the Buying Power of White Evangelical Moms

In 1979, Bob Dylan released *Slow Train Coming*, which was, for all intents and purposes, a Contemporary Christian album. Dylan reported having a mystical experience with Jesus and converted to Christianity. He was mentored by Vineyard luminaries Larry Myers, Bill Dwyer, and Kenn Gulliksen, who had provided spiritual guidance for numerous Jesus-music performers.[1] Dylan developed an apocalyptic imagination about the Second Coming and began telling his fans to get ready for Armageddon and the thousand-year reign of Jesus. *Slow Train Coming* included songs that expressed Dylan's anticipation of the end of time, including "When He Returns."

The conversion of Dylan, considered to be one of the greatest songwriters in American history, was cause for excitement in CCM circles. Many expected that Dylan's conversion would create evangelical revival among the folk legend's fan base. It did not. *Slow Train Coming* did go platinum, however, and it earned Dylan an evangelical fan base and a Dove Award, along with a Grammy.

As enamored as they had been by Jesus music's end-times vision, by the time "America's young majority"—those conservative white evangelicals who fell in love with Larry Norman at events like Explo '72—grew up, got married, moved to the suburbs, and had families, they began thinking about how their children would keep the faith if Jesus did not return soon. Many sought music that did what Jesus rock had done for them: given them credible substitutes for the devil's music. Because, in its early days, Contemporary Christian Music was considered too niche for distribution at Tower Records or Wherehouse Records, the only place most evangelical parents could find CCM was in Christian bookstores.

In 1979, *Billboard Magazine* dedicated fifty pages to the "bullish future" of "Religious Music."[2] *Billboard*'s spotlight covered Black Gospel, Mormon, Catholic, Jewish, and "Messianic Jewish" music industries. But the largest and fastest-growing segment of the industry was CCM: music made mostly by and for conservative white evangelical Protestants.[3] About 80 percent of all CCM sales went through Christian bookstores, as did a majority of live-concert tickets and other merchandise. The sales charts in *CCM Magazine*, by that time *the* industry magazine, were based largely on reporting from CBA bookstores. The industry was driven, therefore, by the buying habits and tastes of Christian-bookstore customers.

Who were those customers? They were mostly white evangelical mothers looking for media to help them raise their children in the faith. "If you want to understand CCM sales," observed Christian marketing and retailing veteran Steve Potratz of the role that evangelical parents played in CCM, "you need to understand one word: legacy." This quirk of CCM's business model—that the bulk of sales came not through mainstream retailers marketing directly to teens, but through Christian bookstores, who marketed primarily to evangelical caregivers interested in passing the faith to their children—became its defining characteristic.

"Christian booksellers don't just market, they minister," observed *Billboard Magazine*'s Anna Sobczynski in 1981, "consequently, any idea conveyed via sound has to be a sound idea in a Christian sense as well."[4] The "Christian sense," of course, was quite specific. It reflected the theologies and tastes of bookstores that were overwhelmingly white-owned, white-serving, and suburban. Those bookstores were also run mostly by white evangelical denominations, or independent devotees with ties to historically white Baptist, Holiness, Pentecostal, and Charismatic congregations and denominations. Many factors, including long-standing redlining practices, which pushed non-white communities away from valuable suburban real estate, the historic whiteness of the Christian Booksellers Association, and the FBI's campaign against Black-owned bookstores in the 1970s, ensured that most Christian bookstore owners were white.[5]

The ministry of Christian Booksellers Association (CBA) bookstores was intertwined with National Religious Broadcasters (NRB), the primary broadcast outlet for CCM, which drove retail foot traffic to bookstores. Like the CBA, the NRB was primarily white, and by 1979 the association had developed from a smattering of radio stations spread across the nation to a flourishing coalition of 1,400 "religious broadcasters" that was adding about one new station per week.[6]

Christian radio stations thrived primarily in suburban areas and secondary cities like Birmingham, Alabama; San Bernardino, California; and of course Nashville, Tennessee. Far from the trend-setting American media centers like New York, Los Angeles, or Chicago, Christian radio tended to reflect established sonic consensus rather than experimentation. Bringing radio to the airwaves meant bringing CCM to vehicles, which, in suburban America, meant inviting CCM artists to be the soundtrack for moms doing school pick-ups and drop-offs, driving kids to soccer practice or art lessons, and, of course, shopping. Thus, as CCM grew with American suburban culture, it came to provide an ambient soundscape for the domestic lives of evangelical families.

For caregivers of very young children, finding music to shape the spiritual and moral lives of their children was fairly simple. Albums like Sparrow Records' *Music Machine* taught little ones about the fruits of the Spirit, while

Marantha! Music's *Kids Praise* records encouraged children to worship God. Buying music for adolescents, who had their own tastes and occupied their own marketing niche, was considerably more complicated. Popular music was, after all, a well-known medium around which young people formed their own identities and differentiated themselves from their parents. If the history of rock and roll was any indicator, parental efforts to successfully curate the musical tastes of American teenagers seemed unlikely to succeed.

Many late twentieth-century white evangelical parents were determined to try, however, because they were convinced that the future of the Christian faith and the social order of the United States rested in no small part on their shoulders. Popular ministries like Dr. James Dobson's Focus on the Family and Bill Gothard's Institute in Basic Life Principles argued that parents were responsible for the future of the nation because the nuclear family was the "divine institution" upon which the United States was built.[7]

Building off their nineteenth-century predecessors, Dobson, Gothard, and others helped make "parenting" a verb and focused much of their attention on the teenage years. Dobson, a multi-generational Nazarene, translated many of the Holiness codes of earlier generations into secular, psychological language. Dobson's best-selling *Preparing for Adolescence*, first published in 1978 as Dobson's "youth course for kids ages 9–14," was a particularly influential guide for parents and children eager to end the "epidemic of inferiority" and "sexual confusion" that Dobson believed plagued American youth.[8]

To lobby for public policy that promoted moral parenting, Dobson created the Family Research Council in 1981. Dobson's Focus on the Family sold a plethora of how-to manuals, videos, and workbooks at bookstores, and also broadcast popular radio programming to guide parents along the way. Many evangelical parents of the 1980s came to view their role through Dobson's lens.

Preparing for Adolescence depicted parents as football "coaches" in a high-stakes, win-or-lose "big game" of parenting. To lose was to undermine the social order and create insecure, drug-abusing young adults confused about their sex and sexuality. To win was to prepare heterosexual young women and men with good values and robust self-esteem. Children of the losers had sex outside of heterosexual marriage. Children of the winners practiced abstinence and were drug-free. If everything went according to plan, young men would be faithful providers and leaders of their household. Young women would be nurturing keepers of the home—and under no circumstances would they be feminists. Together, they would guarantee a preferable, prosperous future for the nation.[9]

As evangelicals sought to shape and discipline evangelical youth toward these ends, they found that while classes and books were good, concrete examples of young people who embodied those evangelical norms were even better. While evangelical parents bought books by Dobson and Gothard at bookstores, savvy CCM marketers found that it made all the sense in the world to pair that purchase with an album that reinforced those values through song. CCM pop stars, therefore, came to be highly valued assets for evangelical media makers and consumers looking to protect the young, promote the virtues of a God-honoring life, and celebrate the prosperity that accompanied the evangelical lifestyle.

Amy Grant and the Model Evangelical Life

Amy Grant was the first true breakout star of CCM and thus the most important role model for evangelicals of the 1980s. Her 1979 album *My Father's Eyes* took the singer to the top of *Billboard*'s best-selling "Inspirational LPs" charts. Soon she was invited to perform at Billy Graham crusades as an opening act for the Bill Gaither Trio. Grant was a natural fit for a Graham revival. Her camera-friendly smile, delicate beauty, and palpable enthusiasm for God and music attracted listeners young and old.

Grant's 1982 *Age to Age* was the first-ever platinum-selling Contemporary Christian album. It firmly established the singer-songwriter as the "Queen of Christian Pop."[10] Grant's star was rising just as music videos were growing in importance, which created new storytelling possibilities. In the video for her 1984 Grammy-winning song "Angels," Grant portrayed a teacher of young children. A picture of virginal innocence and wholesome beauty, Grant sang about how angelic forces kept her from a series of dangers that many parents of the eighties feared: a fast car, a dangerous-looking young man, and a room full of partying sophisticates drinking mysterious green drinks. "God only knows the times my life was threatened just today," she sang, before the chorus comforted her listeners with the assurance that God had protective "angels watching over me, every move I make." Christian television networks launched competitors to "Music Television," aka MTV, a cable channel that broadcast a steady stream of mainstream music videos. The evangelical versions included PTL's "Sound Effects" and TBN's "Real Videos: A Christian Music Video Show," and they put Grant's "Angels" in heavy rotation.

Grant's personal story, as she recounted it, was a testament to the power of legacy. Unlike Larry Norman or Keith Green, she had no dramatic tales of drugs or conversion. Grant grew up as an upper-class Southern white woman in a loving, multi-generational Christian household. She praised her mother as a spiritual mentor who helped her stay away from temptations like marijuana. In an interview with televangelists Jim and Tammy Faye Bakker, Grant dutifully chastised American youth for their unfocused politics and ignorance of biblical prophecy.[11]

Evangelical mass-media makers came to see Grant as an ideal partner for promoting "traditional" womanhood. In 1985, Sweet Publishing released *Amy Grant's Heart-to-Heart Bible Stories*, an audio collection of Bible stories written for young children. Though she had yet to become a mother, the cover featured Grant snuggling with two fair-haired children in a portrait of domestic bliss.[12]

When she married Gary Chapman and had her first child, Robert Schuller's periodical *Possibilities* portrayed the couple as the evangelical domestic ideal. Grant graced the pages of *The Christian Herald*, *Christian Life Magazine*, *Eternity Magazine*, *Today's Christian Woman*, Campus Crusade for Christ's *Campus Life Magazine*, Jerry Falwell's *The Fundamentalist Journal*, and the flagship Pentecostal and Charismatic periodical *Charisma Magazine*. As Christian bookstores expanded their offerings for evangelical women in the 1980s to include Christian romance novels like Janette Oke's *Love Comes Softly* series, stories of Grant's family life were consumed alongside fictional stories of love (without sex), individual conversions to evangelical Christianity, and prosperous, "abundant life."[13]

Mostly unmentioned in evangelical media was the obvious fact that Grant was hardly a stay-at-home mother. She was an industry powerhouse who financially supported not just her husband and children but her band, managers, promoters, and record-label employees. In her 1985 Grammy acceptance speech, Grant seemed to acknowledge these tensions. "[I want to thank] my sisters for staying home and having babies and giving my parents somebody to bump on their knee while I hit the road most of the year," she said, "and I want to thank my husband, Gary Chapman, because he's given me my songs to sing."[14]

If Grant was the evangelical Barbie of CCM, the unattainable ideal of beauty and virtue of her generation, her friend and collaborator Michael W. Smith was the complementary Ken doll. The blond, blue-eyed West Virginian attended Belmont Church along with Grant and was already well established as a songwriter before going out on his own in 1983 with *The Michael W. Smith Project*. One of Smith's biggest early hits was "Friends," which he co-wrote with his wife, Debby, and performed on tour with Grant. Together on stage, Smith and Grant wrapped their arms each other another and sang about the wonders of Christian friendship. The good-looking pair, married to other people, were a portrait of chaste evangelical values in action. Hundreds of youth-group members stared up at them in teary admiration, held hands, swayed to the music, and sang along.

Smith's 1983 "Be Strong and Courageous," which charged believers to live like the biblical figure Joshua, may have appealed to CCM listeners looking for a positive depiction of men doing God's bidding, but it was the warnings to avoid the temptations of the "in crowd" and "sordid street" in songs like "Rocketown" (1986) or "All You're Missing Is a Heartache" (1988) that endeared him to anxious parents. Smith's Dove Award–winning 1986 album *The Big Picture* featured the abstinence anthem "Old Enough to Know," which advised a young woman not to give in to pressure from a man to have premarital sex.

In 1987, Smith—then thirty years old—published his first book, also called *Old Enough to Know*, which was aimed at teenagers. Co-written with Fritz Ridenour, author of evangelical advice books like *How to Be a Christian and Still Enjoy Life* and *How to Be a Christian without Being Perfect*, the book addressed pressing questions that figures like James Dobson believed were facing evangelical youth. "Michael's first book answers your questions," the *CCM Magazine* advertisement for *Old Enough to Know* promised, "about sex, drugs, empty religion, feeling good about yourself, alcohol, fighting with your parents, friends, and what to do with your life."[15]

Grant and Smith were the most prominent of a host of pop music entertainers who, in the eyes of many parents and youth pastors, served as examples of beauty, health, and prosperity. Male artists like Smith, Steven Curtis Chapman, Leon Patillo, David Meece, Bryan Duncan, and Benny Hester, with their denim jackets and skinny ties, were seen as wholesome, healthy alternatives to George Michael, Lionel Richie, or Bryan Adams.[16] Meanwhile, Grant, Debby Boone, Twila Paris, Michelle Pillar, Lisa Whelchel, and Leslie Phillips, with their hair scrunchies and shoulder pads, were modest versions of Madonna or Cyndi Lauper. In addition to visually representing the virtues of evangelicalism, CCM songs often celebrated the personal benefits of the faith. "I never knew I'd receive so much," sang Debby Boone in 1985, "when I accepted you."

Top-selling CCM pop stars of the 1980s embraced certain sounds over others. "Middle of the road" soft-rock sounds that emphasized melodies and harmonies and synthesized piano were common. Disco beats were rare. Disco stars like Donna Summer or the Village People regularly ruled mainstream charts in the late 1970s and early 1980s, but the genre's association with Black and gay culture made it an unlikely choice for CCM.[17]

CCM figures were marketed as public testimonies to the power of the evangelical gospel, which meant that the artists were subjected to an additional level of scrutiny for their conformity to white evangelical ideals. Record labels included morality clauses that would ensure their roster would live up to evangelical moral standards, which usually included faithfulness in marriage, modest clothing, and abstaining from drugs and drunkenness. For bigger acts like Grant, managers curated "image associations" with corporate sponsors that aligned with evangelical mores and steered clear of partnerships with alcohol or tobacco companies.[18] Some complained behind the scenes that the standard for living was impractical and oppressive, but many CCM musicians and artists enthusiastically endorsed rigorous standards for holy living from the stage.

For women in particular, the spotlight of CCM was a dilemma that showed that the industry had not strayed far from its Holiness and Pentecostal roots. On the one hand, to sell records to evangelical consumers, it was important to visibly embody what godly living could do for a believer, which—for a woman—included being seen as marriage material. The ideal CCM star, therefore, would have a chaste, disciplined body that conformed to white middle-class beauty standards. Sparrow Records, for example, featured the music of pop singer (and *The Facts of Life* star) Lisa Whelchel when they produced Stormie Omartian's Christian aerobics videos, which sought to sculpt women's bodies to a petite, wifely ideal.

On the other hand, if one was too attractive, according to contemporary standards, one could be accused of enticing men with sexual worldliness, a violation of Holiness standards of modesty and purity. On the industry side of things, the overwhelming majority of Contemporary Christian decision-makers—record executives, A&R representatives, and bookstore owners—were men, and in most cases, those men were the arbiters of what constituted crossing the line from wifely ideal to inappropriately provocative. Many women of CCM were deemed to be in the latter category.

No one exemplified these tensions more than Amy Grant. As Grant cranked out hit after hit, her body and her body of work became the site for an ongoing conversation among evangelicals. As they talked about Grant, evangelicals considered the right relationship between Christians and mainstream culture in the United States, and the appropriate role of Christian women in the public sphere. When Grant's album cover featured a V-neck shirt with the first three buttons unbuttoned, it scandalized vigilant observers. Grant's album was banned by some bookstore owners who retained Holiness code sensibilities and believed even the suggestion of risqué outer garb indicated inner corruption. The incident became known in certain industry circles as the "Three Button Controversy."

The bigger Grant's fame, the more carefully evangelicals measured her words and actions against their standards of godliness. When Word Records' 1985 distribution deal with A&M Records gave Grant access to mainstream retail outlets, her album *Unguarded* sold more copies outside the CBA bookstore network than inside it, a first for a CCM artist. Grant's management team rejoiced, but some fans were worried that mainstream success brought with it moral and spiritual compromise.[19]

Grant gave an interview in *Rolling Stone* that year that seemed to confirm those fears. The article included vignettes that upheld Grant's status as a wholesome evangelical woman—she was portrayed as a devout member of Belmont Church and was quoted affirming sex within the boundaries of heterosexual marriage. But the interview *also* included stories about how Grant had sunbathed naked and enjoyed sex. "My hormones are on key as any other 24-year-old," she said, and Grant frankly acknowledged that she understood how sex appeal helped her sell records. "I'm trying to look sexy to sell a record," she acknowledged, "But what is sexy? To me it's never been taking my shirt off or having my tongue sticking out. I feel that a Christian young woman in the '80s is very sexual."[20]

CCM Magazine was flooded with letters about the interview. Those who praised Grant argued that a song from a pop star could reach a lot more of the unsaved than any traditional hymn or gospel song could. Those scandalized by Grant wondered whether the singer was "running wild," "too secular," or "too worldly." *Christianity Today* reported that there were many who questioned the wisdom of "Christian singers who try to appeal to a secular audience." "To me," opined Assemblies of God rock opponent Jimmy Swaggart, "Amy Grant's music is a very fleshy, sensual program of music undermining Christianity itself."[21]

For pop rocker Leslie Phillips, life as a moral exemplar was suffocating. "[M]y record company was demanding dishonesty from me, saying weird things like, 'This song just sounds a little too sexy. We don't know why, but you've got to change it,'" Phillips recalled in a 2009 interview. She made up her mind to leave the confines of CCM but was still bound by her contract with Myrrh. Phillips understood how important it was for CCM pop stars to conform to evangelical norms, especially around a woman's sexuality, and used that to her advantage. "There's a moral clause in my contract," she reportedly told Myrrh executives in 1987, "And you know what? I've slept with someone that I'm not married to. And I'm not ashamed to tell anybody about that. And I will."[22] She and Myrrh parted ways that year.

Phillips was not the only one for whom the norms of CCM were too confining. Many CCM songwriters and music critics voiced frustration with the relentless positivity of CCM pop tunes. In 1984, one critic complained that Amy Grant's pleasant performances were "antiseptic"—"just an avuncular God, a steady beat and good lighting." In the pages of *CCM Magazine*, singer-songwriter John Fischer bemoaned the fact that most CCM was fan-pleasing music that upheld the safety and security of the music industry rather than challenging its listenership. Contemporary Christianity in the United States, Fischer warned in 1987, was "at its worst: no blood, no thorns, no cross, no hunger, no pain, no rain."[23]

Fischer's comments were widely disregarded by CCM radio stations and CCM consumers, however, who viewed CCM pop stars as living proof that the evangelical message *worked* in the life of the believer. After all, evangelical tastemakers like Billy Graham, Robert Schuller, Norman Vincent Peale, and James Dobson claimed that living according to evangelical principles would result in tangible secular benefits—a strong democracy, a loving family, a healthy psyche, a happy life. Showing that prosperity to the wider world was a part of sharing the Good News. From this perspective, focusing too much on sin or torment or poverty compromised that public witness. In addition, pop songs were short—usually around three to five minutes in length—which meant that if a song needed to show that Christianity would bring benefits of godly living by the end of the song (or preferably by the bridge or chorus), themes of suffering and death, while historically key to the Christian message, must be skipped or at least curtailed.

For young evangelicals whose parents were wary of the messaging in mainstream culture, pleasing pop entertainers like Smith and Grant were not just moral exemplars but highly prized windows to an outside world. They were cool enough for the kids, but ultimately not too edgy for the parents. "That was the way our parents liked it," observed journalist Tyler Huckabee, who grew up in a conservative home with parents who introduced him to Amy Grant as a substitute for mainstream music, "and the songs were catchy enough that we didn't mind it either."[24]

In 1986, when Grant released a duet with Peter Cetera that topped mainstream charts, CCM listeners were mostly proud of her. The aim of CCM pop entertainers was, after all, to occupy with wholesome evangelical values the same space as any other pop star. By all accounts, Grant's music was meant for stadiums from the beginning. Her management team actively avoided having her perform for churches or youth groups, and, atop the *Billboard* charts, Grant was the undisputed First Lady of CCM pop. But the *CCM* charts revealed that evangelical buyers still had a taste for music firmly rooted in the sanctuary.

Sandi Patty, Special Music, and the Star-Spangled Banner

Amy Grant was not the only chart-topping powerhouse who got her start by opening for the Bill Gaither Trio. Sandi Patty, a studio singer-turned-soloist, whose soaring and acrobatic soprano performances quickly earned her the nickname "the voice," had deep roots in the Holiness songbook establishment. A Church of God (Anderson) music minister's daughter, Patty studied music at Anderson College, the Gaithers' alma mater, and her big voice and big hits like "How Majestic Is Your Name" had her headlining gospel concerts by 1984.

Patty and many other choral singers—Larnelle Harris, Steve Green, Russ Taff—as well as ensembles like the Imperials and NewSong rose up through the ranks of old-school Southern Gospel networks and regularly appeared on *CCM* charts. For the most part, Patty and her colleagues embodied the traditionalism and nostalgia of their Southern Gospel roots. They did not adopt "cool" fashion trends like Michael W. Smith or Amy Grant—they often performed in conservative church dresses or three-piece suits. Indeed, most had no desire to compete with Madonna or Bon Jovi. Rather, like the Southern Gospel quartets that preceded them, soloists like Sandi Patty and Steve Green wowed audiences with inspirational displays of vocal virtuosity.

Southern Gospel quartets were initially vehicles for selling sheet music to church people, and in many ways the vocal acrobatics of Patty, Green, Taff, and others followed in that tradition with updated technology. If a music minister heard an inspirational vocal performance on Christian radio that he or she wanted to replicate, he or she could purchase a cassette tape of a well-known single with the vocal track stripped out, allowing a live performer to sing the song in church. These tapes—known as accompaniment tracks or performance tracks—were sold in several different keys at bookstores, in order to fit the register of the singer. Performance tracks of hits by Sandi Patty, Larnelle Harris, Steve Green, and Russ Taff became mainstays of evangelical worship. The moment in the service when CCM songs were performed came to be known as "special music."

Special music added a moment of entertainment and showmanship to church services and often served as the background for an offertory, for an altar call, or as a sermon illustration. Special music also filled the gap left by church choirs as choral singing gave way to small groups called "praise bands" or "worship bands," who used rock instruments.[25] More and more white evangelical congregations were trading church choirs for praise bands, and

CCM performance tracks gave churches of any size the opportunity to attempt large-scale productions. All you needed was a cassette player and a microphone. Of course, in most cases, the imitators paled in comparison to the original artist, but the prospect of re-creating stirring moments of vocal virtuosity as part of an offertory was a huge thrill.

Top-selling special music tracks often repeated historic Pentecostal, Holiness, and Baptist music themes. Sandi Patty's stirring rendition of Dottie Rambo's "We Shall Behold Him" sold well. Baptist Steve Green's plea for evangelism, "People Need the Lord," was popular. Pentecostal Russ Taff's "We Will Stand," a Second Coming–themed petition for revival and Christian unity, was the soundtrack of choice for many multi-church gatherings.

Steve Green's "Household of Faith," recorded in 1986 as a duet with his spouse Marijean, updated the nostalgia and traditional domesticity of Southern Gospel classics like "My Mother's Bible." Sung between a husband and wife, the song announced the couple's intention to invest in creating a secure nuclear household. "We'll build a household of faith," Steve and Marijean sang, "That together we can make / And when the strong winds blow it won't fall down." The performance track for "Household of Faith," along with Steven Curtis Chapman's 1989 ode to long and faithful marriages, "I Will Be Here," became wedding-ceremony standards.[26]

The Greens' musical affirmation of heterosexual marriage struck a chord with many evangelicals who feared that the "homosexual agenda" threatened the nuclear family and the structures of American public life. "The Christian home is the basic unit of our society," Billy Graham had argued for many years. "Our nation can never rise higher than its home life."[27] In 1986, the Greens joined the Graham crusade in Tallahassee, Florida, and they performed the song together following Graham's "message on the family." In the television broadcast, the live performance of Steve (clean shaven, hair carefully parted on the side, in a three-piece suit) and Marijean (carefully coiffed and wearing a long-sleeved, purple lace gown) singing to each other, hands clasped, is interspersed with footage of the couple playing with their children. To see the Green family in this context was to see hope for the faith, and hope for the nation. "As one in Him we'll grow," they sang, "and the whole world will know / We are a household of faith."

The image of a model household translated into healthy sales for the Greens, but singers like Reba Rambo learned the cost of not conforming to ideal evangelical familial life. In 1979, as she sought to launch a CCM recording career, Rambo and her husband divorced. When the news became public, NRB radio stations pulled her music from their playlists and CBA bookstores removed her albums from their shelves. When Marsha Stevens of the band Children of the Day came out as a lesbian and divorced her husband that year, the band lost their agent and split up. Her CCM career was over.

The degree to which a CCM singer could credibly, publicly represent a rightly ordered household was critical in part because of how that representation tapped into prominent political rhetoric. In the seventeenth century, Puritans had promoted the notion of "visible saints"—Christians demonstrating their salvation through prosperity and rightly ordered, patriarchal households. Thanks to Ronald Reagan's famous 1980 evocation of John Winthrop's exhortation to build a godly society that would be a "shining city on a hill," seventeenth-century ideas about demonstrating the nation's virtues to the world enjoyed a resurgence in the 1980s.[28]

In that context, the Greens' song signaled the fact that their home was a faithful representation of God's plan for the family as well as Reagan's plan for the nation. The wide availability of performance tracks meant that husband-wife duos could replicate this performance in congregations and during wedding ceremonies throughout the nation. Through the Graham organization's media machine, the Greens' exemplary American household was also made manifest to international audiences.

CCM singers helped create the soundtrack of that shining city on a hill. Sandi Patty drew national attention in 1986 when she performed the national anthem as part of ABC's coverage of Liberty Weekend, a celebration of the restoration of the Statue of Liberty. She belted out the anthem over a video montage that included footage of Lady Liberty, Ronald and Nancy Reagan, naturalization ceremonies, aircraft carriers, jets, and fireworks.

CCM writer Clair Cloniger added a new stanza to Patty's version of the anthem that combined the nostalgic love for country that was a hallmark of past Southern Gospel music with Ronald Reagan's apocalyptic argument that it was the duty of the United States to "preserve for our children, this, the last best hope of man on the earth, or we will sentence them to take the last step into a thousand years of darkness." "The lantern of hope from the harbor still shines," Patty sang in an ode to Reagan-era American exceptionalism, "Those who seek freedom's dream, to its light are still turning."[29]

Patty's performance caught the attention of Johnny Carson, host of *The Tonight Show*, and Vice President George H. W. Bush, and she and other CCM figures became leading musical purveyors of American patriotism during the Reagan and Bush presidencies. Michael W. Smith and Kim Boyce kicked off the "Constitutional Bicentennial" celebration at Walt Disney World in 1987. Larnelle Harris' "Mighty Spirit" was chosen as the official song for George H. W. Bush's Points of Light foundation, which encouraged American volunteerism. Patty herself sang the national anthem several times at the

Indianapolis 500 and performed a patriotic medley at Disney's 1987 Fourth of July Extravaganza.

Occasionally, there were songs that chastised American Christians for their uncritical embrace of the United States and its policies. Teri DeSario's "I Don't Want to Be a Soldier," for example, made the charts in 1986.[30] But for the most part, the bigger hits, like Phil Driscoll's Grammy-nominated 1984 album *Celebrate Freedom*, praised the nation as God's gift to the world. CCM that encouraged godly living, national pride, and domestic bliss employed the time-tested notion that Christians could influence the world by living so well, and so prosperously, that others would eventually follow their example. For those who were convinced that families were plagued by drugs, sex, and satanism, however, this seemed like far too gentle an approach. Caregivers looking for a more aggressive repudiation of mainstream culture found just what they needed in Christian rock.

Petra, Rockers, and the War for American Youth

Inspirational 1980s performance tracks from Sandi Patty and Steve Green reigned in church sanctuaries. But church basements were ruled by Christian rock: Petra, Stryper, Mylon LeFevre & Broken Heart, Steve Camp, Bryan Duncan, Rick Cua, DeGarmo & Key, Guardian, White Heart, Bride, Allies, Harvest, and many more. Christian rock was the soundtrack of youth-group meetings on Wednesday nights, of outdoor music festivals, and of boomboxes in teenagers' bedrooms. With electric guitars and drum kits, Christian rockers restated the case made by Larry Norman and other Jesus musicians a decade earlier: rock could be a curse, but it could also be a cure. "You can still rock n' roll," Rick Cua sang in 1982, "if you're singin' 'bout the light."

Opponents of Christian rock like Bill Gothard, Jeff Godwin, and Jimmy Swaggart believed that the form of rock itself—its electric guitars and drums and the pageantry of its stars—was entirely irredeemable. Through detailed dissections of its lyrics, sounds, and aesthetics they argued that rock was psychologically, physiologically, and spiritually harmful to young people. Like the watchdog figures of previous generations, they tied the genre's instruments, rhythm patterns, and vocal stylings to Voodoo and sorcery.[31] "They wanna try to justify their strobe lights and their weird, wild suits and their pink hair and their yellow hair, and singin' a rock songs, and smoke bombs going off as glorifying the Holy Ghost," said Swaggart in 1986, "you can't do that."

Others feared rock not because of its sound, but because they believed mainstream rock culture of the 1980s posed a novel threat to society. As heavy-metal, thrash-metal, and glam-metal bands sold out arenas and topped the mainstream music charts, evangelical consternation grew. Many caregivers of teens were horrified by the gleeful use of the occult, transgressive sex, violence, alcohol, and drugs that permeated the lyrics, live performances, and music videos of chart-topping rock acts like Kiss, Megadeath, Pantera, and AC/DC.

The threat of Satan felt very real in the 1980s. For one thing, social change was afoot, and that often breeds fear. Conservative pundits argued that Satan was tempting children through pop culture and that children were vulnerable because they were unsupervised by their mothers. When feminists and "career women" chose work over being at home full time, they argued, children were susceptible to satanic media. Dobson, anti-feminist activists Mary Pride and Phyllis Schlafly, and moral majority Baptists Pat Robertson and Tim and Beverly LaHaye warned the American public about the fate of "latchkey kids." The children whose parents worked outside the home and left their kids to their own devices behind locked doors—hence the "latchkey"—were at risk psychologically, physically, and spiritually.[32]

Evangelicals were not the only ones who were worried. In horror films like 1987's *The Lost Boys*, latchkey kids were left on their own to fight evil vampires, demons, wizards, or other supernatural dangers. The obsession, paranoia, and fear of the occult was so widespread that it got its own moniker: the "satanic panic." The media spread tall and mostly unsubstantiated tales of Canadian and American children being victimized by daycare workers participating in occult sex rituals. Families blamed role-playing games like Dungeons and Dragons, which included monsters and magic, for creating psychoses in young adults.[33]

But the majority of the blame for satanism—as well as for sex, violence, and drugs—fell on "certain rock music" that glamorized it. In 1985, Pastor Jeff Ling, at the request of Southern Baptist Tipper Gore of the Parents Music Resource Center (PMRC), briefed a United States Senate committee on the "violence and brutal erotica" in rock music. Gore, wife of Tennessee senator and future vice president Al Gore, was one of several spouses of influential men in the United States government known as the "Washington Wives" who led the PMRC. The Wives were concerned about violence, sex, and drugs in rock and pop music. Ling dutifully presented a slide show that cataloged instances of profanity and references to violence, drugs, alcohol, and sexuality in songs by heavy-metal bands like Black Sabbath, Judas Priest, AC/DC, Metallica, Twisted Sister, Great White, and Mötley Crüe, as well as pop artists like Prince and Madonna. Music videos like Twisted Sister's "We're Not Gonna Take It," which featured a young white suburban boy terrorizing his family's patriarch and worshiping the band, posed "new and different" dangers to the American home, Ling claimed.

The Washington Wives wanted (and eventually got) a "parental advisory" labeling system to inform parents if music had references to sex, drugs, violence, or the occult. In California, lawmakers tried to regulate the marketing of "backwards masked" records that they believed were embedded with evil subliminal messages.[34] These efforts, while initially embraced as victories, famously backfired. The advisory labels drove sales among youth who clamored to buy heavy, horror, and glam metal their mothers warned them about. Warnings from the PMRC jumpstarted the careers of formerly little known acts like Bill Lindsey's horror rock band Impaler. Steve and Dan Peters and their Truth About Rock ministries staged a series of televised debates with Lindsey, which propelled book sales for the Peters brothers and album sales for Impaler. Parental indignation and rock-and-roll rebellion benefitted both parties.

Christian rock groups were in a difficult position. On the one hand, rock acts signed to Christian labels like Word, Sparrow, or Benson had the same morality clauses as their pop peers. They could not afford to seriously offend parents, as suburban evangelical mothers were the core customers for Christian bookstores, their major distributors. On the other hand, mainstream rock was credible in part because it offended conservative white mothers in the suburbs. Their status as rockers, therefore, hinged on at least some level of transgression.

Chart-topping CCM rockers were those who could flip the script and reframe traditional white evangelical mores as the *true* form of rebellion. Drugs and alcohol were what followers did—the *real* rebels were Bible-reading, parent-honoring, clean-living, virginal teens. In *Beat the System*, Petra's 1984 album, the band re-tooled anti-establishment, anti-authoritarian concepts from punk and metal and encouraged listeners to resist the "pressure to compromise" their Christian morals and their beliefs and to "hold their ground" and go "against the flow" of contemporary culture.

Petra founder Bob Hartman viewed the group's status as rock stars as incidental to the band's primary calling as Christian ministers to America's youth. Under his leadership, the band created "a curriculum package for church youth groups which utilizes music videos to encourage Christian growth." The curriculum included four Petra music videos but also an introduction to the video by a member of the band, and a "leaders' guide" that included skits, games, and "live simulations." Petra's willingness to function as co-creators with youth pastors expanded their listenership and made them a mainstay in youth ministries. Others, like DeGarmo & Key, as part of a partnership between Benson and Zondervan, worked to promote an NIV Student Bible in 1990.

DeGarmo & Key's "Six Six Six" illustrated how easily the aggression and violence that characterized much of 1980s rock could be channeled toward the enemy of souls. The 1984 music video for "Six Six Six" included cataclysmic images of atomic bombs, warfare, and the supposed Beast from Revelation being set on fire. The video, initially in rotation on the mainstream cable music channel MTV—a first for Christian rock—was soon banned by executives who were not well versed in Christian apocalypticism and interpreted the video as anti-Christian. Rockers were not the only CCM artists to marshal military language against Satan, but the soaring guitars and rebellious posture of rock really hammered the message home.[35]

When it came to 1980s rock trends like heavy metal, glam metal, and thrash metal, however, creating Christianized versions of the sounds and aesthetics was tricky. Stryper—a Christian glam metal band known for yellow-and-black-striped spandex bodysuits, big hair, and guyliner—signed with Enigma Records, a mainstream label. Lead singer Michael Sweet and his brother, drummer Robert Sweet, viewed rock music as a mission field. The brothers had been converted by watching Pentecostal televangelist Jimmy Swaggart on television, and they were not at all subtle about their Christianity. They set out to employ all of the tools of flamboyant glam metal to create overt Christian messages and save the damned. The band was named after Isaiah 53:5, "by his stripes we are healed," and Stryper was an acronym for "salvation through redemption, yielding peace, encouragement and righteousness." Their third album, *To Hell with The Devil* (1986), employed classic Pentecostal hellfire and brimstone. The cover art showed four muscular angels in loincloths, presumably the four members of the band, thrusting Satan into an apocalyptic pit of fire.

Stryper was certainly a Christian band, but whether it was a CCM band was up for debate. The band opened for mainstream bands like Bon Jovi and Ratt, which caused consternation among evangelical parents, who did not want their children to witness the debauchery of arena rock. The Peters brothers created an "interview" special dedicated to discerning whether Stryper was safe for bookstore moms to purchase. In youth-group circles, the band caused a sensation, in part because their glamorous aesthetic seemed so out of place in Christian bookstores. "I remember walking into the Bible Bookstore in Odessa, Texas," said one Christian metal fan, "and it was the most Bible-Baptist-Bookstore you've ever seen, and I walked in and I saw *To Hell with the Devil*—I came unglued."

Of course, not every aspect of mainstream rock could be adapted for CCM audiences. Punk rock's anarchist, anti-government themes were anathema for most white evangelical patriots. Christian metal bands like Bloodgood, Barren Cross, and Bride offered Christianized versions of heavy metal's anti-authoritarianism, affinity for spiritual battles, and appreciation for gore, but they rarely landed at the top of *CCM* or *Billboard* charts.[36] With clear directives like "Accept the Lamb," Bloodgood's 1985 demo, *Metal Missionaries*, summed up the aim of most Christian metal bands.

When it came to the world of Christian bookstores, however, acceptance eluded most Christian metal bands. "Heavy metal subculture" itself—the genre's dark, gory imagery, sex, drugs, and "spirit of antichrist and rebellion"—and the overt, gender-bending sexuality of glam bands like Holy Soldier or Stryper were a stumbling block for some CCM customers.[37] Stryper famously threw Bibles to proselytize their stadium audiences, but the bands' repetition of familiar rock rituals and aesthetics, like the phallic deployment of the electric guitar, their low-cut shirts, spandex, and glam makeup, were all too far from evangelical gender norms to win them enduring CCM acceptance.[38]

Stryper's appeal among evangelical youths was substantial, however, and was based in part on the idea that they had mainstream credibility, in contrast to the mom-approved artists of CCM. Adam Palmer, a young teen in 1980s Owasso, Oklahoma, recalled "the elation I felt the first time a Stryper video was number one on MTV's top ten request show." Stryper had three videos on MTV in the late 1980s, and for many evangelical fans, mainstream popularity was welcome news. "Finally, the music I loved had been dubbed 'cool' by the gatekeepers of cool," recalled Adam, "and I couldn't tell anyone because my parents didn't allow me to watch MTV (though I disobeyed them and still did)."

The band felt the tensions between their work and audience and the conservatism of Nashville-based CCM. "When we went out and we performed at the Dove awards," recalled Michael Sweet of the band's 1986 appearance, "In our costumes in the yellow and black spandex and makeup and big hair, I'll never forget my perception of what was going on around us and the crowd responses: they were horrified, they did not know what to think of us." Sweet noted that some established CCM stars like Sandi Patty, Andraé Crouch, and Pat Boone embraced the young glam band with enthusiasm, but "a lot of people kept their distance." He thought that "they might have been a little fearful."[39]

Stryper was always a bit too edgy, but Petra, by contrast, managed to capitalize on late 1980s rock trends while staying firmly within evangelical gender norms. While their spiritual battles were intense, they lacked the blood and guts of heavy metal. Petra eschewed spandex for t-shirts and jeans. In 1986, the band acquired a new lead singer, John Schlitt, whose soaring tenor vocals helped Petra take on an arena rock sound. That year, the band produced *This Means War*, an album that articulated a combative form of Christian masculinity. Songs "This Means War" and "He Came, He Saw, He Conquered" portrayed Jesus as the ultimate warrior against Satan. "Get on Your Knees and Fight Like a Man" encouraged men to "pull down [spiritual] strongholds" and make the devil "tuck his tail and flee."

While Steve Green embodied the role of genteel, benevolent father, and Michael W. Smith presented himself as the gentlemanly heartthrob, Petra left manners behind in favor of godly aggression. Christian rockers waged unambiguous wars against social ills that conservatives worried would corrupt teens: premarital sex, drugs, alcohol, and mainstream rock. Youth-group kids responded to Christian rock's adversarial message by destroying the music of the devil in favor of the music of the Lord. Inspired by the Peters brothers' ritual, mainstream music burning caught fire in youth groups nationwide. The events functioned like revivalist altar calls. Rather than bringing the sinful self in need of the holy waters of baptism to the front of a sanctuary, participants brought their favorite AC/DC or Metallica albums—a sign of their pre-Christian sinful identity—to a bonfire and burned them in front of their peers as a demonstration of sanctification.

This musical sign of separation from the world was something of a windfall for CCM labels. As the Southern Baptist Convention, the largest Protestant denomination in the United States, grew more politically homogeneous in the 1980s and began cooperating with other conservative white evangelicals, the market for music that reinforced Republican values grew. "Say that a pastor tells a young kid, 'Okay, if you want to get right with God, you have to get rid of your Billy Idol albums, or your AC/DC albums or your Van Halen records or whoever,' and the kid really prays about it and decides he will get rid of his rock albums with nonscriptural messages," Scott Pelking, head of publicity for Word Records, said in 1985. "But he still likes music. So how do you fill that void? With Jimmy Swaggart? With Southern gospel? With the Mormon Tabernacle choir? No way. They're all just totally different cultures. But then along comes Stryper or Servant or Petra or Amy Grant or whoever to replace whatever the kid had to give up. We can fill that void with something that's pro-Christian, something that's pro-moral, something that celebrates life."[40]

While rock stars saw their work as evangelistic, record-label executives like Billy Ray Hearn were more realistic about the majority of Christian rock. "What we're doing is evangelistic in one way in that we are getting some Christian family kids who are reborn," said Hearn, "but I don't think we are going out in the street and grabbing kids and hitting them over the head with Christian rock and roll and winning them over to Christ, at least not very often." "Now every artist I have can tell you stories of that happening," he continued, "some kid who had never been to church wandered into their concert and got turned on to Jesus Christ—but that is such a small margin."[41]

Because youth leaders and parents saw Christian rock as a way to keep Christian children safe from a hostile, spiritually dangerous world, their buying habits reflected an appreciation for certainty over subtlety. Top-selling CCM rock lyrics, band names, and iconography often included on-the-nose references to classic evangelical theological favorites. Petra, Greek for "rock," was a reference to rock music and also to the Apostle Peter as the rock upon which Jesus built the church (Matthew 16:18). Holy Soldier waged war with the devil. The Rez Band was short for "resurrection."

Music critics appreciated bands like the 77s and the Choir, but they rarely cracked the Top 20 of the *CCM* charts. Other critically acclaimed acts, like artists like Charlie Peacock and Steve Taylor, were regulars on the *CCM* charts, but they failed to resonate with many evangelical gatekeepers, in part because their songs were either confusing or offensive to evangelical sensibilities. Charlie Peacock's 1991 "Kiss Me Like a Woman" was an enthusiastic Song of Songs–esque take on the act of marriage, but it turned off radio promoters and parents who felt that an endorsement of the joy of sex *inside* of marriage was confusing the critically important message for teenagers not to have it *outside* of marriage. Steve Taylor's 1987 "I Blew Up the Clinic Real Good," a satirical song condemning abortion clinic bombers, scandalized Christian bookstore owners who mistakenly assumed Taylor was mocking anti-abortion efforts and pulled his album from their shelves.

Peacock and Taylor resisted the typical CCM preference for creating music meant to teach youth-group kids basic principles of evangelical theology and practice. Part of the reason is that they were shaped by the artistic visions of Francis Schaeffer. Known as the conservative Presbyterian "fundamentalist guru" of the 1980s and 1990s, Schaeffer critiqued evangelicals for creating "very romantic Sunday School art." He argued that rather than a utilitarian model that created art for conversion or activism, evangelical Christians should "use these arts to the glory of God, not just as tracts, but as things of beauty to the praise of God."[42]

As a young convert in the 1980s, Peacock was new to the revivalist networks of CCM and was discomforted by the idea that music could be divided neatly between "secular" and "Christian." Schaeffer's thinking was a revelation. "At that time, [Schaeffer's theology of art] was one of the most freeing things you could say to an artist," he said, and Peacock's application of Schaeffer's ideas became a manifesto of sorts. "We are not going to play this game of sacred and secular," he recalled, "We are going to play the game of what is good and right and worthy of our attention—'Christian' or not."[43]

Taylor and Peacock won praise for creating art that aimed to be divinely good rather than supremely useful, but Christian-bookstore moms preferred a more direct approach. The simply stated, overt, muscular Christianity of top CCM rock acts made them ideal sonic partners for the Power Team, which sought to use ideal male evangelical bodies to demonstrate the efficacy of the gospel. Founded by John Jacobs, a six-foot, three-inch, three-hundred-pound bodybuilder and Charismatic evangelist from Dallas, Texas, the Power Team was a group of bodybuilders who waged "war against the devil" by performing feats of strength in churches, community centers, and school gymnasiums. The Power Team used the aggressive, hypermasculine bodybuilding culture of the late 1980s as a metaphor for the Christian life. Dressed in very small tank tops and accompanied by Christian rock like the Imperials' "The Power of God," the Power Team members ripped apart phone books, chopped blocks of wood, and snapped apart handcuffs—all with their bare hands—and shared anti-drug messages with young attendees.

Christian rock was also used for evangelical theatrical productions known as "hell houses." Hell houses were evangelical haunted houses that used grotesque and gory sets to show how sins sent souls to eternal torment. Instead of classic horror images, hell houses depicted bloodied teens who died as a result of drunk driving or young women's botched abortions—complete with bloodied fetuses in a bowl. Using Christian rock as the soundtrack, they tried to scare the hell out of attendees. As natural of a fit as Petra's "This Means War" was for depictions of the cosmic war between good and evil, however, when it came to melodrama no Christian rock or pop star held a candle to the theatrical virtuoso of Contemporary Christian Music: Carman.

Carman and the Power of Pentecostal Theater

Carmelo Domenic Licciardello, known professionally as "Carman," was something of an oddity on the CCM charts. The Charismatic singer-songwriter-actor-entertainer was raised in New Jersey and told dramatic stories of near misses with an infamous crime family. While visiting Disneyland as a young man, Carman converted at an Andraé Crouch concert. He would later combine the sounds of Crouch's Black Pentecostal music, the spectacle of musical theater, a persona as an ultramasculine "Italian Stallion," and the inevitable happy endings of Disneyland into a unique brand of Pentecostal showmanship.[44]

Carman was hardly the only figure in CCM to demonstrate a Pentecostal concern for the work of the Spirit in the world. Amy Grant introduced a robustly Pentecostal account of the world to 1980s CCM audiences. After reading Frank Peretti's 1986 novel *This Present Darkness* in a Bible study, Grant regularly celebrated the work during her performances in the 1980s. Published around the time when Stephen King's *Pet Sematary*, *The Talisman*, and *It* were blockbuster horror titles, Assemblies of God minister Peretti's approach to the horror genre resonated with readers—especially those, like Grant, with a background in Charismatic Christianity.

Set in a small college town in the Pacific Northwest called Ashton, *This Present Darkness* told the story of a two-layered battle between spiritual principalities and local government powers.[45] In the material world, the novel followed devout pastor Hank Busche and skeptical local newspaper editor Marshall Hogan as they uncovered an evil global conspiracy. The Universal Consciousness Society, a New Age cabal led by nefarious corporate overlord Alexander Kaseph and Juleen Langstrat, professor of psychology and New Age philosophy, aims to take over the town, the nation, and then the world. In the spiritual world, mostly unseen (by humans), a battle rages between the forces of heaven and hell.

The climactic battle for the soul of Ashton is waged in the body and soul of Hogan's teenage daughter Sandy. Seduced by Langstrat's psychology courses and meditation practices, Sandy becomes enamored with a "hideous, leather-skinned monster" demon who masquerades as a benevolent spirit guide. Brought to the brink of suicide under hypnosis, Sandy is saved by heavenly forces and her dad's brute force. *This Present Darkness* upheld the notion that Christian men could and should save their young children through prayer *and* fisticuffs. Most of all, the novel explored the idea that the future of the family, the community, and the nation depended on protecting young adults—especially young women—from the spiritual and physical dangers of universities and non-Christian spirituality.

The spiritual world of *This Present Darkness*—wherein Christians aided the work of angels and resisted the work of demons to save their country—was familiar in Pentecostal and Charismatic circles. Grant's pastor Don Finto, along with others like Vineyard pastors John Wimber and Jack Deere, and nondenominational Charismatic Rick Joyner, routinely told tales of spiritual warfare. The demon-slaying and end-times prophesying in Charismatic worship services were a lot, however, for the average Baptist to absorb. Peretti's fictionalized version was more palatable to those outside Charismatic circles. And Grant's pop-princess sheen made it even more accessible to non-Pentecostal audiences.

As Grant endorsed Peretti's work during sold-out concerts, the novel became a bestseller in CBA bookstores, retaining the number-one sales slot for 150 consecutive weeks. Peretti's subsequent novels like *The Prophet* were marketed as dramatizing "the struggle over which vision of moral authority will define our nation."[46]

Many CCM songs, like Debby Boone's 1983 "Wounded Soldier" or Twila Paris' 1984 "The Warrior Is a Child," showed keen interest in spiritual warfare, but Peretti's vast, vivid, and rollicking Pentecostal universe came to life on stage with the most potency through Carman's shows. Part Liberace-esque Las Vegas showstopper, part Billy Graham revival preacher, part Rat Pack crooner, Carman's work might best be categorized as "camp."[47] His theatrical, over-the-top, gaudy, and sometimes grotesque concerts were multimedia evangelistic extravaganzas meant to impress upon attendees their particular role in resisting and rebuking the devil's work.

One of Carman's best-known works, 1985's "The Champion," uses the metaphor of a boxing match to retell the story of the death and resurrection of Jesus. Plotting the passion of the Christ with classic American sports film tropes, complete with *Rocky* anthem sampling, Carman's Jesus dukes it out with Satan and his demons. While Rocky was an underdog, Jesus strides into the ring with swagger; Jesus responds to Satan's taunts with a line from Clint Eastwood's *Dirty Harry*, "Go ahead, make my day!" The crucifixion is a knockout. God the Father, the referee of the proceedings, begins "The 10-count of defeat." When the count reaches one, the Son of God is resurrected in glory.

Carman relied on broad, stereotypical masculinity to create cosmic battles between Satan and the Lord. In one song, Carman engages in a Western shootout ("Satan, Bite the Dust"); in another, a journey into hell ("Revival in the Land"). In each case Carman relished portraying Jesus as a man of action who was victorious over the demonic. The battles Carman fought aligned with those identified by political conservatives as posing a particular danger to the young: drugs, drinking (and driving), gangs, teen pregnancy, television violence, homosexuality, and AIDS. The spoils of that war were souls of the young snatched from these dangers into a victorious Christian life: Carman ended almost every show with a dramatic altar call.

CCM critics complained that Carman's lyrics were cheesy and devoid of nuance, and that, like *This Present Darkness*, his songs built dramatic tension on the idea that the outcome of the cosmic clash between the spiritual forces of Jesus and those of the devil was not quite decided. For those who believed CCM should generate orthodox Christian teachings, this was heresy.

Carman's fans, however, were undeterred. They were there for the battle. And Carman was fighting one they wanted to join. "I acted out a Carman song for my Drama class," wrote Emily Zink Kirchner, who grew up in Mesquite, Texas. "The other groups danced to songs about lollipops, and I was hunting the devil."[48]

Emily was not alone. Carman's campy, cartoonish stories of good guys winning and bad guys being sent into eternal torment were widely cherished by children. Carman founded Carman Ministries in 1983 and began offering free concerts. The offerings collected at Carman events often exceeded average CCM ticket sales, which made good business sense, and for many young CCM fans, free Carman events were their first live-concert experience. For many, the singer's dualistic spiritual vision made a mark. Fans responded theatrically and created pantomimed versions and performed them in church services, outreach events, hell houses, and school assemblies.

Lip-synced adaptations of "The Champion" or "Satan, Bite the Dust" often included elaborate costuming, makeup, lighting, and sound. The effect of these reenactments—depicting Satan and the violence, drugs, alcohol, and sexual temptations he brought to American teenagers being trounced by Jesus, his angels, and the prayers of the faithful in public schools—was profound. "I felt like I was a part of this big work of God," said one reenactor, "and doing things like bringing a Bible to school or saying no to drugs was a part of this war and I was winning it for the Lord."

Carman occupied a singular place in the CCM universe, but he was a part of a growing set of performers who offered theatrical alternatives to mainstream entertainment. *Toymaker and Son*, which *CCM Magazine* referred to as "Godspell & The Nutcracker," presented an allegorical retelling of the creation, fall, and sacrifice of Jesus through dramatic dance, mime, and musical theater.[49] *Hi-Tops*, written by the songwriting duo behind the Kids Praise albums, depicted the spiritual war for the souls of humanity in a 1985 high school setting. Mime ministers like Todd Farley or Susie Kelly Toomey, and puppeteers like Puppet Love Ministry, often used CCM accompaniment music in their performances. Christian illusionists like Michael Winters and Christian comedians like Mike Warnke toured together with CCM artists. Warnke, the Carman of Christian comedy, was signed to Word Records, and stories of his deliverance from a supposedly Satan-worshiping past were joined on bookstore shelves by Carman, Petra, and the many other CCM artists who saw the world as a spiritual battle for believers to wage.

CCM and "The Christian Community in America"

By the close of the 1980s, there was hardly a white evangelical congregation in the United States that had not lip synced to a Carman tune, played a performance track by Sandi Patty, featured Petra at a youth-group all-nighter, or piled kids into a van to go see Amy Grant. CCM's influence over the teens who listened was pronounced. "CCM practically WAS my identity," wrote Robert, a young adult in 1980s Pennsylvania. Sales of these mom-approved entertainers increased as the infrastructure of white evangelicalism grew.

First and foremost, CCM thrived as Christian bookstores expanded into American suburbs and as NRB radio stations began to expand and consolidate. NRB Christian radio stations doubled in number and in market share between 1979 and 1989, and an increasing amount of airtime was dedicated to music. In 1982, evangelical activist Chuck Colson helped fundraise for Christian Media Ministries to create a radio station in San Francisco, California, dedicated to "truth commercials instead of Pepsi and Big Mac commercials."[50] Colson's efforts yielded what became K-Love, a growing group of non-profit radio stations dedicated to broadcasting Christian music, preaching, and news. Stuart Epperson and his brother-in-law Edward Atsinger created a for-profit network of thirteen radio stations dedicated to Christian broadcasting.[51] Epperson, a twice-defeated Republican candidate for the fifth congressional district of North Carolina, was deeply committed to promoting conservative policy on through Salem Communications talk radio, and through the CCM played on his radio station.

Megachurches (congregations with over 2,000 attendees) that catered to increasingly suburban, increasingly wealthy, white, middle-class evangelical families proved to be invaluable partners of the CCM industry. Figures like Rick Warren of Saddleback Church and Bill Hybels of Willow Creek Church utilized Donald McGavran's homogeneous unit principle to great effect, and they were not alone. McGavran's student C. Peter Wagner continued to mentor pastors (including, eventually, Rick Warren) at Fuller Seminary in the ways of church growth, and many found that one way to lower the barrier between suburban white people and the church was by engaging the "younger generation" with "contemporary music to spread godly values." Built to grow like big-box stores, megachurches often functioned as retail outlets for CCM merchandise and as venues for CCM concerts.

When CCM songs were used in megachurch worship services as "special music," other churches would often follow suit. Baptists, Pentecostals, and Charismatics were especially good at building megachurches, and by virtue of their size and mass-media capacities, they served as tastemakers for white evangelical congregations of all sizes. C. Peter Wagner recognized the extraordinary church-growth potential present in Charismatic and Pentecostal circles, and he collaborated with Vineyard's John Wimber at Fuller to teach on the subject. Wagner's colleague pastor Lance Wallnau, along with YWAM's Loren Cunningham, developed what became known as "7 Mountain" theology, which called for Charismatic Christian influence over seven mountains in culture: "religion, education, family, business, government, the arts, and media."[52] In theory, CCM was art and media that promoted white evangelical family values and political agendas, which made it a helpful tool for promoting church growth and cultural influence.

At Wimber's Vineyard church, well-produced worship music was key to growing churches and planting new congregations. Pentecostal and Charismatic megachurches often included songs from Maranatha! and Vineyard. Integrity Music, a company created in 1987 by a "group of pastors," also aimed to give a platform to independent Pentecostal and Charismatic songwriters from around the country and the world. Much of the music from Integrity reflected Latter Rain praise and worship themes, which included an emphasis on "the special period of presence and power of God as king over all the nations."[53] That period of presence was not best felt through the preached word; praise-and-worship songs were where God was enthroned. After the creation of Christian Copyright Licensing International (CCLI), a company that licensed music for use in churches, the song selections of big churches provided songwriters with ongoing financial support in the form of royalties.

Megachurches also had large youth groups full of CCM fans, and *parents* of said fans. Of course, youth groups were not only present in megachurches. White congregations of all sizes poured unprecedented resources into creating entertaining learning and worship spaces and events for young people, and CCM often set the scene for being both "cool" and Christian.[54] CCM acts toured congregations large and small, and by the end of the decade, a kind of farm team system based on church size was in place. Small churches hosted lesser-known acts, and successful acts could work their way up to performing regularly at wealthy megachurches. Working in tandem with suburban churches, parachurch organizations aimed at ministry to middle-class white youth groups—Youth for Christ, Campus Crusade for Christ, Young Life, and Youth with a Mission (YWAM)—also used CCM on stages and for devotional practices. When evangelical youths went to summer camps like Camp Kanakuk in Branson, Missouri, they also enjoyed concerts from aspiring and established CCM bands and singers.

The time-tested method of taking young adults away from their ordinary suburban life into the wilderness for a revival meeting lived on in CCM festivals like Pennsylvania's Creation East; Cornerstone Music Festival in Bushnell, Illinois; Georgia's Atlanta Fest; and the Alive Festival in northeastern Ohio. Part concert series, part old-time revival, part Sunday School, and part evangelical book-promotional tour, Christian festivals built on the success of Ichthus and Explo '72 and galvanized youth-group kids. Often held at the same camp meeting locations where their grandparents held Holiness and Pentecostal revival meetings, Christian festivals attracted a plethora of figures to seek for and save lost youth. Petra encouraged their fans to bring Bibles to public schools and share their faith with their friends. Conservative preachers like C. J. Mahaney led altar calls. Frank Peretti appeared to talk about his latest Christian thriller.

When evangelical young adults grew up and graduated from high school, many went to Christian colleges in the Holiness, Baptist, and Pentecostal traditions. These schools functioned as a talent pool for CCM stars, including a rap and rock trio called DC Talk, which consisted of three young men who met at Jerry Falwell's Liberty University in 1987. Meanwhile, Cam Floria's annual Seminar in the Rockies continued to grow (even expanding into Europe in 1981), and its competitions and workshops drew thousands of aspiring CCM entertainers and artists and hundreds of label executives together in hopes of identifying new stars.

As the industry grew, it consolidated in the print-publishing, gospel-music hub of Nashville, Tennessee. By 1991, Billy Ray Hearn's Sparrow Records had relocated to Music City along with a host of West Coast producers and artists. When book publisher Thomas Nelson bought Word Records in 1992, the music label's headquarters moved from Texas to Tennessee. Nashvillian company Benson Records expanded their Southern Gospel roster by distributing Eddie DeGarmo's new venture ForeFront Records in 1987. Many CCM records were marked by the influence of the famous "Nashville sound"—professionally crafted songwriting; smooth, string-based sounds; and tight background vocals.

As CCM consolidated and honed a patriotic, American-centric sonic canon, its international reach expanded. Part of this expansion came through Spanish-language albums released by artists like Steve Green, which extended CCM's reach into Spanish-speaking communities in the United States and beyond. CCM also traveled outside American settings when US-based congregations sent missionaries to other countries, many of whom found that interpretive dances to their favorite CCM song transcended language and cultural barriers more efficiently than preaching. International growth was also fueled by Christian music festivals that sprang up in Germany, the Netherlands, the United Kingdom, Australia, and other countries. As the faithful gathered around the world, they were exposed to many articulations of the American gospel according to CCM.

The narrow theological palette of CCM in the United States frustrated *CCM Magazine* columnist John Fischer. In 1987, Fischer, a Jesus-music alumnus, critiqued "all of us who propagate and support Contemporary Christian music" for choosing the ideological "safety" and financial "security" of giving evangelicals messages they already believed. "I see a continual rehash of those things that we have already agreed upon," wrote Fischer of CCM's homogeneity, "things we know will be accepted in the Christian community in America."

The homogeneity of CCM artists themselves undoubtedly contributed to the lack of variety in the industry's ideological offerings. Amy Grant and Sandi Patty were two of the genre's biggest acts, but women rarely constituted more than 15 percent of the CCM Top 40. In addition to being male dominated, CCM rarely broke the so-called sonic color line, which segregated most popular music in the United States and racially coded it as Black or white.[55] The CCM album charts were dominated by white artists, who regularly held about 90 percent of the Top 25 slots. Black artists like Leon Patillo, the Winans, Take 6, Larnelle Harris, and Philip Bailey were exceptional; Latin American or Asian American acts were rare.[56] Black singers and artists who cracked the Top 25 often had direct links to white networks: the Winans first appeared on Jim and Tammy Faye Bakker's *PTL* variety television show, Larnelle Harris first appeared with the Gaithers, a young balladeer named Mike Tait and his sister Lynda were introduced to television audiences through Jerry Falwell's Old Time Gospel Hour.

The initial hodgepodge of congregational music, children's albums, Jesus rockers, and sermon broadcasting had been largely refined to polished, marketable entertainers. Singer-songwriter Rich Mullins produced well-known worshipful music and enjoyed moderate success on the charts, but artists who promoted congregational singing known as "worship music" like Dallas Holm and Phil Driscoll charted only periodically. Entries from Jesus musicians like Keith Green, Randy Stonehill, Steve Archer, or 2nd Chapter of Acts, who helped launch CCM as a category, were few and far between by the end of the 1980s. Fischer and others wanted the industry to produce art that pushed beyond white evangelicals' favorite tropes, but audiences wanted the tried and true. This was not bad news to everyone. If CCM represented musical distillation of white evangelical values, then the industry was a promising outlet for evangelical activism.

CCM as Activism

In the 1970s, parachurch organizations like Youth for Christ and Campus Crusade for Christ were quick to see CCM's potential as a tool of evangelism. Music could give evangelists like Billy Graham access to white evangelical youth, and organizations like Allen Weed's Interlinc and Al Menconi Ministries took things a step further and treated CCM as a form of spiritual formation. Menconi compared Christian rock to a vitamin that "should be a part of every believer's spiritual diet."[57] His *The Hot 200: 200 Insightful Profiles from a Christian Perspective of the Hottest Secular Music Artists and Groups* (1987) analyzed "today's entertainment from a biblical perspective" and warned caregivers of any content that conflicted with evangelical values. Weed's Interlinc, initially developed by Weed at Word Records, analyzed the listening habits of young Americans, carefully diagnosed the sinful content present in the music of Madonna and Michael Jackson, and presented the results of their findings—as well as healthier CCM alternatives—to parents and youth pastors. Weed's Interlinc created charts that compared CCM to Top 40 music. "If you like Bon Jovi," the charts would say with confidence, "you'll *love* Petra!"

Savvy evangelical activists recognized that CCM concerts contained within them a powerful tool, a ritual remnant from a past era, for promoting activism: an altar call. CCM concerts often included a moment where the music paused and the singer spoke about the things of God, then called for prayer, reflection, and public response at a small area near the stage. CCM concerts substituted or augmented calls for salvation with calls for public action.

For example, child-relief non-profits Compassion International and World Vision paired needy foreign children with young Americans. Compassion worked with artists like Randy Stonehill, Phil Keaggy, Mark Heard, Daniel Amos, and Ken Medema to create a campaign called "Compassion Reaches Youth" to "educate the youth on the needs of the hungry and oppressed of the world." Many CCM acts toured with photos of children from the majority world and paperwork waiting to be filled out by an American patron. The person-to-person model of mission avoided controversial policies like immigration reform or foreign debt relief, which poverty and hunger activists argued would do more to assist poor children, but which were unpopular among conservatives. The appeal to help one single child also complemented evangelical appeals to Jesus as a "personal Lord and Savior." In many cases, CCM tours were sponsored by Compassion or World Vision and concerts included passionate calls to action.

Mainstream media companies like ABC, NBC, or the Walt Disney Corporation also collaborated with CCM artists in order to access the industry's core suburban evangelical customers. Disney recognized the fact that their clientele overlapped with CCM buyers and added CCM singers to its annual "Candlelight" Christmas processional. In 1982, Derric Johnson of Re'Generation partnered with Walt Disney World and created the patriotic music ensemble Voices of Liberty. On September 10, 1983, Disney, recognizing the popularity of Christian music festivals like Jesus '83 in Central Florida, created "Night of Joy," an evening celebrating Christian music featuring Petra, Sheila Walsh, Shirley Caesar, Benny Hester, David Meece, and Leon Patillo. Disney advertised "a day with Amy [Grant]" through the *New Mickey Mouse Club* in 1990.

Sometimes, CCM was not just an unofficial promoter of American nationalism, but an official one. Television producer George Stevens Jr. had served during the early years of the Cold War as director of the US Information Agency's Motion Picture Service, which was known officially as a vehicle for "public diplomacy" and unofficially as a form of American propaganda. His "Christmas in Washington," a Reagan-era variety show on NBC, unabashedly celebrated the holiday season, the president and first lady, and the United States of America. Stevens Jr. made sure to showcase CCM singers like Debby Boone, Amy Grant, Michael W. Smith, Take 6, and Sandi Patty as headliners, which further drove home the "god and country" message. Smith, who performed for President George H. W. Bush's 1989 Christmas in Washington, struck up a friendship with the Bush family and was one of the first to meet with and congratulate the president on the suspension of combat operations during the Gulf War in April of 1991.

In addition to serving as the sound of American patriotism, CCM artists felt a responsibility to shape the United States through "political and social activism."[58] Christian artists Mickey and Becki Moore created an anti-lottery anthem song, "Stand Up and Say No," and worked to try to prevent a state lottery in Virginia in 1987 (they did not succeed).[59] CCM artists raised money for AIDS patients and Farm Aid, advocated for the end of nuclear armament, and called for an end to US military involvement in Central America.[60]

But their most energetic efforts were those that aligned with the Republican national platform, and no public policy issue of the 1980s galvanized CCM artists more than abortion. The Supreme Court's protection of abortion rights struck at the heart of evangelical ideals about youth, sexuality, parenting, and nation-building through the nuclear family. Many responded through song. Phil Keaggy's 1980 "Little Ones," Andraé Crouch's 1981 "I'll Be Good to You, Baby," the 77s' 1982 "Your Pretty Baby," Pat Boone's 1985 "Sixteen Thousand

Faces," Ray Boltz's 1986 "What Was I Supposed to Be?," Steve Taylor's 1986 "Whatever Happened to Sin," and Michael Card's 1989 "Lullaby for the Unborn" all directly condemned abortion.[61]

The song that became *the* song about abortion was arguably Sandi Patty's "Masterpiece," a musical reflection on Psalm 139 that praised an unborn child as "a new creation He has formed," and it became a rallying cry for American evangelical campaigns against abortion. Patty's tender performance accompanied showings of Shari Richard's 1990 anti-abortion video, "Ultrasound: A Window to the Womb." The song became an unofficial anthem for the Reagan-instituted Sanctity of Human Life Day.

In 1986, Melody Green's Americans Against Abortion placed an ad in *CCM* with a call to concrete political action. Green's spouse Keith had died in 1983, cutting his music and ministry career short, but giving him mythic status as a prophet gone too soon. As his widow, Melody Green had a special place of authority in evangelical circles as the curator of Keith Green's legacy. She committed many of their Last Days Ministries resources to the work of Americans Against Abortion. "We believe abortion to be the taking of an innocent human life," the petition argued, "and therefore a violation of the constitution of this nation."[62]

"Collect signatures at schools, shopping malls, churches, bookstores, businesses, concerts, door to door, or have it printed in your local newspaper," the ad exhorted its readers, "Be creative!" Americans Against Abortion informed readers that Green would personally deliver the petition to President Reagan on the steps of the Capitol Building in Washington, DC. CCM fundraising collaborations with other anti-abortion organizations like the Christian Action Council and Operation Rescue continued throughout the decade.[63] In 1990, Sandi Patty joined over 700,000 anti-abortion protestors at the Washington Monument and closed out the Rally for Life with the national anthem.

All these efforts meant that the consumption of CCM was *itself* a form of evangelical activism. Consumers eagerly supported music that upheld their moral vision of the world, even if the music was not exactly to their liking. They were participating in something much bigger than personal taste; they were changing the world.

Ritualized productions of CCM hits, like Carman's 1989 "Revival in the Land," gave consumers the chance to frame their activism not only as building up the "city on a hill," but also as a cosmic battle between Jesus and Satan. In the music video for "Revival in the Land," Carman narrated a supernatural story before a live audience. Satan and an injured demonic imp (both in elaborate costuming and voiced by Carman) discussed abortion alongside a litany of conservative Protestant public-policy hot-buttons like prayer in public school and teen pregnancy. "We kill 4,000 unborn a day," he reported to Satan, "through, shall we say, surgical removal." Satan may have won a few battles, Carman rap-sings to the crowd, but the "sanctified . . . blood-bought, spirit-filled, saints of God actually presently on their knees in prayer" were destined to win the war. As youth groups and church drama teams replicated Carman's theatrical song, they, like Carman's revved-up video audience, enacted the Pentecostal notion that their everyday actions and activism were part of a vast spiritual war for the cause of Christ.

The fact that most top-selling CCM activism aligned neatly with Reagan Republicanism did not sit well with John Fischer. In the pages of *CCM Magazine*, he warned that synergies of profit and politics in CCM were signs of danger. "When Christianity gets votes, it pays," he argued. "When Christianity aligns itself with a growing socio-political power that is already moving the mountains of big government, it pays. When Christianity feeds the fire of a public and militaristic righteous indignation, it pays. When Christianity provides a scapegoat for personal guilt by attacking the moral ills of everybody else, it pays."[64] Fischer worried that the industry's profitability would lead to unsavory alliances between Christians and their business and political partners. "When Christianity pays," he wrote, "any opportunist can show up to collect. You can be sure they're here."

In terms of dollars and cents, Fischer was certainly right; CCM's homogeneity, consolidation, and conservative activism paid off. Major CCM labels were raking it in. Billy Ray Hearn's Sparrow Records was twice the size in 1990 as it had been in 1987; independent labels like Briar Patch or Pan-Trax Records were also growing.[65] *Billboard* noted that the growth of Christian bookstores; collaborations in print publishing like Melody Green's publication of Keith Green's story, *No Compromise*; and Menconi and Weed's CCM music replacement recommendations were key to CCM's success. CCM's development networks were producing new artists like soulful pop singer Crystal Lewis, who was cast as a teenager in *Hi-Tops*. Mainstream record labels like Warner Brothers and Mercury Records recognized this growth and created CCM labels in 1989. *Billboard*'s 1990 Spotlight on Gospel Music painted a rosy picture of CCM's sales growth and market penetration.

CCM Crosses Over: Amy Grant and the Ascent of Evangelical Entertainment

It was clear by the end of the 1980s that CCM had accumulated the kind of core consumer base, talent roster, and mainstream distribution partnerships to make a serious crossover attempt into mainstream Top 40. In 1991, Amy

Grant's *Heart in Motion* did just that. Six years earlier, there was a lot of skepticism about whether it was possible to create Contemporary Christian crossover artists. "You couldn't take an Amy Grant, for instance," Billy Ray Hearn said in 1985, "and have her appeal to non-Christian audiences."[66] Grant had proven in the 1980s, however, that her brand transcended the evangelical subculture; she appeared in *Parents Magazine* and *Ladies' Home Journal*, where she stood out to the editors as a "welcome relief" of wholesome normalcy. Grant and her fans bridged the distribution gap between CCM radio and bookstores and mainstream outlets with a real-deal pop music hit.

Heart in Motion was made without Grant's former youth leader Brown Bannister as sole producer and without her husband Gary Chapman as executive producer, and was nearly exclusively about romantic love. Top 40 hit singles like "Baby, Baby" and "Every Heartbeat" were seen as wholesome and middle of the road in the general market. In evangelical circles, they were, predictably, controversial.[67] In the music video for "Baby, Baby," a *Billboard* Hot 100 chart-topping song that Grant was inspired to write when looking at the face of her newborn daughter, Grant flirted, danced, and canoodled with an actor who *was not her husband*. Compared to Madonna, "Baby, Baby" was tame, but in the eyes of some fans, Grant had compromised her status as a public witness of ideal evangelical domesticity. Concerned fans wrote disapproving letters to the *CCM Magazine* editors, and a few bookstore owners refused to carry *Heart in Motion* on their shelves.

Grant's stated motives for making the album, however, were in line with CCM's overall philosophy. When CCM-alumna-turned-televangelist-hostess Sheila Walsh asked Grant why she made a mainstream pop record, Grant answered that she made the record for her nieces and nephews and their friends. "I know a lot of kids who love the Lord," she said, "that don't like Contemporary Christian Music." Grant argued that her album was meant to engage those young people and to reflect the pop music of a more innocent time, such as when the Beatles were topping the charts. The Beatles were, of course, quite scandalous at the height of their fame, but a quarter of a century after they shocked her parents' generation, the band signified to Grant more wholesome mainstream sounds. "Our culture has gotten so lineless," she lamented, "everybody has crossed every line now and I really think it's the responsibility of the Christian songwriters and singers to provide some atmosphere music for people."[68]

Most CCM consumers agreed with Grant. The album sold over five million copies, proving that excitement about Grant's music far outweighed any misgivings voiced by her detractors. Grant's sizable CCM base saw her album as a triumph of the wholesome influence that CCM could have on the outside world. Evangelical mass-media makers interpreted the success of *Heart in Motion* as a major victory in the war to win the nation for God. Seeing Grant on *Good Morning America* or Oprah or *The Arsenio Hall Show* was a thrill because it signaled that evangelical media makers were just as cool and trendy as anyone else. It also meant that their values were present in mainstream media. Figures like Pat Robertson saw Grant's success as a public legitimization of evangelical values. As a sign of this seal of approval, when Grant promoted *Heart in Motion* on *The 700 Club*, Pat Robertson introduced her in order of true fundamentalist gender hierarchy: "she's a wife, she's a mother, she's a superstar."

Grant's triumph meant that, at least in theory, many others could follow suit. With a strong talent pipeline, an energized consumer base, and a legitimate crossover star, most CCM industry executives regarded the future with optimism. Many of CCM's architects viewed sales as an indication of God's work in the world. "We sold 700,000 copies of one record," recalled one CCM marketer, who concluded that the sales represented "700,000 souls reached for Christ." This idea, that product distribution was tantamount to soul-winning, was not universally embraced, but it was also not uncommon. As CCM headed into the 1990s, the decade seemed full of promise and prosperity. "It'll be interesting to see what happens," said Roland Lundy, head of Word Records, "as we all work to tickle a nerve in the church market."[69]

5

"Jesus Freaks"

Youth-Group Bands and the Power of Christian Rock (1992–2000)

"What will people think," Toby McKeehan, Michael Tait, and Kevin Smith asked thousands of young evangelical fans in 1996, "when they hear that I'm a Jesus Freak?" This trio of young men "on fire for God," who performed as DC Talk, were the biggest thing in CCM in the 1990s. Their 1995 album *Jesus Freak* portrayed conservative evangelical youths as rock-and-roll rebels. "Welcome to the Freak Show," the *Jesus Freak* tour, filled stadiums, and their high-energy, slickly produced concerts were teaming with screaming devotees. Fans pointed up to the sky as the band sang, "Jesus is the way," in a throwback to the Jesus-freak revivals of their parents' generation. DC Talk's sold-out shows gave conservative evangelical activists hope for the future of the nation.

Jerry Falwell Sr.'s Moral Majority dissolved at the end of the 1980s, but Pat Robertson's Christian Coalition filled the conservative activism gap, and organizations intent on realizing the Christian Coalition's political agenda saw CCM as a powerful instrument in the fight for the future of the United States. DC Talk had formed at Falwell's Liberty University, and while on tour in 1992 the band received blessings from Falwell, Jesus-music legend Larry Norman (they covered his "I Wish We'd All Been Ready"), and Billy Graham. Graham, by that time the elder statesman of evangelical mass media, invited the young men to appear at a Crusade and thanked God for DC Talk, "this tool of evangelism."[1]

The years between 1992 and 2000 were the peak of DC Talk's career—and of CCM as an industry. Utilizing Graham's longstanding media networks and energized by fresh articulations of end-times urgency, CCM became the soundscape of evangelical public action. Youth-group bands like DC Talk, pop artists like Rebecca St. James, and singer-songwriters like Steven Curtis Chapman filled the charts with pop articulations of white evangelical ideals. "It was such a formative movement for so many of us," noted Carrie Daukas, who grew up in Tempe, Arizona, in the 1990s, "It told us what were appropriate values, and what lines we should never cross." Even as sales reached their zenith, however, there were signs that the world of evangelical entertainment was under threat.

Christian-Bookstore Mothers Make a Great Nation

CCM boomed in the 1990s, as evangelical media makers like Graham and James Dobson brought conservative white evangelical ideas to the forefront of American public life, and energized white evangelical consumers purchased musical renditions of those visions.[2] Suburban youth pastors and parents (especially moms) remained Christian bookstores' primary customers, and, by extension, CCM's. Marketing techniques also got much more sophisticated in the 1990s, thanks to digital tools like Soundscan, which most Christian bookstores had adopted by around 1994. Retailers and marketers were able to study the buying practices of evangelical caregivers with greater accuracy than ever before, and thus to cater to their tastes with increased precision.

Christian bookstores expanded rapidly, which was good news for CCM sales.[3] Joshua Harris, who sold homeschooling literature for his father, Gregg Harris, attended the Christian Booksellers Association (CBA) annual trade gatherings in the 1990s, and he was astounded by the scale and glamor of the music promoted there. "It's hard to believe how big it was," he said, "the hype at CBA was incredible; there was so much money that these publishers and music houses put into things."[4] CCM was central to the hype. "Being someone that listened to only Christian music," recalled Harris, "that was a badge of merit—it was a huge part of everyone's lives." At the CBA, sales and salvation were intertwined. "It was like a mall of mini temples," recalled Harris of the lavish displays for Christian music and books.

In Christian bookstores, the target customers were churchgoing moms. They were meticulous mothers, who cared about bettering themselves and their children through evangelical media, even if fewer of them were stay-at-home moms than in previous decades.[5] Staying home remained the preferred option in Focus on the Family circles, but bookstores served moms in and out of the workforce. The ideal Christian-bookstore mothers came from well-to-do suburban areas. They worshiped at megachurches with premium services for young people, including expansive youth groups that played Contemporary Christian Music alternatives to mainstream, "secular" music. They bought Christian aerobics videos, chaste Christian romance novels, and Bible studies for themselves, and Christian pop music for their children.

Christian retailers were not the only ones doing market research on evangelical caregivers. The church-growth advocates were doing so as well. A growing group of white evangelical leaders, building on Donald McGavran's homogeneous-unit principle of church growth, targeted white evangelical parents. Rick Warren's Saddleback Church, for example, developed their target parishioners based on meticulous market analysis of Orange County, California. "Saddleback Sam" and "Saddleback Samantha," along with their two kids (Steve and Sally), were the ideal attendees of Warren's church. Together, the well-off, healthy, and educated Sam and Samantha embodied the tastes, consumption patterns, and conservatism of the Orange County residents whom Warren's team hoped would be drawn to Saddleback.

As church audiences grew, and bookstore sales increased, Christian radio audiences expanded alongside them. The Telecommunications Act of 1996 deregulated the radio industry and allowed for massive corporate buyouts of small radio stations. Non-profit K-Love expanded, as did for-profit Salem Communications, which eventually rebranded its newly acquired stations as "The Fish." Salem also purchased *CCM Magazine* in 1999, consolidating the industry's leading periodical under the conservative umbrella organization, and became a publicly traded company that aimed to expand its reach to digital platforms once the internet came along.

Mainstream music conglomerates like EMI, BMG, and Warner recognized CCM's market potential and purchased labels like Benson, Word, Sparrow, Forefront, Starsong, and Reunion. By 1997, *CCM Magazine* reported that "Christian music is no longer owned by the church, financially speaking."[6] Some were critical of the model that gave rise to such a prosperous endeavor. The 1980s rocker Steve Camp argued that such profitable business partnerships had secularized CCM to its spiritual detriment. Camp, depicting himself as the Martin Luther of CCM, published "107 Theses" and argued that "current CCM labels" should divest themselves and "return all the money they have received to their respective secular counterparts that purchased them and divorce alliances with them."[7]

Singer-songwriter Rich Mullins, for his part, was critical of CCM's prosperity and its "little niche in the world where you can live with your perfect little wife and your perfect little children in a beautiful house where you have no gays and minority groups anywhere near you." For the most part, however, Camp's recommendations and Mullins' admonitions went unheeded. Under Salem's management, *CCM Magazine* faithfully promoted artists who reflected the "little niche in the world" that insulated white evangelicals in their conservative suburban enclaves.[8] In fact, rather than arguing that CCM labels had sold out family values, most Christian retailers celebrated the growing profitability of CCM as a form of evangelism.[9]

Even those who believed in the evangelistic work of CCM thought it happened in large part through osmosis. As Christian music played through daily errands, church services, and youth-group meetings, the logic went, the hearer would be transformed. "CCM was part of the brine," said Patti Gibbons, a youth pastor in the 1990s, speaking about the ubiquity of CCM in her work, "we used to say that youth ministry was the brine and the kids were the pickles and we were trying to soak them in something that would make them different from the cucumbers around them."[10]

To make pickles in a sea of cucumbers, youth-oriented church was the place to start. Evangelicals, especially Southern and Midwestern evangelicals, far outstripped other religious groups when it came to youth groups and youth attendance; around 74 percent of children raised in evangelical homes attended in some shape or form.[11] In addition to church youth-groups, parachurch organizations like the Billy Graham Evangelistic Association, Youth Specialties, and TeenMania's Acquire the Fire also recruited top-selling CCM acts as aspirational entertainment. Denominational meetings and evangelical nonprofits did the same.

Christian music festivals also expanded. *CCM Magazine* regularly published tour schedules, which illustrated how the time-tested routes of Southern and Midwestern revival networks had grown into CCM tour itineraries. Festival attendees often arrived in family units, with grandparents, parents, and children in tow to enjoy wholesome music, encouraging preaching, and altar calls. Creation Festivals claimed to host hundreds of thousands of festival goers from around the country every year. Greg Laurie's annual Harvest Crusade in California brought in a reported 125,000 annually. JPUSA's Illinois-based Cornerstone attracted around twenty thousand fans per year to its lineup of quirkier, edgier Christian music.

By raising their children in a supposedly discreet bubble of consumption and entertainment, evangelical parents who purchased CCM and drove their youngsters to Christian music festivals were influential—albeit often unrecognized—CCM gatekeepers. This made them, along with youth pastors, key arbiters of white evangelical ideas about the good news. "Whether they're tuning in to the radio, watching a video show, or purchasing a concert ticket or a CD," noted Charlie Peacock in 1999, CCM consumers "are voting on both the music and its lyrical content."[12] More than any record label or artist, the ideological commitments of evangelical caregivers are what made CCM, CCM.

An enduring concern from Christian bookstore moms was whether or not a song was "Jesus-y" enough.[13] Observers wryly referred to a song's "JPM," or Jesus Per Minute. The humor of the JPM joke hinged on the fact that some fans, and many evangelical tastemakers, wanted CCM songs to mention Jesus or God, by name, at least once per song. In 1997, for example, *Christianity Today* chronicled an "identity crisis" in CCM, as demonstrated by Amy Grant's *Behind the Eyes*, which, to the frustration of certain fans, included "no evangelical bent, no mention of God." Zero JPMs.[14]

Salem's concise 1999 marketing slogan, "Safe for the whole family," showed that CCM consumers also wanted radio to protect their children. In addition to sufficient JPMs, music should feature clean language, positive themes, and sound ideologies. In July of 1999, the Christian Booksellers Association gathered to celebrate fifty years of business, and they had suburban white evangelical women to thank for it. "Christian bookstore mothers" fueled an almost 25 percent increase in sales between 1997 and 1999. In 2000, CCM sales grew to a reported $747 million—and when concert ticket sales and other merchandising was figured in, industry experts estimated that CCM revenues were closer to $900 million or, by some estimates, $1 billion.[15]

When asked to comment on the growth of evangelical bookstore sales, CBA president Bill Anderson summed up the theological and political ideas that brought Christian bookstore moms through their doors. First and foremost, the "born again" consumer base of baby-boomer moms wanted help raising their children. Anderson also cited the "premillennial build-up that raises questions of eternity," and "the realities that we need to return to some of the fundamental values that have made America a great nation," or, as Sandi Patty put it, a "lantern of hope" for the world.[16]

Adult Contemporary Puts God in "America Again"

America's greatness seemed secure when, in January of 1992, Ronald Reagan's successor George H. W. Bush declared that, "by the grace of God, America won the Cold War."[17] Winning the Cold War, however, turned out to be a mixed blessing for evangelicals in the United States. On the one hand, for a Baptist like Billy Graham, defeating communism was an unqualified theological and political victory. For US-based evangelical organizations, the fall of the USSR was an opportunity to flood the former Soviet Union with missionaries and Bibles.

On the other hand, communist atheists—real and imagined—had fueled the patriotic fervor of 1980s evangelicals. The end of the rivalry between the United States and the USSR meant the loss of an energizing foreign enemy. Conservative activist and one-time presidential candidate Pat Buchanan argued before voters at the 1992 Republican National Convention that the nation faced an existential threat at home that was just as critical as the Cold War was abroad. "There is a religious war going on in this country," he said; "It is a cultural war, as critical to the kind of nation we shall be as was the Cold War itself, for this war is for the soul of America."[18] Buchanan's claim made it clear: only voting Republican would save the soul of the United States. "We must take back our cities," he said, "and take back our culture, and take back our country."

Democrat William Jefferson Clinton, however, held the Bush presidency to just one term. It seemed that evangelicals had lost the first battle in Buchanan's culture war, but they actually gained a domestic opponent who galvanized conservative media makers. Clinton entered office bearing a liberal agenda—at least, it looked liberal to conservatives—a feminist First Lady, and the stench of sexual impropriety in the form of a long-term affair with Gennifer Flowers. All were anathema to conservative, nuclear-family-centric evangelical media makers. Throughout the Clinton years, Pat Robertson, James Dobson, and Jerry Falwell kept their evangelical audiences informed about every salacious detail of Clinton's sex-scandal-ridden presidency—particularly his sexual relationship with intern Monica Lewinsky—along with a host of conspiracy theories about the Clinton administration. Together, they bemoaned the role that Bill and Hillary Clinton played in "America's Moral Crisis."[19]

Publicly, most CCM artists and entertainers, along with their fan base, sided with the Christian Coalition. In the runup to the 1996 presidential election, *CCM Magazine* observed the political uniformity of the industry and asked: "Where are the Democrats?" To that query, a reader angrily responded, "I seriously hope that Christian music does not represent a cross-section of the body of Christ if it means that it must embrace the liberal ideas and propaganda that we get bombarded with every day."[20]

Much of the top-selling CCM aimed at adults reflected the idea that American patriotism and social conservatism were synonymous with Christian orthodoxy. Southern Gospel, the genre that specialized in rose-colored visions of the American Christian past, enjoyed a surprising revival during the Clinton era. Bill and Gloria Gaither's *Homecoming* VHS video series re-created the Southern "homecoming" services—special gatherings wherein current and former attendees celebrated the church community together through song. The Gaithers recruited Southern Gospel legends of yesteryear who sang revivalist hymns as well as warm renditions of "America, the Beautiful" and "The Star-Spangled Banner."

Country music—another overwhelmingly white, patriotic, Nashville-centric genre—topped 1990s mainstream charts with artists like Garth Brooks and Shania Twain. And country-tinged pop acts like 4Him, Susan Ashton,

Steven Curtis Chapman, and Geoff Moore climbed the *CCM* charts with tales of the good Christian life and comforting Americanisms.[21] Steven Curtis Chapman's hit "The Great Adventure" portrayed the Christian's triumphant journey using cowboy imagery. "Saddle up your horses," sang Chapman in 1992, "we've got a trail to blaze." The Christian in this case was in a cosmic Western, about to gallop off to "the wild blue yonder of God's amazing Grace." Geoff Moore and the Distance's signature song "Home Run" (1995) and its accompanying video used baseball to depict the Christian life as a win-or-lose game (complete with the national anthem) between the believer and "the big guy, the prince of darkness." Much like Jarrell McCracken's "Game of Life," God was a coach, Satan was the opposition, and the fans were the communion of saints "Saying 'go, go all the way!' "

American patriotism combined with end-times rapture at Jesus Northwest, a Christian music festival in Oregon in the early 1990s. There, Frank Peretti recalled how Baptist minister and conservative activist Tim LaHaye approached him about creating a series of novels about the rapture and America's special role in the end times. Peretti demurred, however, because he thought that a novel about the rapture was a tired idea, and also because, as an Assemblies of God pastor, he disagreed with LaHaye's staunch premillennial dispensationalism.[22]

LaHaye ended up finding a more suitable partner in Moody Bible graduate and fellow dispensationalist Jerry B. Jenkins. Together, Jenkins and LeHaye created *Left Behind: A Novel of the Earth's Last Days* in 1995. The novel was, in essence, an updated version of 1973's *A Thief in the Night*, which was a fictionalized version of Hal Lindsey's *Late Great Planet Earth* (1970). In a departure from Lindsey's idea that the United States had no special importance in the end of days, however, *Left Behind* placed the United States at the center of the global conflict for the fate of the world. The faithful Christian resistance to the evil European Antichrist was located primarily in the United States. Jenkins and LeHaye cranked out a book or two a year, many of them bestsellers. A direct-to-video film adaptation starring former teen heartthrob Kirk Cameron was eventually also given a theatrical release. Reunion Records released *Left Behind: The Movie Soundtrack* featuring Michael W. Smith, Bryan Duncan, and Rebecca St. James.

Ray Boltz's 1994 "I Pledge Allegiance to the Lamb" epitomized this blend of 1990s nationalism and premillennial dispensationalist angst. The music video featured a Christian father and son, persecuted for confessing Jesus Christ, mourning the 1962 Supreme Court decision banning school-sponsored prayer in public schools and "political correctness" as inciting incidents of the apocalypse.[23] Feeling bereft of school-sponsored public prayers and monitored by the liberal "thought police" in "PC" American media, many evangelicals coped by praying publicly. See You at the Pole (SYATP), a Baptist-sponsored annual event that encouraged school-age evangelicals to pray at flagpoles before school, enjoyed plenty of CCM support. Steven Curtis Chapman endorsed SYATP right away, Al Denson wrote its theme song in 1992, and CCM songs became a regular part of SYATP meetings.

The National Day of Prayer had become a highly cherished moment of public devotion to the Christian Coalition, and Focus on the Family's Mrs. Shirley Dobson, chair of the 1993 National Day of Prayer Task Force, introduced Michael Card's official theme song for the event: "Heal Our Land." Card's "Heal Our Land" borrowed language about ancient Israel from 2 Chronicles 7:14 and applied the prayer to petition God for "the future for the land we love, our life, our liberty." "Give us eyes to see," Card sang reflecting on American prosperity, "that you alone make things new and the blessings of the land we love are really gifts from you."[24]

Conservatives were distraught when Clinton won a second term, but that did not stop Sandi Patty, Steven Curtis Chapman, BeBe and CeCe Winans, and many other gospel and CCM artists from performing at his 1997 inauguration. When asked about his participation in the festivities, BeBe Winans noted that he was not "into politics." But, "when the most powerful organization in the country is calling upon us to be a part of something like this," Winans reasoned, "it just signifies the growth of Christian music and how far we've come."

That year, Sparrow Records released *Let Us Pray: The National Day of Prayer Album*, a compilation album that gave Carman's bombastic 1993 "America Again" the last word on the subject.[25] Carman explicitly stated what a lot of CCM implied: the fate of the nation depended on ending divorce, abortion, homosexuality, and premarital sex as well as restoring "prayer in public schools," ridding schools of drugs and guns, and reviving interest in Bible reading.[26] "Send the alarm from the Church house to The White House," he told an audience of over 71,000 at Texas Stadium, "and say, 'We want God in America again.' "[27]

When it came to putting God back in America, the first order of business was to build up the evangelical home. Shirley's husband Dr. James Dobson argued that healthy nations were built on families in which husbands enjoyed respect as the divinely ordained head of household, and wives—their natural subordinates—received love and romance in return.[28] Adult Contemporary Christian artists did their part to encourage evangelical women and men to follow this model.

Steve Green supported Promise Keepers, an evangelical parachurch organization created in 1990 in part to promote benevolent American patriarchy. Green promoted the organization by promising, in polished tenor tones, "to nurture our children and love our wives." The ideal man, according to the Promise Keepers organization, was a man who was willing to fight for his wife and his children, but he was not a brute. Green embodied the "tender warrior" who would offer gentle protection and manly support of his family.[29]

Sheila Walsh and Kathy Troccoli toured with Women of Faith, an organization that catered to evangelical women with conferences celebrating motherhood and healthy family life. There they sold music as well as books like Walsh's *Gifts for Your Soul* (1997) and Troccoli's *Different Roads* (1999) to "touch the feminine heart." At bookstores, music for adult evangelical women sold alongside women's Bible studies, like Lifeway's hugely popular series by Southern Baptist Bible teacher Beth Moore, and Christian romance novels, a rapidly expanding publishing genre. As they listened to the sweet sounds of CCM songs of family and fellowship, they read The Heritage of Lancaster County series, an enormously popular trilogy about Amish people written by an Assemblies of God woman named Beverly Lewis. The series gets a lot about Amish life wrong, but the heroine has a personal relationship with Jesus and a fulfilling romance, both treasured by evangelical wives.[30]

In 1995 Heather Whitestone, a young Baptist woman from Alabama, competed in the Miss America pageant. Whitestone had lost her hearing at eighteen months of age, and she spoke openly during the pageant about ballet as an act of worship. When it came time for the talent portion of the competition, she chose Sandi Patty's crucifixion-themed "Via Dolorosa" as the soundtrack for her dance. Dressed in a flowing white gown, Whitestone's routine was a picture of feminine grace and perseverance through suffering. She won the title of Miss America, and when she did, the former Kathie Lee Johnson—known as television talk-show host Kathie Lee Gifford—was there to serenade her. "There she is," Gifford sang to audiences around the country, "your ideal."[31]

The pressure on CCM artists to serve as symbols of family values was intense. Many struggled privately. Russ Taff turned to alcohol abuse to deal with childhood trauma. Ray Boltz hid the fact that he was gay from his family and his fans. Rumors were rampant in and around Nashville about those who veered away from the strict holiness codes that were spelled out in recording contracts. The financial stability of the industry rested largely on CCM figures serving as public moral examples, though, so—even though gossip was supposed to be a sin—open secrets about the personal lives of CCM stars were commonplace in and around the industry.

When high-profile CCM marriages fell apart, however, there was no hiding it. The two leading ladies of CCM divorced in the 1990s, and a lot of ink was spilled in evangelical medias as a consequence. *Christianity Today* broke the shocking news that Sandi Patty, "American Christendom's public bastion of family values," had divorced her husband in 1992 because she had been sleeping with backup singer Don Peslis.[32] *Media Update* denounced the singer (along with a long list of other divorced CCM figures), and CBA bookstore owners withdrew her catalog from their shelves. Patty's tour was canceled. Her 1995 album recording halted, and she resigned from her partnership with World Vision.

Amy Grant and Gary Chapman divorced in 1999. They had publicly acknowledged difficulties in the past—especially surrounding Chapman's use of cocaine and marijuana—but they stuck it out for seventeen years. Grant announced she was dating bluegrass singer-songwriter Vince Gill, whom she would marry in 2000. Grant's newly blended family infuriated many CCM listeners who had watched Grant and Chapman on stage, bought their albums, and purchased magazines with smiling family photos.[33] *Christianity Today* writer Wendy Murray Zoba was troubled that instead of acknowledging "the tragedy of two failed marriages," Grant's image was being marketed as the ubiquitous queen of CCM. "I open a catalog from a Christian retail chain," Murray Zoba wrote, "and there she is again—ever smiling, ever promoted."[34]

For lesser-known 1990s CCM women like First Call's MaraBeth Jordan, whose highly publicized affair with Michael English was exposed in 1994, extramarital affairs were devastating career-enders. Grant's and Patty's extensive catalogs were fixtures in so many evangelical households, however, that fans ultimately acclimated to their new families, but it took a while. "I remember when Sandi Patty had an affair, and also when Amy Grant got a divorce," recalled one young woman growing up in 1990s Alabama, "That was confusing—I didn't yet have categories for Christian performers who weren't necessarily role models."[35] Patty married Peslis in 1995 and relaunched her career by singing the Star-Spangled Banner for Bill Clinton's 1997 inaugural gala. Grant continued to release cozy Christmas albums and had a baby with Gill, and the two became ensconced among Nashville's beloved elite.

Critics were quick to blame the descent of CCM divorcees on the corrupting power of fame, but Patty, Grant, and many others were among a much larger cohort of non-famous Americans divorcing in the 1980s and 1990s.[36] Murray Zoba herself went through a divorce a few years later, and she shared her painful experiences with Christian bookstore customers in memoir form. Rather than representing an untarnished ideal, Patty and Grant demonstrated the reality that evangelical marriages in the United States—the foundation of the City on a Hill—sometimes fell apart.

CCM sales grew in spite of the marriage melodramas, in part because the prized audience for both American marketers and evangelical media makers was not married adults. Teenagers were the consumers of the future, and, for Graham, Dobson, and others, evangelical youths were the future hope of the nation. Dobson thought that raising well-disciplined, happy evangelical adolescents of the 1990s was a "delicate art" that required moms and dads to bear responsibility for "family life, spiritual training, education, sex education, discipline, sibling rivalry, responsibility, hyperactivity, adolescence, and television."[37] As he identified ever-expanding domains of parental expertise, Focus on the Family cranked out a steady stream of advice via radio, film, and books. To counter the mainstream dating and sex advice in *Teen Vogue*, Focus on the Family created *Brio Magazine* for girls; for assistance raising healthy boys, they created a companion periodical, *Breakaway*. For advice on the critical issue of music for American adolescents, Dobson turned to Interlinc and *Media Update*.

Rockstar Rebels with a Cause

Al Menconi's *Media Update* argued that "the rock star" met three basic teenage needs that ought to be met by God and parents: unlimited time, unconditional acceptance, and "understanding and interest." "If we see rock music as a problem," he advised his readership in 1995, "we need to understand that teens see it as a solution and a friend; it meets their needs!"[38] Menconi and others like Allen Weed at Interlinc understood that the theatricality of Petra and Stryper was out of date by the 1990s, and they studiously analyzed mainstream rock trends in order to recommend safe and healthy alternatives. CCM, it was believed, could impart "Godly self esteem" to teenagers, if the right song were applied in the right sort of way.[39]

The guy-lined, big-haired, glam rock of the late 1980s gave way to a grimier aesthetic as so-called grunge bands in Seattle like Pearl Jam, Soundgarden, Alice in Chains, and Nirvana employed raw, mournful vocals and "dirge-like" guitar riffs on early 1990s radio.[40] Influenced by anti-authoritarian punk and heavy-metal predecessors, 1990s rockers like Rage Against the Machine regularly criticized American capitalism, law enforcement, and the US government. Richard Linklater's 1990 film *Slacker* would lend its name to the flannel-clad, stereotypical "slackers" dramatized in films like *Singles* (1992) and *Reality Bites* (1994): young men who embraced grunge and showed disdain for outward markers of achievement or prosperity.

Slackers, especially male slackers, worried evangelicals who sought to raise "noble men, gentle men, men of valor, principled men, *knights*."[41] Pot-smoking skateboarders who did not care whether they were going to get into a good college were not the youths that Dobson-following parents imagined raising. Menconi woefully observed that "secular rock music" was "more aggressive, more bold."[42] If slacking was a sickness, evangelical ministries like Focus on the Family bet that Christian rock stars could deliver a cure. Dobson argued that boys needed physical aggression to learn how to be proper men, so, in theory, aggressive rock, in the right doses, administered through youth group, could benefit young men and hold back "moral erosion."[43]

The Youth-Group Bands

DC Talk was *the* youth-group band of the 1990s, in part because the trio's malleable style was a dream come true for the creators of "comparison charts," which told listeners that if they loved secular artist X, they would really love CCM artist Y. The group was both racially and musically diverse, with a white rapper (Toby McKeehan), an African American singer (Michael Tait), and a white singer (Kevin Smith). McKeehan's rap and hip-hop sensibilities meant that they could stand in for A Tribe Called Quest or the Beastie Boys at youth events. Tait's soulful sounds made DC Talk a credible substitute for boy bands of the decade like New Kids on the Block, Boyz II Men, and eventually the Backstreet Boys and NSYNC. And Smith's gutsy solos allowed the band to ride the grunge wave.

Toby McKeehan was the mastermind behind much of the group's catalog, and right away fans learned that he "luved" rap music. McKeehan believed rap could teach America's youth to live chastely and to tackle timely issues like: "family harmony, materialism, the right to life, and racial harmony."[44] Rappers topped mainstream charts in the 1990s, but the historically Black musical art form was met with predictable suspicion by most conservative white parents. The twenty-eight-year-old white rapper McKeehan appeared one afternoon at Interlinc's 1992 "Talkback Sessions" to let concerned evangelicals know that while he believed rap had descended into excess, abuse, anger, and vulgarity, he was convinced the genre could be redeemed to make a difference in the world. "I went to school [and] I wanted to be in politics," McKeehan said, "I never in a million years thought I would be doing hip hop."[45]

In many ways, McKeehan and DC Talk were able to do both. DC Talk's first albums featured a lot of McKeehan's rhymes, which shocked and delighted CCM listeners. Earlier attempts, like Daniel Amos alum Terry Scott Taylor's The Rap'Sures, had fizzled out soon after they started. Stephen Wiley's 1980s Brentwood Benson rap albums did not get a wide hearing. And CCM labels overlooked other Black Christian hip-hop artists like Sup the Chemist. In 1989, ForeFront Records released music from two promising "Christian rap" groups: E.T.W. and DC Talk. Given white evangelicals' historic aversion to music associated with Black culture, it was not surprising that E.T.W. ("End Times Warriors"), a Black hip-hop trio from Tulsa, Oklahoma, did not find a wide audience on Christian radio. In the end, it took a white rapper from Liberty University in Lynchburg, Virginia, to bring rap to the top of the CCM charts. DC Talk, a group born at a center for white evangelical political activism, became superstars.

Nu Thang (1990), DC Talk's second album, earned the band a coveted spot opening for Michael W. Smith, and together they toured with a catalog that concisely reflected and distilled white evangelical social concerns during the Clinton era. DC Talk's next album, *Free At Last* (1992), topped the *CCM* charts. The Dove-award-winning single "Socially Acceptable" set Jerry Falwell's jeremiad about the state of the nation to music. "Times are changing," they sang mournfully, "with morals in decay." "Children (Can Live without It)" (1990) decried abortion as murder.

The handsome young trio sang enthusiastically about not having sex. The virginity anthem "I Don't Want It," a seemingly direct response to George Michael's 1987 "I Want Your Sex," told young women that "I don't want your sex . . . for now." "She's That Kinda Girl," elevated female virginity and demonized female sex appeal and sex drive. Men should instead desire "a lady" who was "virtuous in every way." For Carrie Daukas, a teen growing up in Tempe, Arizona, in the 1990s, DC Talk's abstinence anthems had the desired effect. "My first crushes were the DC Talk boys," Daukas remembered, "When they told me the type of girl they were looking for was a modest virgin, I assumed that's what all hot godly guys wanted, and since all I wanted was to marry a hot godly guy, modesty and virginity became my number one priority."

On July 29th of 1994, an organization called True Love Waits invited DC Talk to the National Mall to give a concert promoting virginity among young evangelicals. From that iconic location at the heart of the American government, the Southern Baptist group opposed the Clinton administration's AIDS-era "safe sex" policies, which emphasized condoms and sex education in public schools.[46] Instead of learning to use condoms or birth-control pills, participants signed pledges "to God, myself, my family, my friends, my future mate and my future children to be sexually abstinent from this day until the day I enter a biblical marriage relationship."

DC Talk performed before representatives from the Wesleyans, Assemblies of God, Church of God (Cleveland), and Youth for Christ. Together, True Love Waits organizers displayed an estimated 210,000 chastity pledges on the Mall.[47] Alan Weed of Interlinc created a compilation album of songs in honor of the day, including "I Don't Want It" and Michael W. Smith's well-worn "Old Enough to Know." The 25,000 attendees enjoyed performances from Steven Curtis Chapman, DC Talk, and DeGarmo and Key.

In attendance that day was Joshua Harris, the teenaged homeschool publishing scion from Oregon, and the experience left a mark on him. "That moment of seeing those cards," he said, "I really took that to heart. It really shaped my sense of my generation. We made these promises, we've got to follow through with this! IF this really matters, and we are going to keep these promises, we can't keep putting ourselves in this position [dating]." He went home and started thinking about how he could put his thoughts on the experience to paper.

In addition to mobilizing for virginity, DC Talk's "racial harmony" songs like *Nu Thang*'s "Walls" showed how CCM audiences were adjusting to thinking about race and racism in the 1990s. The longstanding segregation between the predominately white CCM and Black Gospel market niches usually went unsaid on Christian radio waves, just as it did in white evangelical congregations.

But, by the early 1990s, white evangelicals were ready to talk about racism—in their own way. Ending racial prejudice was a core component of multiethnic Promise Keepers gatherings. The events included passionate appeals for "racial reconciliation" and "racial unity." At Promise Keeper events, white Pentecostal Jack Hayford and Black Baptist E. V. Hill encouraged American men to be saved, and "there'll be no difference between us on the basis of race." Promise Keepers introduced many white evangelical men to Black preachers like Hill and T. D. Jakes. But, while they watched Jakes on television, bought his books, and worshiped alongside Black attendees at the events, by and large, their home churches remained racially and ethnically homogenous.[48]

For many CCM music makers, the Promise Keepers brand of racial reconciliation fit with a Clintonian form of "racial universalism," which downplayed race and racial difference in favor of social unity and depicted racism as a problem for society to "get beyond."[49] Michael W. Smith's 1992 "Color Blind," for example, appropriated Rev. Dr. Martin Luther King's famous 1963 "I Have a Dream" speech. Dr. King's famous line, "I have a dream that my four little children will one day live in a nation where they will not be judged by the color of their skin but by the content of their character," became, in Smith's song, a call to solve racism by not acknowledging racial difference. "We could see better," he sang earnestly, "if we could be color blind."

Three months after "Color Blind" landed in stores, DC Talk's breakout album *Free at Last* further riffed on Dr. King's speech. For many, the sight of the group with one African American singer and two white singers using Dr. King's famous words was proof that white evangelicals had come a long way from their segregationist past. After all, a generation earlier, Jerry Falwell Sr. had warned that King was an insincere "left-wing" political activist who brought "more hate than help."[50] Falwell's argument against King's peaceful protest was that "good relations between the races" would be realized only when the "individual life" became a "messenger of God's love."

For the most part, *Free at Last* aligned with Falwell's logic. "I'm free," the group sang, "from my past." The album's title track applied the language of "shackles" and "oppression," not to the institution of slavery, but to the negative consequences of personal sin. The expansive social gospel of King's "I Have a Dream" speech became an expression of personal evangelical conversion and freedom from transgression.[51] Racial prejudice, in DC Talk's catalog, was certainly a sin, but one that could be overcome by accepting Jesus Christ.

Thus, while the album used King's words, the lyrics of *Free at Last* reflected an individualistic gospel more akin to that of Falwell or Billy Graham than to that of King. On Martin Luther King Jr. Day of 1993, DC Talk sang "Free at Last" with Black Gospel legends the Mighty Clouds of Joy on the *Arsenio Hall Show*. An eighteen-second filler track that they sang to promote their appearance summed up the group's approach to race and racism. "We're just two honks and a negro," the trio sang cheerfully "serving the Lord." By equating the words "honk" and "negro," the group implied that racism in America was a two-way street, a problem for which whites and Blacks were equally to blame. Musical calls to end prejudice that placed no particular burden on white Christians to respond to the problem of anti-Black racism were warmly welcomed on Christian radio stations and at Billy Graham Crusades.

For some young adults raised in white evangelicalism, DC Talk's music was their entree to thinking about race and racism in the United States. "One of the most profound moments for me was when I first heard DC Talk's [1995] song, 'Colored People,'" recalled Justin Hartpence, "I learned what melanin was from that song." As a young evangelical with Native American ancestry raised in Oklahoma, discovering a language for thinking about and discussing racial identity was a revelation. "Growing up in a predominantly white culture it ["Colored People"] deeply shaped my view on diversity," he wrote, "I'm not sure if I can overemphasize the importance of that song for me in my teen years—I really don't think that I would be in an interracial marriage with a passion for multiethnic ministry if it wasn't for that song."[52]

DC Talk was number one in terms of sales and cultural cachet, but they were hardly alone. The Newsboys, an Australian pop-rock group, rose to prominence in 1992 when lead singer Peter Furler's affection for hard-hitting evangelical messages met with Steve Taylor's quirky sensibilities in their fourth studio release, *Not Ashamed* (1992). Songs like "I'm Not Ashamed" (1992), "Shine" (1994), and "Take Me to Your Leader" (1996) used offbeat imagery to encourage youth-group audiences to share their faith publicly. Audio Adrenaline, a power-pop band formed at Kentucky Christian University, specialized in simple, straightforward songs that made easy-to-teach Bible lessons like 1993's "Big House." "Come and go with me," lead singer Mark Stuart paraphrased the Gospel of John 14:2, "to my Father's house." The Big House was a vision of an eternal home created by Southern white men right out of college and, as such, reflected their favorite things. Heaven had a big yard. People played football. There was plenty of food. Heaven sounded a lot like the ideal youth-group retreat for well-adjusted, popular, middle-class kids. The song, which summed up an idealized evangelical teen experience so well, was ubiquitous in youth groups around the nation.

Stuart's passion for missionary work was evident in many Audio Adrenaline songs. Songs like the band's 1999 hit "Hands and Feet," for example, drew on 1 Corinthians 12, which compared Christians to the body of Christ (his hands, head, feet, etc.) and exhorted youth-group kids to engage in the work of Christ abroad. In the music video for "Hands and Feet," the young band members were filmed in front of huts, along with non-white children who held signs encouraging the youth-group audience viewers to go where God sent them. When it came to applying the lessons of "Hands and Feet," or most other missions-oriented CCM music, the betterment of the youth-group listener often received priority over the communities supposedly receiving aid. Centering white evangelical youth-group teens as the beneficiaries and protagonists of mission trips was so pronounced that in Christian college admissions circles, essays discussing how applicants' lives had been changed for the good on a "mission trip to Mexico"—without mentioning the impact of that work (for good or ill) on the societies that constituted the "mission field"—became something of a cliché.

These straightforward messages from youth-group bands were invaluable resources for youth pastors of the era. "I basically led a youth group for three years based around CCM," recalled a youth pastor ministering in Pennsylvania, "Wrote my own lessons, usually based around a song or album with biblical connections." In light of the youth-group success of DC Talk, Newsboys, and Audio Adrenaline, record labels of the 1990s stocked up on bands that countered 1990s slacker culture by presenting earnest, clean cut, well-adjusted young men who wanted to sing about the Lord. Reunion Records signed Third Day, youth-group-kids-turned-Southern-rockers from Marietta, Georgia. Caedmon's Call, folk rockers from Texas whose founding members included the son of Southern Baptist mega-church pastor Ed Young, signed with Warner Alliance. Forefront signed hard rockers Skillet from Memphis, Tennessee. Essential Records signed FFH (Far From Home), a band formed at the Methodist Rawlinsville Camp Meeting in Pennsylvania, and Jars of Clay, from Free Methodist Greenville College in Illinois.

Jars of Clay and Jesus Freaks

From the outset, Jars of Clay looked poised to be the next big youth-group band. Members Dan Haseltine, Steve Mason, Charlie Lowell, and Matt Bronleewe grew up as youth-group kids and formed the band at an evangelical college. The band's name came right out of the New Testament, and they attracted CCM attention at a Gospel Music Association competition. Jars of Clay signed with Essential Records, a relatively small label in Nashville, and after touring a bit with PFR, they landed a spot opening for Michael W. Smith.

Jars of Clay's self-titled 1995 debut album, however, was distinct from typical chart-topping CCM. For one thing, the moody, restless lead single "Flood" scored very low on the JPM index. "My world is a flood," sang Haseltine, making no mention of Jesus, "slowly I become one with the mud." *Jars of Clay* proved that while Christian meditations on suffering and sorrow were typically unpopular on Christian radio, plenty of general market listeners had ears to hear them. In addition, Essential had access to mainstream *and* CCM distribution through Silvertone Records, a subsidiary of Zomba/Jive Records, and so could introduce the band to both CCM and mainstream radio audiences without the lag time of crossing over from the evangelical market to the mainstream.

Soon, Jars of Clay was opening for Smith in the early evenings and, after the church crowd went home, playing a set in a club. Bars and clubs were unfamiliar territory for the band, but it did not take long to adjust. "You watched God move into this place," said Haseltine of the mood in a club after the band performed in San Francisco, "we all looked at each other and said, 'Ok, This is where we're supposed to be right now.'"[53]

For a short while, Jars of Clay had two discrete audiences: CCM and mainstream alternative-rock concertgoers. As the band climbed the charts, however, those audiences converged. Evangelical youth groups descended upon unsuspecting bars and clubs across the country. As youth-group leaders and parents brought van loads of kids to see their new favorite CCM band, a territorial dispute of sorts ensued. Evangelical caregivers complained when opening acts like the Samples swore from the stage. They accused the band of not being Christian because they did not perform altar calls at bars. Sometimes, when they waited for Jars of Clay to appear, youth pastors found creative ways to sanctify alcohol-serving spaces and make their presence known. "We love Jesus, yes we do," they chanted back and forth across the room, "we love Jesus, how about you?"

Their actions horrified the band. "My blood would grow cold and my heart would sink," recalled Haseltine, "when, from somewhere else in the room, another voice would repeat the call—the worst was when it grew to include what I could only assume were church groups shouting back and forth at each other."[54] In many ways these pre-concert rituals summed up a certain evangelical philosophy of public life. As Carman advised, in order to protect the young, every space in society was meant to be occupied, cleansed, and sacralized by devout caregivers: school, government, and entertainment spaces.

The CCM-versus-mainstream turf war over Jars of Clay extended to merchandising too. Through Silvertone Records, Jars of Clay albums appeared in mainstream retailing spaces, but CCM marketers preferred that Jars of Clay was sold under the category of "Contemporary Christian" or "Christian" or "Inspirational" music rather than the general market category of "rock." On the CCM side of things, the hope was that by reporting a *Jars of Clay* sale as CCM, the proverbial rising tide of Jars of Clay would help lift all boats in the category. When it came to "artists like DC Talk or Jars of Clay," noted A&R and marketing director Brad Moist, "any time an artist is just really punching through outside of just their small bubble, it helps everybody."[55]

Less than a month after the debut of *Jars of Clay*, DC Talk released *Jesus Freak*, an album with plenty for those who relished the bookstore bubble to love. The album's title was a clear callback to the legacy of the Jesus rockers, the music of evangelical parents' youth. True to the CCM model, *Jesus Freak* borrowed heavily from Nirvana and Offspring, a few years after grunge peaked. Redirecting the rage of early 1990s grunge, DC Talk argued that *true* 1990s freaks were not the "over-bored and self-assured" youth of Nirvana's "Smells Like Teen Spirit," but those who had been "apprehended by a spiritual force." The real rebels read their Bibles, they rejected racism, drugs, and extramarital sex, and they relished being outcasts for the Lord.

The "Jesus Freak" music video visually repeated the martyrdom themes of Ray Boltz's "I Pledge Allegiance to the Lamb." As Kevin Max sang, "people say I'm strange / does that make me a stranger / that my best friend was born in a manger?" images flashed over the well-coiffed, stylishly dressed trio. Those images—Nazi salutes, communist party symbols, civil-rights protesters in the American South—compared the life of a young American evangelical to the life of someone living under persecution from fascists, communists, and segregationists. Christian teens who listened to CCM were not just geeky youth-group kids, the video suggested—they were rebels fighting against immoral, oppressive mainstream culture.

Framing conservatism as rebellion connected with evangelical audiences right away. *Jesus Freak* shot to the top of the CCM charts and debuted at number 16 on *Billboard*; 90 percent of those sales came from CBA bookstores. Bethany House Publishing released *Jesus Freaks* (1999), an accompanying book in partnership with Voice of the Martyrs, a parachurch ministry that supported persecuted Christians. The album sold over two million copies and garnered the band Dove Awards for rock album and artist of the year.

On the strength of *Jesus Freak* sales, DC Talk signed a distribution deal with Virgin Records in 1996, and hopes were high that 1998's *Supernatural* would follow in the footsteps of Amy Grant's crossover sensation *Heart in Motion*. In spite of their energized base, national exposure, mainstream distribution, and multiple, record-setting chart performances on *CCM* charts, however, DC Talk's crossover never materialized. The group was clearly branded as a youth-group band, and that association undermined any shot at credibility in mainstream circles.

Indeed, DC Talk's failed crossover attempt highlighted an ongoing conundrum facing CCM rock bands who hoped to enter the mainstream. Many started out in youth-group circles, and being associated with evangelical networks paid the bills. The aesthetics, ideologies, and overall earnestness of evangelical culture, however, had limited appeal in the mainstream. Jars of Clay, after all, succeeded by *not* crossing over in the strict sense of the word. They connected with mainstream audiences before they were widely known as a CCM band.

In fact, in most mainstream music publications, Contemporary Christian Music was widely panned by critics. *Rolling Stone* reviewed *Supernatural* and gave the band credit for creating "likeably earnest" music that would likely garner the band "a few converts," but most estimations of CCM were quite poor. "Most Christian releases," observed *Spin Magazine*, "struck outsiders as dull, out-of-touch—neatly re-styled hair-metal, or Richard Marx synth-pop, where the Lord's message beggared the music."[56]

Being associated with youth-group culture became a nagging source of embarrassment and frustration for many CCM artists and their fans. Youth-group kids tried to convince their friends that "*Jesus Freak* was as good as Nirvana," but *Rolling Stone* dismissed DC Talk and all of Christian rock as "simply riding on the coattails of secular bands," which summed up a growing consensus among evangelical teenagers as well as "secular" fans.[57] Many teenagers in homes with a "CCM rule," wherein parents allowed only Christian music, rebelled privately or publicly and listened to the music of the mainstream. Some got creative and used the CCM comparison charts to reverse-engineer their listening tastes. "The charts said I would like Audio Adrenaline if I liked the Beastie Boys," said one CCM listener. "That's how I fell in love with the Beastie Boys."

Teenage Politics of the West Coast

By 1993, Brandon Ebel, a West Coast pastor's kid raised in a conservative home, was tired of hearing music aimed at the listening tastes of suburban moms. A regular Cornerstone Music Festival attendee, Ebel found most of CCM to be cheesy and out of date, and he was sure he was not alone. The shiny, happy music of Christian bookstore moms was inauthentic to many of their children's ears. "There was this huge need," recalled Ebel, "for people that were Christian at the time to have options, because their parents didn't let them listen to secular music."[58]

To meet that need, Ebel borrowed money from his grandfather and started Tooth & Nail Records in Southern California, and then quickly resettled in Seattle. Comparison-chart-publishing, Nashville-based CCM dominated bookstore sales and Christian radio airwaves for years, but the West Coast Calvary Chapel youth-group music scene had continued to develop long after Jesus music had faded from the charts. They lacked national exposure, but by the 1990s, the children of Jesus-loving hippie rockers of the 1970s had developed underground Christian punk, metal, and ska communities through word of mouth, underground rock magazines, all-ages clubs, and touring West Coast youth groups. Foursquare and Vineyard Churches, non-denominational Charismatic churches, and especially Calvary Chapels filled youth rooms, skate parks, and gymnasiums from Bremerton, Washington, to Carlsbad, California, with lo-fi, DIY sounds of teenage youth-group rockers.

Once he settled in Seattle, Ebel began collaborating with Christian rockers at Calvary Fellowship Seattle. The music scene at Calvary Fellowship included singer-songwriters David Bazan of Pedro the Lion, Damien Jurado, and producer Aaron Sprinkle, a pastor's kid who, along with his sister Jesse, had a band named after C. S. Lewis' *Chronicles of Narnia*, Poor Old Lu. Tooth & Nail's early releases included West Coast alternative rockers like Starflyer 59, power pop/punk like Plankeye, punk bands like Blenderhead, post-hardcore groups like Frodus, electropop groups like Joy Electric, and ska rockers the O.C. Supertones.

Two years after Tooth & Nail began, Frank Tate, who managed Californian Reunion Records' underground rockers the Prayer Chain, came to the conclusion that Nashville-based CCM was not keyed into grunge-influenced youth culture. "Nirvana's *Nevermind* came out and all of the sudden, it was fastest [pop culture] pivot I'd ever seen," he joked about the transition from '80s pop to '90s slacker culture, "all of the sudden, dancing was stupid and everyone was wearing flannel and saying success is failure." After encountering an early Green Day performance, Tate saw in punk rock "the voice and the vocabulary to give the hope of the gospel to kids."

For Tate, an alumnus of Oral Roberts University, punk themes of rebellion were not counter to Christian theology. "I think Jesus is pretty punk rock," he said, but Reunion Records was not interested. In 1995, Tate went out on his own and created 5 Minute Walk Records, which signed Vineyard house band My Brother's Mother, Five Iron Frenzy (a ska band from Denver), and The W's (a ska and swing revival band from Corvallis, Oregon).

Tooth & Nail and 5 Minute Walk's rosters challenged the aesthetics and emotional range of major-label CCM. The frantic pace of ska, and the distorted guitars and screamed lyrics of punk, served as sonic deterrents, leading evangelical moms to ban the music from the minivan. "They were listening to us in their rooms," noted Leanor Ortega Till of Five Iron Frenzy, "or even better, on headphones."

Violent, gory, horror-inflected depictions of Christian concepts pervaded many West Coast metal songs. The Crucified's 1991 "Mindbender" characterized people who watched too much televisions as being "Slowly raped though they can only feel the tickle in their ears," and as "A nation of puppets / Who worship a beast / Who drinks the blood of their souls." In theory, evangelical moms might have agreed with the idea that "the media's children" were under the influence of deleterious mainstream influences, but they did not want to listen to lyrics about blood-drinking and sexual violence while they ran errands. In addition, Christian metalcore bands like Zao, who sang about suicide, veered outside the positive emotional boundaries of CCM. Evangelical mothers wanted to raise well-adjusted teens, and they preferred the cheery, heavenly God of "Big House" over wrenching despair and grief.

In some cases, anti-authoritarian, anti-nationalistic messages found within Christian punk directly challenged the stalwart patriotism of major-label CCM. Tooth & Nail's MxPx, a group of young punk rockers from Bremerton, Washington, released *Teenage Politics* in 1995, with songs that repudiated "Americanism, nationalism, bow to the flagism!" "They're lying when they tell us / This is the home of brave and land of the free," they sang before decrying "Militaristic, egotistic, high class and capitolistic!" culture in the United States. In contrast to Steven Curtis Chapman's Christianized cowboy life in "The Great Adventure," Five Iron Frenzy's 1997 "The Old West" was a take-down of Manifest Destiny. "West or bust, in God we trust," they sang adopting a first-person imitation of an American frontiersmen, "Let's rape, let's kill, let's steal / We can almost justify anything we feel."

Some late 1990s Tooth & Nail listeners had vigilant moms who—to the disappointment of their offspring—went the extra mile to protect their children from musical harm. When Justin Ruddy of Scranton, Pennsylvania, ordered an album from the Cootees, a band that featured two MxPx members, his mother insisted on reading the album liner notes. "She sat down and read the lyrics to 'School Girl Fantasy,'" he recalled, "and gave it a hard 'no.'" Ruddy's mom went a step further to protect other teens from the effects of songs about dream girls "clean off the cover of a magazine." "She called up Tooth & Nail mail order to complain," he remembered. Teenaged Ruddy was mortified. "As a teenager who was in a punk rock band and dreamed of being signed by Tooth & Nail someday, I almost died."[59]

Ruddy's experiences were hardly unique. Fortunately for him and many others, a lot of metal, hardcore, and punk bands offered lyrics that conformed to conservative evangelical values. Metalcore band Underoath's "Burden In Your Hands," for example, was a sharp denunciation of abortion. "You should of [*sic*] thought about the baby before you had sex," they sang, "Because you have destroyed a gift from God."

If it were up to evangelical moms, the more transgressive offerings from metal, hardcore, and punk bands probably would not have found nation-wide audiences, and, in the end, few West Coast bands ascended to the heights of the *CCM* charts. Tooth & Nail and 5 Minute Walk still thrived, however, because their business model was not as heavily dependent as other forms of CCM upon selling to bookstore mothers. They focused on young men who *rebelled against* the music of their mothers.[60] This gendered marketing strategy meant that they sold music mostly to young evangelical men (and some women) through performances at small venues, and niche periodicals like

HM Magazine or *True Tunes News*, or through compilation albums, like *7ball Magazine*'s popular *Gas Collection* sampler series. The punk, ska, and metal that was distributed through CBA bookstores was often curated by young men who sold directly to their peers. Thus, while Christian punk and metal rebelled against many aspects of white evangelical culture, gender distinctions were not usually among them.[61] Most Tooth & Nail fans were *dudes*, first and foremost.

The success of the label proved that there were "Tooth & Nail Kids" (and "5 Minute Walk kids") in youth groups around the country, not just on the West Coast, looking for music that "reconciled Christianity and DC Talk versus Pantera."[62] Teen listeners in cities and small towns had to work to find their favorite bands, which added to their desirability and increased their fans' dedication. In some ways, the greater the obscurity of the band, the better.

Being less tied to the branding of major-label CCM meant that many groups had a more porous relationship with general market music. MxPx played churches and Christian festivals like Cornerstone, but they also opened for mainstream ska-punk-alternative band No Doubt. In 1998, they signed with A&M Records and landed a coveted spot on the Warped Tour, the largest and one of the most influential mainstream rock tours in North America. Five Iron Frenzy joined the "Ska Against Racism" tour of 1998 with the aim of educating the predominately white, male American ska listenership about the anti-racist political roots of the bouncy, horn-driven Jamaican genre.

Many Tooth & Nail kids exalted at the mainstream success of their favorite bands, but MxPx took a lot of Tooth & Nail's profits with them into the general market, which made the label's financial future precarious. In the end, a ska band that evangelical moms loved, the Orange County (O.C.) Supertones, became the top-selling band of the West Coast indie scene. Their lighthearted sound played a role in broadening the appeal of the band from the underground scene to suburban commuter cars. "If you're able to show parents and families and kids," noted Jason Carson of the Supertones, "something with incredible Christian content and it's fun and danceable with horns, it's perfect—It played a big part in [the Supertones] becoming one of those big youth group type bands."

The band's methods also aligned with those of Nashville-based corporate-owned CCM. The Supertones welcomed moshing—the frenetic, often violent dancing favored in punk, alternative, and metal music scenes—*and* altar calls at concerts. Like Petra and Audio Adrenaline, they helpfully provided youth-group leaders with literature and study guides for their meetings. They toured with Audio Adrenaline and recorded a duet with Crystal Lewis. They used their platform to condemn drugs and pornography, sang a lot about evangelism, and preached during concerts. As the safe alternative to ska punk bands like No Doubt or the Mighty Mighty Bosstones, they garnered invitations to perform at Billy Graham crusades.

At the end of the day, as MxPx and the Supertones demonstrated, the financial stability of the business depended on CBA bookstore sales. The youth-group basements along the California coast may have allowed for tattoos, piercings, and mosh pits for (mostly male) teens to dance out a bit of their aggression, but longstanding lines around clean living could not be crossed. The closer to Nashville, the greater the pressure to conform. "I remember when we would visit Nashville," recalled Heather Hellman, who married the W's saxophonist Valentine Hellman and sold merchandise on the road with the band, "we had to make sure to clean things up—no swearing, no alcohol, *no* co-ed sleeping." West Coast efforts to subvert the role of evangelical caregivers in shaping youth-group music had mixed results. The sales and marketing industry that served Christian-bookstore moms was always around, ready to offer support, but always with conditions.

Re:thinking, Reforming CCM

In the late 1990s, Charlie Peacock and Steve Taylor set their sights on reforming the theology and business of Christian music. In addition to being influenced by Francis Schaeffer's theology of art, Taylor and Peacock were shaped by the thinking of Bob Briner, an Emmy Award–winning television producer, executive, and sports manager who disagreed sharply with the way evangelical caregivers used media to withdraw from mainstream culture and protect the already saved. In his 1993 manifesto, *Roaring Lambs: A Gentle Plan to Radically Change Your World*, Briner argued that evangelicals ought to engage the world as "movers and shakers" who make a "deliberate, strategic decision" to "effectively infiltrate" mainstream culture with "the salt of the Gospel."[63] Accordingly, Peacock and Taylor sought to build a "creative environment for Christians in the pursuit of artistic excellence" that would fill mainstream spaces with "things of beauty" that drew listeners to the Divine.[64]

To infiltrate the world with beauty, Peacock founded re:think Records in 1996. The label signed Sarah Masen, a singer-songwriter from the suburbs of Detroit, and three surfers from North Coast Calvary Chapel in Carlsbad, California, who had a band called Switchfoot. In 1997, Taylor founded Squint Records and signed Sixpence None the Richer, an alternative rock band featuring lead singer Leigh Nash and guitarist and writer Matt Slocum, who had met at a church retreat. The aim, from the get-go, was not necessarily to create CCM stars who crossed over into the general market, but to launch new music distributed in the mainstream as well as through CCM networks.

Sixpence None the Richer and Sarah Masen, along with the rest of the re:think and Squint rosters, wrote songs with few to no JPMs. They had little to say about abstinence or abortion or Christian marriage or gender roles or the sad state of the nation. They did not create songs that would pair easily with youth-group Bible studies, but they wrote fervently about love, doubt, pain, and the healing power of beauty. Squint and re:think placed music in mainstream spaces right away. Sarah Masen's 1996 song "Flames of Truth" was featured on the 1998 teen drama television show *Dawson's Creek*. Sixpence's "Kiss Me" became a smash hit as the theme song to *She's All That*, a 1999 teen romantic comedy starring Rachel Leigh Cook and Freddy Prinze Jr.

Peacock had similar general market plans for Switchfoot, but, as Brandon Ebel had discovered, independent labels were expensive to start and maintain, even with early success.[65] Without the personal wealth to sustain dual marketing plans, Peacock was unable to maintain re:think independently. He sold the label to EMI/Sparrow in 1997. For Switchfoot, it meant that their debut album, *Legend of Chin*, was released on Sparrow Records and distributed to mainstream retail and radio by parent company EMI, as well as the well-trod CCM outlets of CBA bookstores and NRB radio.

The members of Switchfoot were well positioned for Christian rock. Jon and Chad Foreman's father pastored a large Calvary Chapel, and their drummer Chad Butler's father was lead singer in the Jesus-music band Parable. The rockers received a warm welcome among CCM listeners, but lead singer/writer Jon Foreman was frustrated. "When Sparrow bought re:think Records, it was evident that our music wasn't going to be in the hands of everybody," he recalled in a 2006 interview with *Christianity Today*; "As a Christian, I have a lot to say within the walls of the church. But also, as a Christian, I've got a lot to say just about life in general."[66]

In spite of Foreman's discomfort, Switchfoot ascended into the stratosphere of youth-group bands. Their reluctant success demonstrated how very hard it was for evangelical rockers to shed the cultural distinctions of conservative white Protestantism and embrace coolness and rock rebellion. CCM rockers found that the ideological commitments that sustained the industry—patriotism, abstinence, temperance, and respecting one's parents—were irreconcilable with being an American rock star in the '90s. Those who were held up by Jerry Falwell as ideal young men would *not* be praised by *Rolling Stone*.

Christian rock may not have been cool, but it was very popular in 1990s youth groups. Sales soared throughout the decade, even as mainstream rock sales declined precipitously.[67] As pop, R&B, and hip hop took over the general market, however, a new generation of CCM pop stars hoped to assume the mantle of Amy Grant.

6

"God" Pop and the "Personality Trend"

CCM Youth Culture Goes Mainstream (1992–2000)

Britney. Christina. Celine. As the 1990s progressed, pop was increasingly supplanting rock at the top of the charts. Women were the primary consumers of pop music, and that was no less true of Christian pop, so youth leaders of the 1990s often turned to pop artists to shape young women and girls. While Whitney Houston, Mariah Carey, and Wilson Phillips' polished productions played on Top 40 radio stations, balladeers like Point of Grace, CeCe Winans, Crystal Lewis, and Nicole C. Mullen sang about Jesus, the Second Coming, and the resurrection.

In terms of marketability at Christian bookstores and listenability on Christian radio, however, Rebecca Jean Smallbone, known professionally as Rebecca St. James, was the obvious heir to Amy Grant. St. James was the daughter of a Christian music promoter in Sydney, Australia, and she had opened for Carman as a child. She and her family moved to the United States, she signed with Forefront Records, and in 1994 released a self-titled debut.

With vocal inflection similar to Alanis Morisette's 1995 alternative pop breakup anthem "You Oughta Know," St. James' 1996 breakout album proclaimed the existence of "God." St. James bore a passing resemblance to Grant, and she shared her predecessor's adaptability when it came to style. When Morisette's rock angst gave way to Britney Spears' polished tunes, St. James released "One," in 2000, a single sonically similar to Spears' 1999 megahit ". . . Baby One More Time." St. James was eager to use her platform to urge young women to "make a difference" in the world—to give up alcohol, drugs, and especially sex outside of marriage. She wrote devotionals for evangelical publisher Thomas Nelson in the late 1990s, and *CCM Magazine*, and *Campus Life*, the Youth for Christ periodical, named her their favorite female artist.

While finding "the next Amy Grant" seemed crucial to the future of Contemporary Christian Music (CCM), it was not necessarily the numbers that dictated that priority. If the goal of CCM was to sell the most records to the most devout evangelicals, the industry might have looked beyond its traditional strongholds. Demographically speaking, Black and Brown Americans were the future of the country, and Black and Brown Protestants demonstrated high levels of church attendance. Latin music and R&B-influenced pop were on the rise. A completely new market might have opened up. It was St. James, however—a woman of European descent who conformed to traditional Western beauty norms—who captured the hearts of Christian Booksellers Association (CBA) bookstore customers and achieved sustained CCM stardom. Meanwhile, CCM labels made only halting steps toward embracing new listeners.

As pop grew in the late 1990s, sisters Lisa, Andrea, and Danielle Kimmey drew attention from Benson Records, but they hit a snag when the label did not know how to categorize them. The young Black women wanted to be a CCM group, but Benson executives expected them to do Black Gospel music. "I never understood how a childhood of [listening to] Sandi Patty, Steven Curtis Chapman, and BeBe and CeCe Winans led to our unique style of pop and R&B," recalled Danielle Kimmey Torrez, "but that's the music God placed in our hearts." Established labels lost interest, but Toby McKeehan was intrigued. Determined to work with them, McKeehan and his cousin Joey Elwood created Gotee Records in 1994, signed the Kimmey sisters as Out of Eden, and took them on tour with DC Talk.[1]

Myrrh Records released *Heavenly Place*, the debut album from teenage Jaci Velasquez, a singer from Houston, Texas, in 1996, and it was a hit. The "Latin explosion" of the 1990s put Latin American music at the top of mainstream charts, and Velasquez, described in promotional materials as "a dark-haired beauty of Mexican, Spanish, and French heritage," had "pop and Latin sounds."[2] She also had serious CCM bona fides. Velasquez was a Southern Gospel legacy (her father won a Dove Award in 1970 as a member of The Four Galileans), and she was raised in the Assemblies of God. "Un Lugar Celestial (A Heavenly Place)" was released in English and Spanish, which her label hoped would expand her Spanish- and English-speaking audiences. Velasquez was recommended on CCM comparison charts for fans of pop stars like Mariah Carrey or Gloria Estefan.

Jim Chaffee of Myrrh records summarized the CCM appeal of Velasquez and her pop singing colleagues in 2000: "parents want their kids to be like her, boys want to date her, and girls want to be her."[3] Velasquez found that being deemed "dateable" came with drawbacks. Like so many women who went before her, Velasquez received constant feedback on her appearance, sexuality, and sex appeal. "Ever since I was a little girl," she told *Billboard*, "I've always had people in the studio tell me to watch myself so that I didn't sound too sexy." "I've gotten letters about it," she added, "and about the outfits I wear."[4]

Like Rebecca St. James, Velasquez and Out of Eden were avid supporters of virginity before marriage. Both sang chastity songs ("I Promise" by Velasquez and "There Is a Love" by Out of Eden). True Love Waits brought both on tour. "I have made a commitment to keep myself pure until the day I am married," Velasquez told the *Baptist Press*, "I hope and pray that every single person will make this commitment."[5]

By the late 1990s, however, mere abstinence from sex was no longer as far as a young person could go when it came to purity. Joshua Harris helped change that with his 1997 blockbuster advice tome *I Kissed Dating Goodbye*. Harris, building on his experiences in Washington DC, and his father Gregg Harris' Advanced Homeschooling Workshop "Arranged Courtship for a Lasting Marriage," argued that virginity was not enough for the truly devout. The "seductive spirit of impurity" was present even in the act of dating, he argued, and that as an " 'on-ramp' of impurity," it ought to be abolished.

Harris landed two major endorsements for the book: Elisabeth Elliot, author of *Passion and Purity*, a book about chastity published in 1984, and his friend Rebecca St. James, who wrote the foreword to the book. "Christian artists who were famous," Harris said of what it meant to have James' support—"They had another level of influence and coolness in terms of the crowd they drew and everything." At Harris' request, St. James crafted a catchy ode to waiting for marriage in 2000. "Wait for Me" became a staple at gatherings of True Love Waits and its sister organization Silver Ring Thing, and the tune was nominated for a Dove Award.

For Danielle Kimmey Torrez of Out of Eden, *I Kissed Dating Goodbye* seemed a bit extreme. "I believe in purity before marriage," she said, "but I'm fine with dating too." As CCM fans sang along to St. James' visions of sexual purity, however, they participated in increasingly dramatic rituals meant to ensure the holiness of unmarried adolescents before their heavenly and earthly fathers. Youth-group sermons portrayed female sexuality as a flower with a finite number of petals—every kiss, every held hand, every embrace was a deployment of a precious petal. The ideal scenario for women was to present themselves to a spouse as a fully petaled flower.

Youth pastors often found that attractive young CCM artists made the best messengers when it came to teaching about purity culture. "I remember going to a Rebecca St. James concert where she extolled the virtues of *I Kissed Dating Goodbye*," wrote Ryan Lytton, who grew up in Virginia in the 1990s. "My youth pastor later castigated us for being so enthusiastic about it, because he had been teaching us the same thing for months and to his mind none of us had taken his advice to heart."[6]

On paper, sexual purity applied to both women and men, but most applications of "purity culture," as it came to be known, disproportionately emphasized women's sexual purity. "Purity balls," events wherein dads (or prominent male caregivers) brought their post-puberty daughters together to dance to CCM virginity anthems, sprang up around the country, propelled by endorsements from Focus on the Family.[7] Fathers at purity balls were called upon to do on a micro level what CCM listeners regularly did on a macro level to female stars: praise young women for being beautiful, sexually viable young women, while warning them that any sexual act outside of marriage would end in ruin.

Singer-songwriter Jennifer Knapp was flummoxed by the relationship between CCM and abstinence activists. Knapp, an adult convert to Christianity, was unfamiliar with the social norms and implicit expectations that young evangelical women learned from CCM. The Midwestern guitarist sang poignantly of her spiritual journey from sin to salvation, however, which caught the attention of Gotee Records. After signing with Gotee, Knapp released *Kansas* in 1998, and she was plunged into youth-group culture as an opening act for Audio Adrenaline.

Like Grant's earlier "Three Button Controversy," Knapp's body was closely monitored for evidence that she crossed the carefully delineated boundaries of white evangelical sexual ethics. She was first introduced to bookstore moms through a compilation CD, but retailers worried that when evangelical caregivers saw the *Kansas* cover, which included the singer posing with a guitar strap resting between her breasts, customers would feel that the album was too sexy. Knapp's powerful stage presence and proficiency with the guitar—a longstanding phallic symbol for male rockers—was also deemed too seductive for the overwhelmingly male Audio Adrenaline audiences.

Knapp could not control how she was received by youth-group boys, even though she was held responsible for it. She diligently set out to reject "worldly ways of cursing and drinking and, of course, absolutely no sex," however, and as she toured the country, Knapp saw firsthand the power of CCM to incite action. "Music [is in many] ways just as potent as drugs and sex," she observed; "it can move us with pleasure and command our attention."

Kansas sold over 500,000 copies, and as Knapp sang of the impurities of sin and sanctifying work of Jesus, marketers saw an opportunity to promote purity culture through her work. The more experience she gained in CCM, however, the more Knapp feared that the web of evangelical activist partnerships that upheld much of CCM amounted to a "trojan horse for propaganda." When purity-culture activists suggested that she could tap teen girls who did not fit the "St. James market," Knapp declined.

Knapp resisted, but with prominent purity advocates like St. James and Velasquez, CCM pop stars of the late 1990s proved that music could be an invaluable tool in forming young evangelical bodies. Altar calls that promoted faithfulness to a future earthly spouse became standard components of many CCM pop concerts. By the close of the twentieth century, mainstream pop stars raised in conservative white evangelical culture began translating the sexual politics of CCM to Top 40 charts.

The Pop Stars that CCM Made

Two Southern Baptist girls, Britney Spears and Jessica Simpson, brought the tensions within evangelical purity culture of the 1990s to the general market. The notion that young female entertainers must be simultaneously tantalizing and sexually withholding to men long predated the 1990s, but Spears and Simpson brought specific purity-culture signifiers like promise rings and public declarations to "wait for marriage" to the mainstream. Spears' 1998 debut, ". . . Baby One More Time" visualized the contradictions of American purity culture. In the hit video, she performed dressed in a school uniform associated with parochial school, and she added a dose of sex appeal by tying her shirt in a knot, exposing her midriff, and wearing thigh-high socks. Following that performance, *Rolling Stone* sent adult men to profile Spears in her childhood bedroom in Kentwood, Louisiana. David LaChapelle photographed the seventeen-year-old Spears in her underwear. Journalist Steve Daly carefully described Spears' "honeyed thighs" and "ample chest," before explaining that Spears "cleaves to the Baptist faith."

Abstinence rallies helped launch Jessica Simpson as a CCM upstart, until her body got in the way. Simpson's father and manager, Joe Simpson, was a Texas-based Southern Baptist minister whose frequent appraisal of his daughter's large breasts and sex appeal made many interviewers cringe but would not necessarily have been out of place at purity balls. Joe Simpson raised his daughter to sing special music in church, at youth events, and at purity gatherings. In 1996, Simpson landed a spot in an all-star choir performing Andraé Crouch's "My Tribute" and recorded one ill-fated CCM album. But being a beautiful, young, curvaceous, teenage blonde was a liability in church circles, which, by extension, made her a potential liability in CCM. Simpson recalled that when she was just in seventh grade her breasts drew men's attention when she sang special music, and she was scolded for eliciting lust from the congregation. "Anytime I sang [in church]," Simpson recalled, "I covered myself."[8]

Sex appeal was far less of a liability on Top 40 radio, and Simpson's 1999 mainstream pop debut, *Sweet Kisses*, enjoyed respectable sales and produced a couple of charting singles. The ascent of Spears and Simpson as virginal sex symbols showed how conservative white evangelicals were influencing pop culture and not just lagging behind it. Spears and Simpson, steeped in white Southern Baptist conservatism, combined evangelical norms about female sexuality with Disney levels of polish, and became household names.

Evangelical caregivers, as a rule, did *not* approve. Focus on the Family complained that the Britney's "bare midriffs and boy-toy overtones" were dangerous for young ears. The newly categorized "tween"—children between the ages of eight and twelve who were the primary consumers of pop princess music—were, according to many in 1998, the cause of America's "downward march." "They are the vanguard of a new, decultured generation," bemoaned one culture critic, "isolated from family and neighborhood, shrugged at by parents, dominated by peers, and delivered into the hands of a sexualized and status- and fad-crazed marketplace."[9]

CCM answered by fighting fire with slightly more modest fire. In response to scantily clad girl groups like The Spice Girls, Sparrow Records' signed ZOEgirl. The trio, formed in 1999 and including Jesus rocker Chuck Girard's daughter Alisa, became one of the fastest-selling groups in the label's history. ZOEgirl's debut video included aerobic dancing reminiscent of the Spice Girls, but without the short skirts and hip thrusts. Stacie Orrico, who was discovered at Seminar in the Rockies at thirteen years of age, signed a record deal with ForeFront Records and released *Genuine* the same year.

For the young women of CCM, adhering to the standards of modesty and sexual purity was a big part of their marketability. When Nikki Leonti, a pastor's daughter from Corona, California, won a CCM singing contest at age thirteen, she received a record deal from Pamplin Records and released a hit 1998 record, *Shelter Me*. Leonti grew up going to True Love Waits events and eagerly sang for thousands while promoting the abstinence-only message. She even carried a decorative key, meant to be given to her future spouse, along with her virginity. But according to Leonti, she went on tour without her parents, and she was unprepared for how her teen body would be sexualized by the men around her. "Married Christian men," she recalled, "would call me 'eye candy'—I was fourteen or fifteen years old." Leonti's looks, powerful vocals, impressive record sales, and embrace of the abstinence message landed her on the cover of Focus on the Family's *Brio Magazine* at age seventeen. She was portrayed as an example of Christian teendom. "I was always asked the purity questions," she recalled of those days, "and I was sixteen or seventeen and I believed in all of that."

Just after her eighteenth birthday, however, Leonti found out, to her surprise, that she was pregnant. She had been raised with a strict True Love Waits approach to teen sexuality, but she had been given little education about the mechanics of sex and conception. "I had no idea about how sex worked," recalled Leonti, and when a twenty-one-year-old guitarist told her she was not engaging in behavior that would lead to pregnancy, the seventeen-year-old trusted what he said. "He said we weren't doing anything that would get me pregnant," she recalled, "and I believed him."

But, just as the *Brio* cover story was released, Leonti disclosed the pregnancy to her fans. Leonti's concerts were canceled, her music was removed from Christian bookstore shelves, and she was left without financial means to care for herself or her child. She felt utterly alone. "In that world, I was the most visible teen pregnancy," Leonti remembered, "and no one had any resources or help to give me." Like the many women of CCM who had faced scandals about their sexuality before her, the posture she was expected to take was apologetic. So, Leonti married the father of her daughter, said she was sorry, and hoped to start again in CCM. "I tried to come back," she said, and along the way, she fielded pointed questions from evangelical media outlets about the nature of her sexual life. "After I had my daughter, the interviewers asked detailed questions about how I got pregnant," she remembered, "I felt so uncomfortable about that, that people felt they could ask those questions."

Leonti faced an uphill battle. She was a talented singer and songwriter, but there were other young evangelical teen girls who were marketed as the pure, pop-star ideal. When fourteen-year-old Orrico performed her single "Don't Look at Me," at the Dove Awards, the singer wore a more conservative version of Spears' low-cut jeans and tight t-shirts. Her midriff was firmly covered; she barely moved her hips and did not touch her body suggestively. "Don't look at me," she sang, surrounded by backup dancers, bright lights, and glittering makeup before pointing up to the great beyond, "look at Him." Even though she told them not to, CCM fans *did* look at Orrico, and they bought a lot of her records.

Not to be outdone by the pop princesses of CCM, as the Backstreet Boys and NSYNC succeeded Boys II Men on the Top 40 charts, CCM answered with Plus One. Like Plus One's female counterparts, the band was expected to be the group that parents wanted their boys to be like, and that young women would want to date. Because their presumed fan base consisted of straight young teen and preteen girls, Plus One was tasked with being ideal youth-group boyfriend material, and their status as evangelical sex symbols sometimes complicated their Christian messaging. "Sometimes they don't listen," said singer Nathan Walters, "at first it might just be a bunch of screaming because we look good and dance well."[10]

By 2000, the booming, well-established model of clean-cut, moral entertainment obscured almost entirely the roots of CCM in revival-meeting music. In the congregations that promoted CCM, a decades-long artistic war over congregational music was being waged that rarely appeared on sales charts. By the end of the decade, that musical victor's influence grew beyond congregational skirmishes and began a campaign to take over all of CCM.

The "Personality Trend" in Worship

Maranatha!, Integrity, and Vineyard produced a steady stream of profitable praise-and-worship albums in the early 1990s that rarely sold enough to chart in *CCM Magazine*. In the early 1990s, they were made mostly by and for Pentecostal and Charismatic congregations. As such, they had limited appeal to Baptists or Presbyterians. Nondenominational Charismatic congregations, tied together loosely through worship-music networks, were growing quickly, however, and C. Peter Wagner argued in the 1990s that the future of Christianity itself was Charismatic and "Post-Denominational." Wagner's argument for independent Charismatic congregations led by "modern-day apostles," which Wagner dubbed a "New Apostolic Reformation," was not accepted in all corners of Pentecostal or Charismatic Christianity, but there was no denying that the music of Charismatic congregations was spreading far beyond denominational boundaries. As Pentecostal and Charismatic worship styles steadily won the "worship wars," which pitted liturgical norms of hymnals, congregational choirs, and organ music against rock band instruments and sensibilities, their influence expanded.

CCM entertainers were mostly white, male, and from the United States, but top-selling worship albums captured transnational, multicultural Charismatic fervor and stylistic variety. Black Gospel choir sensation Kirk Franklin and the Family brought "new traditional gospel worship and praise" from Fort Worth, Texas, to the number one spot on the *Billboard* Christian music charts.[11] Ron Kenoly, a Black Charismatic worship leader based in California, had a string of 1990s worship hits that transcended racial and denominational boundaries. In *Rejoice Africa* (1993), Lionel Peterson, a Black South African worship leader at Rhema Bible Church in Johannesburg, triumphantly celebrated the end of apartheid and the Second Coming. The Toronto Vineyard Church's 1994 "Pour Out My Heart" updated the Jesus people's hippiezed desire for intimacy with God and became a standard in evangelical services. In

1996, "Shout to the Lord" took Assemblies of God triumphalism from female worship leader Darlene Zschech and "Hillsong," the worship band at Hills Christian Life Centre in Sydney, Australia, to the United States and beyond.

They were missing from the US-centric *CCM* charts, but Charismatic and Pentecostal praise bands had been for decades steadily taking over Protestant worship in the Americas, thanks to rapidly developing worship networks between predominately white, United States–based Charismatic Bible colleges and congregations, and Latin American practitioners. Guatemalan worship leader Juan Carlos Alvarado began producing successful Spanish-language albums in the 1980s as music minister at Palabra En Acción in Quetzaltenango, Guatemala, a congregation pastored by Wes Spencer, graduate of Rhema Bible College in Broken Arrow, Oklahoma. Mexican worship leader Jorge Lozano was introduced to praise bands in the 1970s as a student at Christ for the Nations, a charismatic Bible college in Dallas, Texas.

Lozano mentored Marcos Witt, a child of white American Pentecostal missionaries to Durango, Mexico, who brought high-production-value, rock-driven praise music to Spanish-speaking audiences in the 1990s with praise-and-worship albums like *Proyecto Alabanza y Adoración* on Word Records and *Te Exaltamos (En vivo)* on Hosanna! Integrity. Prior to the arrival of praise bands, Spanish-speaking Pentecostal and Charismatic communities in Latin America worshiped mostly with *coritos*, choruses that were easy to learn and simple to play on the guitar. Flashy, rock-inflected music required specialized skills.[12]

Marco Barrientos, another graduate of Christ for the Nations, created influential worship albums and instructional books and sermons on "prophetic flow" through song throughout the 1980s and 1990s. In 1994, Witt founded Centro de Capacitaciones y Dinámicas Musicales, Asociación Civil, a worship training school in Durango, which expanded quickly to train Spanish-speaking worship leaders in Argentina, Guatemala, Colombia, and the United States. Portuguese-language worship networks in Brazil likewise grew in the 1990s. Worship bands like Diante do Trono, led by Christ for the Nations alumna Ana Paula Valadão, created contemporary worship sounds at Lagoinha Church, a Charismatic Baptist congregation in Belo Horizonte, in southeastern Brazil.[13]

Charismatic worship leaders from around the world were trained at Rhema Bible College and Christ for the Nations, as well as at International House of Prayer (IHOP) in Kansas City, Missouri; Bethel School of Supernatural Ministry in Redding, California; and Brownsville Revival School of Ministry in Pensacola, Florida. Alumni created catalogs of new worship songs and translated English-language hits from the likes of Hillsong and Bethel. Their music crisscrossed the globe as Charismatics in Brazil, Mexico, Guatemala, Colombia, Honduras, Australia, South Africa, the United States, Canada, and many other nations sang new songs of praise.

Through transnational gatherings like Praise Marches, Charismatic worshipers of the 1990s sang songs like "Shine, Jesus, Shine" in multiple languages, in transnational public marches. In events like the March for Jesus, Charismatics all over the world marched in their respective cities and towns. As they did so, they made the public spaces around them their own public congregation, and they declared that the ground under their feet was part of God's kingdom.[14]

Rock-oriented worship music from abroad often returned to the United States, as well as Europe, through immigrant communities, who formed churches wherever they made a home.[15] There, worshipers learned how to grow big churches with elaborate rock-concert-style worship experiences. The bigger the music, the bigger the church, the logic went. And the more prosperous the ministry, the more it was clear that the Spirit was in fact inhabiting the praises of God's people.[16]

In 1996, Lindell Cooley of Brownsville Assembly of God in Pensacola, Florida, released *Revival at Brownsville* on Hosanna! Music, which captured the spirit of predominately white Pentecostal worship.[17] The boisterous enthusiasm and ecstatic practices of Brownsville, along with catchy rock tunes depicting spiritual warfare, brought curious revival tourists from around the world to Brownsville's revival school. There, worshipers sang about King Jesus as an end-times warrior "leading the armies all across this land" to Pentecostal and Charismatic congregations all over the world.

Building on the displays of Zionism made popular in 1970s Charismatic churches, worship services at Brownsville also included enthusiastic appropriations of Jewish rituals. One evening, Messianic Jewish Evangelist Dick Reuben sounded the shofar and afterward encouraged Christians in attendance to use it. The story of Gideon from Judges 6–8, Reuben reasoned, should guide twentieth-century use of the traditional Jewish instrument. Gideon won the battle, Reuben argued, but not with the sword. His weapon was the sound of a shofar.

As Reuben led the congregation, he explained how the shofar worked as a weapon of spiritual warfare. "There's something about the enemy's camp," he told the Brownsville audience, "That, boy, when we sound the shofar, we go right in his [the devil's] face. We stomp on him, and we take back what was stolen from us!" Reuben's rhetoric built in intensity as the music swelled around him. "Let the devil hear you," he yelled after blowing the shofar, "It's war! It's war!" The audience roared and wept in reply.

Reuben went on to call out witchcraft, drugs, addiction, sickness, homosexuality, and violence as demonic powers he believed were afflicting the faithful. The grand finale of the shofar worship service was a call for God to save the United States. "Lord, we're believing you for the government of the United States of America," Reuben said to the cheering crowd, "We're believing you for Congress. We are believing you, Lord, for the White House!"[18]

Reuben's claims for the nation stood in contrast to the historically predominant Baptist notions about God and country favored by the likes of Billy Graham and Jerry Falwell. America was important, not necessarily because God birthed the nation, as Graham and others argued. Rather, as Hal Lindsey reasoned, the United States was *a* nation that supported *the* nation of Israel, which would usher in the ultimate reign of King Jesus. Worship services featuring shofars, paired with the Stars and Stripes, showed support for both. Many powerful pastors in Charismatic and Pentecostal worship circles—like Don Finto, Jack Hayford, and Michael Brown—also subscribed to this theory of the end times.[19]

In the United States, the Brownsville revival's eccentric, ecstatic expressions of praise were considered pretty fringe in the late 1990s, even if their music sold well. But the sensibilities that allowed for robust support for one's nation of birth (wherever that may be) and the nation of God's choice (always and forever Israel) translated well across national boundaries. Juan Carlos Alvarado's "Jehová Edifica Jerusalén" in Guatemala, and American worship pastor Paul Wilbur's *Levanta-te Jerusalém!*, encouraged the worshiper's identification with Israel, while not ruling out patriotism for their homelands. White, English-speaking, North American institutions and industries had significant influence over these theological conversations. Due in large part to United States–based financial and mass media resources, these transnational musical communities expanded rapidly throughout the decade. Their absence from the CCM charts demonstrates, however, that this growth was mostly unrecognized by media-making evangelical networks in North America.

Worship songs of the 1990s rarely charted on Christian radio, in part because the lengthy recordings and eclectic musical styles were out of sync with the sounds of the general market. CCM rockers Petra fused their stadium rock sound with radio-length worship music when they released a follow-up to their successful 1989 album *Petra Praise: The Rock Cries Out* in 1997. Covering worship standards like "Lord I Lift Your Name on High" breathed new life into the band's flagging career and also showed that rock shows made for appealing worship experiences among white evangelical audiences.

An English youth-ministry band called Delirious? crossed the pond with a worship album, *King of Fools*, in 1997, which brought modern British rock to

American evangelical audiences. Stuart Garrard, aka Stu G, was an admirer of Queen's famous performance of "The Champion" at Wembley Stadium in 1986, and when the band led worship songs at "Champion of the World," a youth rally and worship concert attended by over 50,000 at Wembley Stadium in 1997, it was a dream come true. The successful fusion of British rock from Delirious? and fellow Englishman, worship leader Matt Redman, was, for American CCM, a British invasion.

"I Could Sing of Your Love Forever" by Delirious? and "Better Is One Day" by Redman quickly became mainstays in evangelical worship services. As videos of thousands of young, predominately white, English people cheering and praying along to modern rock songs like "Shout to the North and the South" arrived in the United States, white evangelicals began to create their own worship bands. In 1998, *Billboard* reported on the healthy sales of worship music.[20]

The trend of the Anglicized rock-band model, along with stateside Vineyard worship leaders like Darrell Evans and Kevin Prosch, prioritized the worship leader and deemphasized the role of the congregation. Emphasizing a particular worship leader was a departure from earlier Vineyard albums, which showcased a worship experience from a specific congregation. The model of the rock star meant that any given worship leader could travel to any given location—a congregation, a theater, a stadium—and deliver a worship experience with or without a specific congregation or preacher or any other trappings of liturgy. Many worship acts chafed under the label of "artist" or "entertainer," preferring instead the title of "worship leader," but there was no doubt that worship leaders were the stars of the show.

Nashville-based CCM Americanized British mod-rock worship when founding members of the band Zilch, which included members of DC Talk's backing band, traveled to the raucous Brownsville Revival. While in Pensacola, they attended services featuring Vineyard worship leader Andy Park, and their lives changed forever. As Zilch, the band's sales had been, zilch; as a newly formed worship band, they would go on to create a "sonic flood" of God's presence in the world in partnership with independent artist Jeff Deyo. The band renamed themselves Sonicflood and released a praise-and-worship rock album in 1999.

Sonicflood's hits included "I Want to Know You" by Andy Park. The jangly ode to intimacy with God included, in the Sonicflood version, a spoken-word exhortation about the state of the nation. "You can't move away from that foundation without destroying the nation," said the outro, "The only truth that founded this nation, we left a country of tyranny for religious freedom to worship." Without context, musings on the constitution and religious freedom seemed out of step with the intensely personal spirit of the song. When seen as a part of CCM's ongoing concern for the moral and spiritual foundations of the United States, the Brownsville Revival attendees' words made sense.

Well-produced, high-energy rock worship music played by professional musicians became standard practice for megachurch congregations, many of which, like Brownsville, were Pentecostal or Charismatic. Whereas earlier generations of megachurches, like Robert Schuller's Crystal Cathedral, spent money on orchestras, operatic soloists, or theatrical props, megachurch pastors of the new millennium invested in expensive guitars, rock lighting, and fog machines.[21] When Charismatic pastor Joel Osteen inherited his father's pulpit in 1999, the first hire he made was Cindy Cruse-Ratcliff of the Cruse Family, who honed a bombastic worship rock sound known by the name of the church: the Lakewood Sound. Cruse-Ratcliff and Israel Houghton, who was hired in 2001, wrote jubilant songs of Pentecostal exultation.

The worship band Passion baptized modern worship music into Neo-Reformed and Southern Baptist college ministries. As an outgrowth of his college campus ministry at Baylor University, Louie Giglio's Passion Conferences aimed to instill quality teaching from prominent Neo-Calvinists like firebrand John Piper and buttressed those messages with worship music extolling Reformed doctrines about the sovereignty of God. Based in Giglio's hometown of Atlanta, Passion conferences launched worship rockers like Texan Chris Tomlin, along with worship duo Nathan and Christy Nockels.

Chris Tomlin's early work showed a typical CCM interest in the fate of the United States. Tomlin's 2000 album *The Noise We Make* included a musical take on 2 Chronicles 7:14. Like Michael Card's "Heal Our Land," Tomlin's "America" reappropriated the exhortation from the ancient nation of Israel to the twenty-first-century United States. "The Lord is coming," he sang triumphantly, "Coming to America." Tomlin and the Passion band toured the nation, interceding on its behalf on the same Christian college circuit that had launched so many CCM artists. While white rock bands were a declining presence on mainstream Top 40 radio, Tomlin and Passion showed they had durable appeal in white evangelical worship spaces.

Brewing Trouble for the "Church Market"

By 2000, CCM was the fifth-highest-selling music genre in the United States and by some growth estimates was outpacing general market music sales.[22] *Rolling Stone* and *Spin* thought CCM was hopelessly uncool, but major corporations with overlapping suburban white customer bases like Target,

Disney, Great America, and Universal Studios eagerly sought out CCM partnerships. Fueled by multiple generations of eager evangelical consumers and riding high on the cultural capital associated with born-again evangelicalism, CCM sales soared. Fundamental cracks in the foundation of the industry appeared, however, even when sales were at all-time highs.

Digital tools helped refine CBA bookstore marketing practices. In the new millennium, aided by internet technology, a figure known as "Becky" materialized in the collective imagination of CCM marketers. Becky (or, by some accounts "Lisa") was a data-driven composite sketch of the typical buyer of CCM—a suburban, middle-to-upper-middle-class straight white woman who raised her kids with the help of Contemporary Christian Music. As the Digital Age progressed, bookstores and radio stations honed their portrait of Becky. They knew what Becky drove, where she lived, her marital status, the size of her household, where she went on a special night out for dinner, and where she took her children to the drive thru. In fact, in some marketing circles, Christian punk and metal developed its own composite figure: "Todd," the sons who rebelled against the Beckys of CCM.[23]

Understanding Beckys paid off on the airwaves. "Since employing that research and data," remarked radio promoter Chris Hauser, "Christian radio audiences went through the roof."[24] But, the same year that the CBA rejoiced at its record sales, several small businesses were founded with the aim of circumventing bookstores as distributors of CCM through the internet. Startups like MusicForce.com, Club Fish, and Crosswalk.com vied for CCM customers. Competition was fierce, however, as five-year-old bookseller Amazon.com recognized the potential in CCM sales, to the frustration of Christian music startups.[25]

The idea that CCM customers could purchase with no curation from a Christian bookstore or website meant that some of the final theological gatekeepers—the bookstore buyers—would lose their status as curators of CCM theology. Beckys had worked in close partnership with CBA retailers, but thanks to the rise of Amazon, the role of bookstores began to diminish. The advent of online file-sharing was another monumental threat to CCM. Musicforce and Club Fish were selling physical products in competition with brick-and-mortar stores, but file-sharing platforms like Napster (released in 1999) allowed listeners to share music via digital files, which meant that the internet had the potential to make the profitability of recorded music a thing of the past.

Tech-driven innovations challenged the entire recorded music industry, but CCM faced particular existential threats at the end of the century. The fact that some of the most successful artists of the decade like Jars of Clay,

Switchfoot, and Jennifer Knapp—along with their substantial fan bases—expressed ambivalence or outright anger about being used as "tools of evangelism" for conservative white evangelicals called the future of the evangelization through osmosis into question. Christian-metal-rap-rock band P.O.D. (Payable on Death) further demonstrated the potential irrelevance of CCM as a niche when the band signed with Atlantic Records and released "Rock the Party (Off the Hook)," a single that topped MTV's influential *Total Request Live* music video countdown in 2000.

In many ways, P.O.D.'s "ministry," as they called it, was recognizably evangelical. Lead singer Sonny Sandoval brought straightforward messages about the love of God to MTV. He appeared on *Politically Incorrect with Bill Maher*, where he earnestly spoke about his love for the Bible and shared the story of his conversion to Christianity. But P.O.D. was decidedly outside traditional CCM in other ways. None of the band members were white, they did not form at an evangelical college, and they did not develop on a Nashville-based CCM label. P.O.D. proved that a group of devout young rockers did not need the mechanism of CCM to be rock stars for God.

Other rockers followed in the footsteps of P.O.D. Scott Stapp, the frontman of Creed, was raised in a Pentecostal church, and the band's 1999–2000 hit "Higher" reflected the "golden streets" where "blind men see" of generations of heavenly minded Pentecostal songwriters. Creed was signed to a mainstream label (Wind-up Records), however, and Stapp insisted that the group was not specifically "Christian," which in Stapp's imagination would make the band's music didactic. "A Christian band has an agenda," Stapp argued on the band's website, "to lead others to believe in their specific religious beliefs. We have no agenda!"[26]

Musicians were not the only ones to leave the CCM fold. As young white evangelicals grew up, many felt that the positive distillations of white evangelical truths that dominated CCM charts were unsatisfying. For Bethany Erickson, who grew up making up dances to Carman songs in Jackson, Tennessee, in the late 1990s, CCM was "emotionally constricting." "Some feelings and desires were simply not allowed to be expressed," she noted, "Better to stick with the sanitized version, all 'positive and encouraging.'" When Erickson became an adult, her world expanded. "My college roommate introduced me to Black Gospel music, and I found a genre that expressed suffering without resolution," she recalled; "that was better."[27]

In addition to philosophical challenges, the future of CCM was in peril because of simple demographics. CCM was built on the purchasing power of white suburban boomers, but boomers did not replicate the birth rates of their parents. The overwhelming market advantages for white-owned bookstores meant that, by the 1990s, white Christian bookstores were the only place where many non-white evangelical communities shopped for books, Bibles, music, and other merchandise. For young people like Korean American Daniel Lee, who grew up in a Full Gospel Church in New York with parents who would not let him listen to U2, CCM was the only option. "A lot of the CCM music was a safe place," he recollected, "Korean parents were ok with teenagers listening to it." CCM inspirational songs were standard in his church. "We had a lot of Steve Curtis Chapman," he recalled.

There were simply not as many white evangelical consumers coming of age in the new millennium, while Asian and Latino/a Americans made up the fastest-growing segments of evangelicalism in the United States.[28] To expand their customer base, CBA bookstores began "targeting Hispanics" and established CCM stars like Carman and Steve Green recorded in Spanish. Toby McKeehan's Gotee Records promoted and platformed many of the Black and Brown artists who charted on *CCM*, like Out of Eden, hip-hop duo GRITS, and Samoan-American Assemblies-of-God boy band the Katinas.[29] Top 40 radio and *Billboard* Hot 100 charts featured more and more Black hip hop, rap, and pop artists and entertainers, but week to week and year to year, Contemporary Christian charts remained around 75–90 percent white.

The whiteness of the business was a problem for the long-term viability of CCM, but it was an asset for Republican activists of the 1990s. Michael W. Smith and DC Talk sang before 20,000 at the US Capitol with True Love Waits in 1994, as evangelicals protested condoms in public schools. Third Day accompanied Jerry Falwell Sr. and Pat Robertson to Washington DC while they preached against "laziness called welfare," "abortionists," and "homosexuality" at the "Washington for Jesus" rally in 1996. The Maranatha! Promise Band of 1997 led a crowd of between 600,000 and 800,000 predominately white men in worship as the Promise Keepers denounced racism, promised to love their wives, and prayed for the United States on the National Mall. Wherever the evangelical fight for public policy went, CCM was likely to follow.

The Music of Mini-Martyrdoms

Carman's over-the-top militant metaphor for taking over public spaces with weaponry was realized in a gruesome, literal manner on April 20, 1999. Two heavily armed teenagers from Littleton, Colorado, attempted to bomb Columbine High School and in the process shot and killed twelve students and one teacher and injured another twenty-one. Their actions shocked—and fascinated—the nation. The twenty-four-hour cable news cycle and emerging online culture created an endless appetite for details about the troubled duo and students they killed.

Two young white evangelical women whose lives were cut short captured the imagination of conservative Christians in the days that followed. Rachel Joy Scott, an outspoken Christian and pastor's daughter who died as the first victim of the shooting spree, was memorialized as a "modern-day martyr." Cassie Bernall's reported confession of faith with a gun to her head, however, became an evangelical phenomenon. After a gunman asked her if she believed in God, the young woman was said to have responded with "Yes," before the gunman "blew her away."

"Yes." The legend of the girl who said "yes" to God—and "no" to the atheism of a public-school killer—enchanted white conservatives. For activists like Joseph Bottum, the Columbine horrors had an upside. Bottum argued that future generations would remember her death as the beginning of a revival of "the American soul" comparable to the Great Awakening of the eighteenth century. "To picture her standing there trembling in the school library, with a gun to her head, the question 'Do you believe in God?' hanging in the air," wrote Bottum, "is to believe that a change of heart is possible, that God may be loose in America again, that the pendulum may have finally begun its long arc back."[30]

The only sticking point was the fact that Cassie Bernall was almost certainly not the evangelical girl who said "yes."[31] Another young woman, a Catholic student named Valeen Schnurr, had a well-corroborated conversation with the young man who shot her. In response to the question "Do you believe in God?" a bullet-riddled, bleeding Schnurr responded "Yes" and survived. The facts, however, were quickly subsumed by an eager evangelical media. Franklin Graham spoke at the memorial service in Columbine. Amy Grant and Michael W. Smith added special music. Nonwhite pastors and non-Christian religious leaders in the Denver area noted with frustration that although the victims included a cross-section of the local community, the event was "too evangelical and too white." No people of color spoke or sang at the memorial, and all speakers were Christian.[32]

Four months after her daughter died, Misty Bernall published a memoir of her daughter's life and death. *She Said Yes: The Unlikely Martyrdom of Cassie Bernall* spent five weeks on the *New York Times* bestseller list. Five Iron Frenzy—whose band members were related to a young woman trapped in a choir room during the Columbine shootings—wondered in "A New Hope," "what made the human mind dark enough to kill?" but most CCM songs took Bernall's imagined response and created a story of triumphant martyrdom.

Rebecca St. James released "Yes, I Believe in God" as a tribute single that year. In November of 1999, Michael W. Smith released *This Is Your Time*, his fourteenth studio album (along with a co-authored companion book *This Is Your Time*, released the following year). The title track was inspired by the story of Bernall. The music video for "This Is Your Time" included footage of Cassie Bernall talking about how she wanted to share her faith with others. DC Talk repeated the Bernall myth and compared her death to the early Christian martyrs in Rome in their co-authored *Live Like a Jesus Freak: Stories of Those Who Stood for Jesus, the Ultimate Jesus Freaks*.

The Center for Reclaiming America, founded by dance-instructor-turned-televangelist D. James Kennedy, saw an opportunity in Columbine to take their messages against abortion, the "homosexual agenda," and public schools to broad audiences through song. The organization recruited Rebecca St. James as their spokeswoman for a new "Yes, I Believe in God" campaign, the aim of which was to inspire students to bear witness to the importance of religious liberty in public schools by forming "Bible clubs" on campus. "People have tried to remove God from the classroom," the national director Janet Folger told Liberty University's periodical in 1999. "The time has come for the youth of America to rise up," wrote Folger, "and boldly declare, as Cassie did, 'Yes, I believe in God.' "[33]

Eventually, when Valeen Schnurr shared her story of being a Catholic spared from death, she was derided as a copycat, and Columbine became for young evangelicals a Clinton-era myth of resisting encroaching secularity and liberalism. "I wish it could happen to me," said one enthusiastic evangelical teen, reflecting on Bernall's death.[34] "I was obsessed with [This Is Your Time]," wrote Cindy, who as a teen in the early 2000s came of age during the aftermath of Columbine "and often wondered if I'd be willing to sacrifice my life for Jesus." As an adult, Cindy now sees things differently. "Adults asking teens these sorts of questions," she notes, "instead of making policy changes feels absurd to me now (many, many school/workplace shootings later)."[35]

To the relief of many, the likelihood of evangelical high school students dying in a school shooting by an anti-Christian atheist was low. "The guns pointed at the Columbine students' heads were literal," mused Michael W. Smith in *This Is Your Time*; "Our guns will usually be figurative." In lieu of guns to the head, Smith advised students to seek out lower-stakes "mini-martyrdoms." Smith noted that being excluded from the popular crowd at school or maintaining conservative sexual ethics could serve as a form of public self-sacrifice.[36] In the end, the public prayers at flagpoles and confessions of virginity before marriage became, for many young people, a much more achievable form of self-denial than martyrdom.

After eight years of Clintonian politics, evangelicals were hopeful for a change. In the weeks leading up to the presidential election, as Clinton's vice president, Democrat Al Gore, campaigned against Republican legacy George W. Bush, the Call DC, a co-ed version of Promise Keepers, brought several hundred thousand energized evangelicals to the US Capitol. At the September 2, 2000, gathering, participants rallied for "reconciliation between children and parents, an end to abortion and sexual immorality, and the return of school-sponsored prayer." Attendees prayed, wept, danced, waved American flags, and renounced demonic curses over the nation to worship music that celebrated Jesus as king.

The Call DC was predominately white, but it was noticeably more diverse than evangelical trips to Washington of the past, a reflection of growing white, Latinx, Black, and Asian Charismatic worship networks. Attendees received exhortations from up-and-coming young white preachers like Judah Smith and Charismatic evangelists like Korean American Ché Ahn, who predicted "a revolution" in American society. As the guitars strummed, anti-abortion preachers passionately argued against "women who have given in to the culture of death that has arisen in our country." Michael W. Smith led the audience in a worship tune.

Rachel Joy Scott's father also appeared. "Two thousand years ago, a teacher and twelve students had a powerful impact on this world and they started a revolution," he said, "two thousand years later at Columbine high school, another teacher and twelve students had an impact on this nation once again, and they are the seeds of the revolution we are seeing take place right here today." Michael Brown of the Brownsville Revival built on the language of revolution and spiritual warfare that had fueled his Florida meetings. "If you are absolutely serious about enlisting in the army, if you are absolutely serious about giving your life for a Jesus revolution," Brown said, "I want you to stand to your feet right now, cry out!"[37]

A month later, *CCM Magazine* surveyed artists about which national political issues mattered to them. "Music and its dance with politics continues today," Gregory Rumburg of *CCM Magazine* noted, and CCM artists did their part to get out the vote. No one endorsed George W. Bush explicitly, but Michael Tait of DC Talk stayed true to his Liberty University conservative roots and argued for "less government and more privatization." Phillip LaRue of LaRue criticized Bill Clinton as someone who had "not been a very good definition of what a president should be," and Rebecca St. James said that "I admire a politician who takes a stand against abortion." When George W. Bush won a hotly contested and bitterly disputed presidential election in 2000, he invited his longtime friend—another "W" by the name of Michael W. Smith—to perform "Above All," a worship song, at the 2001 inaugural prayer service in Washington DC.

7

"God's Not Dead"

The Waning of CCM and the Waxing of Worship (2001–2012)

Michael W. Smith's album *Worship* was released on Tuesday, September 11, 2001. That morning, however, the usual album-launching festivities were cut short by the worst terrorist attack in American history. As the nation grieved, Smith visited his old friend, President George W. Bush. "Hey W," George W. said to Michael W. in his retelling, "I think you need to write a song about this." "There She Stands," Smith's tribute to the American flag raised by firefighters in the rubble of the World Trade Center, became an unofficial soundtrack to the Bush administration's "War on Terror."

In the aftermath of 9/11, conservative white Protestant Americans found something that they had lost after the fall of communism: a foreign, non-Christian threat to the United States. The enemy was perhaps not so well defined as the USSR, but the fact that the attacks were carried out in the name of Islam gave evangelicals an enemy of the faith as well as of the nation. The War on Terror's focus on the Middle East also reinvigorated longstanding evangelical visions of the end times. With a clear ally in conservative evangelical President George W. Bush, Smith and other CCM luminaries sang songs praising God—and soldiers of the United States—for waging a righteous war against an international "axis of evil."

All of the patriotic fervor and end-times energy in the world, however, could not stop the business of CCM from descending into freefall. Internet streaming and file sharing pummeled the entire recording business. But CCM's descent was arguably much steeper and faster, because the scaffolding that supported it collapsed. While the mainstream recording industry eventually found a new financial normal, CCM's recovery stalled, and white evangelical political power seemed destined for the same fate. When Barack Obama became president in 2008, many speculated that a growing multiracial electorate would usher in a political revolution. Even as pundits predicted the end of white evangelical power in American public life, however, CCM stars defiantly insisted that God—and conservative evangelical activism—was not dead.

"Battle Cry"

To many, 9/11 felt like the end of the world. More often than not, white evangelicals were keen to interpret the attacks as a sign that the rapture was near. *The Late Great Planet Earth* author Hal Lindsey argued that the events of 9/11 were an indication that "America will be destroyed as a world power," but Lindsey's pessimistic vision of the fate of the United States did not resonate with a nation preparing for war. Americans were much more attuned to Tim LeHaye and Jerry Jenkins' *Left Behind* series, in which the United States remained a nation of eschatological consequence, and Americans were cast as an "embattled minority of fringe survivalists" resisting the evil, pacifist Antichrist.[1] For their part, LeHaye and Jenkins saw 9/11 as a "foretaste" of the coming end of days calamity.

To the delight of many CBA booksellers, consumers turned to *Left Behind* for help interpreting the times. Jenkins was pleased that 9/11 brought interest in the series, and that the tragic events had rekindled a robust love of God and country. "It took something like these attacks to all of a sudden make God 'okay' again," he told *CNN*; "Senators are singing 'God Bless America.'"[2]

Senators were not alone. Jaci Velasquez sang "God Bless America" to George W. Bush and members of the 101st Airborne Division in 2004, proclaiming that "their fight against terror and for America's freedom makes me proud to be an American!" Fledgling pop ensemble Jump 5 re-released their debut album and included a rendition of Lee Greenwood's "God Bless the USA." CCM luminaries also created a flurry of original patriotic responses. Carman's "Red, White, and Blue" was a bombastic ode to American exceptionalism. DC Talk's "Let's Roll" took its name from the famous last words of Tod Beamer, an evangelical Christian who died while stymieing the hijackers of United Airlines Flight 93, and seamlessly blended patriotism and piety. "Let's roll, let's fight," they sang in the midst of the American war in Afghanistan, "let's show the world what's right." Sparrow Records' "In God We Trust" brought Amy Grant, Michael W. Smith, DC Talk, Rachel Lampa, and many more to sing the official motto of the United States. Rebecca St. James' 2003 "I Thank You" featured audio footage of President Bush praising soldiers and Americans ensuring members of the military that "we stand with you—more importantly, God goes before you."

While Beckys sang along in support of American soldiers abroad, at home their eyes were on their pocketbooks. The prosperity gospel—the belief that God provides material abundance to the faithful—was on the rise, and no book did more to promote this idea than *The Prayer of Jabez*. Written by evangelical parachurch leader and Dallas Theological School graduate Bruce Wilkinson, *The Prayer of Jabez* applied a short passage in 1 Chronicles about an "honorable" man named Jabez to American evangelicals at the turn of the twenty-first century. Pray for "enlarged territory," Wilkinson advised, and God will give blessings to you.

In 2001, ForeFront Records released *The Prayer of Jabez*, a Dove Award–winning compilation disc filled with offerings from CCM mainstays like Margaret Becker and Geoff Moore. Pamplin Records partnered with Rebecca St. James and Nicki Leonti on *The Jabez PrayerSong*, a collection for children. MercyMe, a band of Southern Baptist worship rockers from Highland Terrace Baptist Church in Greenville, Texas, released their first single, "Bless Me Indeed (Jabez's Song)," asking God to "Let your hand keep me from harm and pain." *The Prayer of Jabez* and related music encouraged Beckys of the new millennium to embrace the notion that the God of Israel wanted to bless them with enlarged "territory" in the here and now.[3]

At first glance, these two ideas seemed contradictory. *Left Behind* claimed that the world would soon be a terrible place for Christians. The *Prayer of Jabez* said that God would make His people rich and powerful. Bookstore buyers, however, reached a higher synthesis. Their mission was to protect their children from impending doom and also to increase their inheritance. Energized by a climate of apocalyptic fear, they grew determined to battle for their children's future. Every space in society, from the Capitol Mall to public schools to clubs and bars, was meant to be occupied and cleansed by the devout, and CCM music played a leading role.[4]

The Terrorist Threat

The post-9/11 militarization of American society extended to youth groups, where attendees playacted as the army of God. Some youth groups hosted events wherein members were bombarded by figures dressed as "terrorists" demanding that they renounce Jesus. Others created musical marches in formation to DC Talk's "Let's Roll," wearing camouflage and singing, "let's fight / let's show the world our light." In most cases, those portraying terrorists had only vague notions about Islam or "Sharia Law." The version of Islam in these games may have been a figment of the evangelical imagination, but for many attendees the terror was very real.

Soon enough, evangelicals began to see the threat on their doorsteps. No one did more to make this threat seem real than Teen Mania's Ron Luce. Luce, a longtime collaborator of Carman's, shared the entertainer's love of bombast. He warned that "virtue terrorists" were attacking the youth of the United States. "They're raping virgin teenage America on the sidewalk," said Luce in a rant about sex, drugs, violence, and secular music, "and everybody's walking by and acting like everything's OK. And it's just not OK." Luce, like many youth ministers of the decade, held fast to the notion that "music is the most significant inroad of the Christian faith into the life of the youth," and he formulated a music-driven response to the threat of so-called virtue terrorism.[5]

Luce created *Battle Cry*, a manifesto for the youth of the new millennium. "Just as the events of September 11, 2001, permanently changed our perspective on the world," he wrote, "so we ought to be awakened to the alarming influence of today's culture terrorists." In the mid 2000s, Luce began holding Battle Cry events—two-day concerts in partnership with Christian heavy-metal band Pillar. Battle Cry aimed to create "potent Christians" who were protected from "heterophobia," abortion, porn, and "media influence." Luce had explicit political aims for the United States. Bemoaning the fact that "our nation has fallen from core, evangelical, Bible based beliefs," he established Battle Cry "to publicly let legislators know that Christians will not stand idly by while being bombarded with legislation that attacks the core values of believers."

Stadiums full of rowdy teenagers screamed along with Pillar's "Frontline," which Luce picked for the gathering's theme "We fight to live, we live to fight / And tonight, you'll hear my battle cry." Being called "Christian fascists" by protesters in liberal cities like San Francisco only added fuel to their fire. Like the small squad of American rebels in the *Left Behind* series, Battle Cry teenagers were encouraged to see themselves as underdogs. Promotional materials for Teen Mania's Battle Cry events included Psalm 144:1: "Praise be to the LORD my Rock, who trains my hands for war, my fingers for battle." According to Luce, Battle Cry was an effort to mobilize young people to fight "political correctness," ecumenism, "civil initiatives promoting gay marriage," the removal of the Ten Commandments from public spaces, and—most critically—immoral film and "an increasingly perverted music industry."[6] Teen Mania's Acquire the Fire concerts (ATF for short) sought to provide young people with wholesome alternatives to the supposed perversity of Top 40 mainstream music, and the events sold books, music, and other merchandise as weapons of war.

"Porcelain Heart"

The "virtue terrorists" identified by Ron Luce were after a lot more than sex, but in the war for American youths, sexual purity remained a frontline issue. The reigning CCM queen of all things purity was Rebecca St. James, and in 2002, she published a book companion to her hit song "Wait for Me," entitled *Wait for Me: Rediscovering the Joy of Purity in Romance*. Praised by the likes of pastor Eugene Peterson and her friend Joshua Harris, St. James filled the book with rapturous dreams of "a powerful stallion carrying a tall, dark, handsome rider" and advice for how to resist Satan by remaining abstinent. To support young women who found it hard to wait for the stallion and his rider, St. James published the *Wait for Me* journal, which prompted young women to write letters to their future spouse. "As you live in sexual purity," St. James wrote to her fans, "enjoy dreaming and sharing those dreams with the one you are waiting for."[7]

In 2004, St. James co-wrote *SHE: Safe, Healthy, Empowered—The Woman You're Meant to Be*, which argued that "Satan's lies" and the "failure of the feminist movement" were making women depressed and unhealthy.[8] St. James labeled her approach "new feminism." The "new feminist" was not preoccupied with making strides in the workplace. She embraced purity and sought a "knight" who would protect her feminine virtue. Practical advice included avoiding "mind sex" and masturbation. Such a woman would find happiness, health, and power. St. James expressed pity for Britney Spears, and disapproval. "When you are wearing very promiscuous clothing and you're showing a lot of flesh," she reflected on the pop icon, "you're really asking for sex."[9]

St. James and many other young women in CCM aimed to show that chastity was the *real* way to be sexy. They took great pains to display their bodies in "stylish yet non-revealing stage clothes" while singing "songs of sexual purity."[10] Their visual virtue was praised alongside their musical abilities. "What is extraordinary about Out of Eden," wrote Tony Cummings for CCM periodical *Cross Rhythms*, "is that they've been able to sell half a million albums, with each album selling more than its predecessor, without taking progressively more and more clothes off."[11]

Cummings may have been surprised, but anyone marketing to Beckys in the 2000s knew that pop songs about modesty and sexual abstinence were good business. ZOEGirl's "Good Girl" praised young women who were "not about miniskirts," while members of the group refused to dress provocatively and put "morals before popularity." ZOEGirl anchored a Women of Faith–sponsored tour for "Girls of Faith," which stressed "sexual purity, friendship and family issues."[12] Superchick, a female-fronted alternative-rock band, released "Barlow Girls," a 2001 song about girls who refused to perform "sexual hypnosis by being a hottie" and instead chose modesty and chastity. "All the guys in the band want a valentine from a Barlow girl," they sang, "boys think they're the bomb 'cause they remind them of their mom." In other words, they were marriage material.

In real life, those Barlow girls were Alyssa, Lauren, and Rebecca Barlow, a rock trio of sisters known as BarlowGirl. Raised in the evangelical media hub of Willow Creek Church, where their father was a pastor, the young women competed at the Seminar in the Rockies and eventually signed a record deal with Nashville-based Fervent Records. At their concerts, BarlowGirl harnessed the rhetoric of rebellion. "We tell people, 'You can be a rebel in a good way,'" noted a then-twenty-year-old Lauren Barlow.[13]

BarlowGirl gave a metaphorical valentine to abstinence advocates and the Disney Corporation with their 2004 song "Average Girl," which connected date-free, pure living with the happiest place on earth: "no more dating, I'm just waiting like Sleeping Beauty, my prince will come for me." BarlowGirl was featured at Disney's Night of Joy and on the official Disney Parks blog.

Billboard proclaimed BarlowGirl the most successful CCM act of 2004. As they crisscrossed the country, their concerts were punctuated by impassioned calls to rebel against the ways of the world by embracing holiness codes. First, clothing needed to be modest. "We need to respect ourselves and we need to cover up," they told their fans, arguing that modesty had the added bonus of "protecting ourselves." Second, interactions with men needed to be carefully regulated. The sisters were fastidious in their efforts. "We've never held a guy's hand," they told the young women and evangelical caregivers who attended their concerts—"we've never kissed a guy." To promote their brand of virtue, BarlowGirl collaborated on books like *Six Ways to Keep the Little in Your Girl*, a handbook for enhancing "parent-child connectedness" and preserving female chastity.

BarlowGirl was joined in their public calls for abstinence by purity-ring-wearing Disney Channel–singing mainstream superstars Miley Cyrus, Selena Gomez, Hillary Duff, Demi Lovato, and all three of the Jonas Brothers. The 2007 *American Idol* winner Jordin Sparks wore one too. Purity rings took center stage at the 2008 MTV music awards when comedian Russell Brand roasted the Jonas Brothers for their public declarations of virginity. Jordin Sparks jumped to their defense. "It's not bad to wear a promise ring," she said, "not everybody—guy or girl—wants to be a slut."

Sparks' categorization of young people as either virgin or slut went over well with many abstinence advocates, who were cautiously optimistic about their teen-idol allies. "The Jonas Brothers, Jordin Sparks, Miley Cyrus—they are doing a great job," Silver Ring Thing founder Denny Pattyn told *Reuters*, "so far."[14] Patton's hesitation was an implicit acknowledgment that marketing purity culture was a risky venture. Living by purity-ring branding sometimes meant dying by it.

When pop stars—particularly female pop stars—who rose to fame as teen icons of abstinence embraced overt celebrations of their sexuality, or had sex before marriage, they were discarded. When Disney-child-star-turned-pop-idol Justin Timberlake announced on national radio that he had sex with Britney Spears, it was she who was tarred as an enemy of sexual purity and a symbol of the depravation of American society.

In 2008, CCM singer-songwriter Bebo Norman felt compelled to repent on behalf of American culture for the woes of former abstinence advocate Britney Spears. Spears had gone from a virginal sex symbol to a divorced mother of two. She had been in and out of rehab and was struggling to maintain custody of her sons. Twenty-seven-year-old Spears was, in Norman's rendering, not a mother enraged by the paparazzi and scared to lose her children, but a lovelorn female child, a fragile creature, ravaged by consumer-driven American society, experiencing a "fall from grace." "We sell the beauty," he said, "but destroy the girl."

Of course, Britney Spears was hardly the first student of purity culture to have premarital sex. Most young evangelical women and men of the new millennium had sex before they were married. A 2001 survey of Southern Baptists, the denomination that gave the world True Love Waits, revealed that 70 percent of frequent churchgoers had premarital sex; 80 percent of those reported feelings of regret about it.[15] The concerts and pledges and workbooks and conferences and dress codes did not lead to abstinence—they led to shame.

The BarlowGirls proudly remained abstinent. They also remained girls with "porcelain hearts" in need of protection for their future spouses long after they left their teen years behind. "We're all in our 20s and we've never had a boyfriend," Lauren Barlow told fans in 2009, and she acknowledged that the idea that God instructed the band to "commit to never date until you meet the one I [God] have for you" would puzzle many.

Francesca Battistelli, a pop singer who became Dove Awards Female Vocalist of the Year in 2010, celebrated personal imperfections like "dents in my fender," and "rips in my jeans." But she also made sure, as a married woman, to celebrate young couples who "waited for love and it was worth it." Rebecca St. James eventually found her knight in her thirties. When she announced her engagement to Jacob Fink, a missionary-kid-turned-indie-rocker, she congratulated all young women who waited for sex until marriage.

"It's a pretty well-known fact that guys would like to marry a virgin," she claimed; "I think the whole idea that a girl is singing that song ["Wait for Me"] and is waiting really appeals to them too and helps them to strive to be men of honor."[16]

St. James was triumphant, but for others, life as a symbol of the pipeline from virtue to wedded bliss was exhausting, and eventually, unsustainable. After landing a role in a mainstream film that included themes of infidelity, drinking, and sex, Jaci Velasquez found herself facing the ire of CCM audiences. "People started canceling events," she said, "radio stations started dropping my music"[17] In part to cope with the stress of her career woes, Velasquez married in 2003, but divorced in 2005. Velasquez's divorce was, predictably, disruptive to the starlet's career, and devastating to Velasquez herself. "I felt guilty that I let people down," she recalled, "The little girls that used to want to be like me when they grew up." Velasquez remarried Nic Gonzales of the band Salvador in 2006, had children, and, like Sandi Patty before her, went on a redemption tour of sorts, but never regained her former stature in the industry.

Velasquez's divorce no doubt hurt her CCM sales, but she was not the only married mother to face an uphill battle on the charts. Full-grown women like Natalie Grant, Sara Groves, or Ashley Cleveland rarely outsold abstinence icons like St. James or BarlowGirl. "Someone like Ashley Cleveland was so incredibly talented," noted journalist Laura Jenkins, "but she was an adult grown woman singing about adult things and that wasn't what many of the record companies wanted."[18] When married mothers did have hits, they were often framed first not as artists, but as mothers and wives who upheld traditional family structures.

When thirty-year-old singer-songwriter Groves was profiled in *CCM Magazine* for her 2002 album *All Right Here*, the article emphasized Groves' status as a pastor's granddaughter with "strong family roots," and her role as "wife, mother, and minister." One word from "Fly," a track written to her husband Troy, caught the attention of *CCM Magazine* because of its potential to "raise eyebrows" of CCM listeners: "afterglow." Groves noted that the song was written as an "outpouring of her life as a worshiper, not just as a wife," but the article highlighted the "sensual" nature of the song and Groves' status as an ideal evangelical woman who fulfilled her husband's desires. "Life may be almost too perfect for Groves," it concluded, "a beautiful family, a successful ministry, and a husband who lingers in the 'afterglow.'"[19]

Looking back on that interview, Groves acknowledged that the stories she shared in the interview for the feature—stories of her grandfather, of welcoming her son home from the hospital—probably came in part from her own discomfort with being a woman with a career in conservative evangelical circles. "I had a fear of being seen as a neglectful mother," said Groves, "so I did so much framing nearly everywhere I went, 'What this? . . . this isn't a career, it's just this thing I do at night sometimes.' "[20]

The reign of virginal CCM pop starlets was eventually threatened, however, by a teenage singer from West Reading, Pennsylvania, named Taylor Swift. Swift was a pretty, petite blonde teenager who wore modest clothing and wrote chaste country songs with plenty of adolescent longing and Christian imagery. Swift's third single, "Our Song," depicted two teenagers who refrained from kissing and made sure to pray every night. "I think the real end for a lot of pop CCM was Swift," observed former Forefront A&R representative Mark Nicholas; "the same moms who brought their daughters to CCM concerts felt comfortable bringing them to a Taylor Swift show."[21]

Whether it was the fault of the Swifties or not, women of any age singing about anything at all were rarer and rarer on sales charts and Christian radio in the early 2000s. Women had always been underrepresented in CCM, but as rock-oriented worship music rose in prominence, their numbers dwindled further.

"Rock and Worship Roadshows"

Male worship leaders, dominated the *CCM* charts of the early 2000s. Michael W. Smith had reignited his career with worship albums. Sonicflood had a gold record and reached number two on the *Billboard* Heatseekers charts.

As worship music rose, the biggest youth group bands of the 1990s were in transition. DC Talk, the biggest youth-group band in the business, released another Grammy-winning album, *Solo*, but the album was a sendoff for the group. *Solo* featured individual offerings from Michael Tait, TobyMac, and Kevin Max. Max released *Stereotype Be* in 2001, but the album sales were disappointing, and he was dropped from Forefront Records. As TobyMac, McKeehan went on to release several solo albums about racial tolerance and being "[a]rdently enthused about God." Michael Tait created a band named Tait and released albums in 2001 and 2003, but he ultimately landed as the new lead singer of Newsboys, after lead singer Peter Furler. In 2006, Audio Adrenaline announced that they would be retiring the band the following year.

Bands that either began as worship groups or easily made the transition, like Third Day and MercyMe, carried on. MercyMe's "I Can Only Imagine," a meditation on heaven written by lead singer Bart Millard after the death of his father, had potential to be used in congregational worship, as special music, or as music for Beckys driving around suburbia, which made it an ideal fit for early aughts Christian radio. Two years after its 2001 release, a mainstream rock station in Dallas played it by request, and "I Can Only Imagine" became a general market hit. MercyMe's subsequent songs about heaven, prayer, and personal holiness hit all the right notes for youth groups, and the group's past life as a worship band meant that they could do double duty as a band. MercyMe toured with Michael W. Smith on the longstanding CCM star's twentieth-anniversary tour in 2003, and tour promoters teased that Amy Grant would join the tour as a "surprise guest" on select dates. CCM labels continued signing bands that fit the worship-and-rock entertainment niche: Casting Crowns (2003), Tenth Avenue North (2008), or Rebecca St. James' brothers' band For King & Country (2011).

In 2009, MercyMe began an annual concert series called "The Rock and Worship Roadshow," which featured what remained of the youth-group bands, especially those with worship chops. Shows included worship leaders like Matt Maher and introduced newcomers like Tenth Avenue North for a night of "family-friendly and Christ-centered entertainment that will uplift people and not break the bank." For just ten dollars per person, evangelical families could see a conglomeration of what they heard on the radio: rock and worship. It was a great deal for CCM fans, and it was a well-attended, profitable tour.

Much of the chart-topping worship music heard on Christian radio emerged not from Nashville-based labels, however, but from Louie Giglio's Atlanta-based Passion conferences as well as a constellation of Reformed organizations like Together for the Gospel, the Acts 29 Network, the Gospel Coalition, and John Piper's Desiring God Ministries. Passion created sixstepsrecords and signed affiliated acts like Chris Tomlin, the David Crowder Band, and Matt Redman. Passion artists Christy and Nathan Nockels landed their own record deal under the name Watermark with Michael W. Smith's Rocketown Records.

Passion musicians were guided in their musical direction by the teachings of John Piper, a patriarch of the "New Calvinists," a group of young conservative white evangelical men—including pastors like Mark Driscoll and Matt Chandler—who were set on reviving sixteenth-century Calvinism in the twenty-first century. Piper placed enormous value on the power of the preached word. He had spent time around Vineyard churches in the 1990s but warned his people about being "swept away" by charismatic practices like falling down under the power of the Holy Spirit during praise and worship.[22] Piper understood that worship music had the capacity to move hearts, and, if the lyrics of a song differed from the theological message of a sermon, songs could challenge the preacher's authority.

Piper's decades-long interest in creating a reformed vision of worship took form in the sixsteprecords roster. Worship through song could not be utilitarian. Worship, in Piper's view, should not inspire a person to give money or pledge virginity or support an orphanage. Worshiping God was an end in and of itself. Piper instructed worship band leaders to be vigilant and guard the hearts and minds of the faithful from what he regarded as poor doctrine. In this case, poor doctrine meant any theological ideas that steered attention away from the sovereign kingship of God, as discerned by Piper and his associates and expressed musically in Tomlin's 2004 megahit "How Great Is Our God."

Piper and his mentees sought to rebel against musical pragmatism that erased theological boundaries and aimed to reassert the importance of theological difference in worship and practice. Loosey goosey songs about human choice from hippie Charismatics engaged the hearts and minds of the faithful, even in Piper's home of Minneapolis. Through preaching, and by carefully regulating who sang what, the New Calvinists sought to reestablish strict boundaries around Neo-Reformed ideas about the mechanisms of salvation.

Whereas music produced by Vineyard writers in the 1990s emphasized mystical personal experiences, New Reformers were adamant that worship music was an intellectual, theological enterprise meant to be an extension of the preached word, and as such fell under the God-ordained purview of men. "We need to make sure that the [musical] accompaniment is suitable to the truth that we're saying," Piper advised his acolytes, "and that we go through the sound and through the truth to God himself."[23]

Piper's Young, Restless, and Reformed acolytes threw themselves into this project. Like their Reformed progenitors, they believed that the written word was key to theological formation; unlike Calvin and company, the Young, Restless, and Reformed network had access to new forms of writing like email, social media, and blogs. Soon, theological musings and full-blown arguments about music and much more were flourishing on big, popular websites and blogs like *Desiring God*, *The Gospel Coalition*, and John Piper's personal site.

Young Reformers rejected the "sea of often over-simplified contemporary praise choruses," in favor of songs "full of biblical, rich, and powerful truth, truth that is all too often absent from modern worship songs."[24] For Reformed people, that often meant music written by modern European Calvinists, but it also included modern music from Passion musicians like Tomlin's "Famous One" or "How Great Is Our God."

The big and famous God of Chris Tomlin was, in many ways, better suited to large arenas than was the Calvary Chapel and Vineyard music of the 1990s, which focused the nearness and accessibility of God "in the secret, in the quiet place." For the evangelical readers of *Christianity Today* in the 2000s, Passion music was "touchstone of modern worship." In 2006 *Christianity Today* put the Young, Restless, and Reformed movement—along with a man wearing a "Jonathan Edwards is my homeboy" t-shirt—on the cover. The headline claimed that Reformers new and old were "shaking up the church."

Shaking up the church, according to the New Calvinists, meant restoring biblical mandates about women and men. Congregations had become unduly influenced by women, *The Gospel Coalition* regularly argued. Women had stepped out of their places as natural subordinates to men and had taken on a "mantle of authority" by preaching. They needed to return to their rightful position, and the New Calvinists aimed to put them there.

Music was key to these efforts. Mark Driscoll, who made male dominion and female submission a core component of his preaching, classified his version of the good news as "Punk Rock Christianity." When Driscoll wanted to bring his hypermasculine messages to the masses, he recruited the head of Tooth & Nail A&R to help him "take over Christian radio and give an alternative to prom songs for Jesus."[25]

Rock-inflected worship music was the preferred mode of theological discourse for the Young, Restless, and Reformed, but Lecrae Devaughn Moore, a Black rapper, singer, songwriter, label owner and producer who performed as "Lecrae," also enjoyed a wide hearing among the New Calvinists of the early 2000s. Lecrae was one of a number of Black Christians who networked with white Calvinist congregations in online spaces and through Neo-Reformed conferences. His early music, highly influenced by John Piper, was welcomed among the predominantly white networks of the Young, Restless, and Reformed. Given the historic whiteness of CCM charts, and of the New Calvinist movement, Lecrae's rise seemed unlikely. But in a way, rap was a natural genre for Reformed theology. Rap's rapid-fire lyrics and history of confrontational social commentary made the genre seem well suited to a movement known for wordy, heated theological disputes. For many predominantly white Reformed figures, Reformed rap also represented an opportunity to "bring a Black art form under its sway."[26]

Lecrae rapped about fatherhood, a welcome topic in a movement intent on upholding distinct gender roles in the family and the church. He appeared on *The 700 Club* and shared his story of finding God as Father, which fit well with the patriarchal aims of the New Calvinists. Lecrae's ode to John Piper's famous sermon, "Don't Waste Your Life" (2008) was a Reformed-theology tour de force: it emphasized the fact that humans were made from dust, elected by God, saved by God, and instructed his listeners to "Magnify the Father." The music video, produced by Piper's Desiring God ministries, dramatized the life of a young Black man in trouble with the law who was connecting with a pastor while incarcerated. White Neo-Calvinist audiences welcomed Lecrae's depiction of himself in prisoner's garb in need of a savior, and Lecrae reached number 2 on the *Billboard* Christian Music charts.

Neo-Reformed ideas about gender grew in popularity along with the sounds of the Passion Conferences, the Gospel Coalition, and other Reformed networks. Many evangelical organizations, including Christian radio stations, began using gender hierarchies as a litmus test for Christian orthodoxy. "When John Piper started banging the drum about complementarianism," recalled Sara Groves, "we started getting calls before we went to events: are you complementarian or egalitarian?" Initially, Groves, a multi-generational member of Assemblies of God, dismissed the questions "as a tertiary issue." Indeed, in Pentecostal denominations like the Assemblies of God, and in most holiness denominations like the Nazarenes, it was. What Groves found out, however, was that the ascent of the New Calvinists had made male headship and female submission a central tenet of the evangelical faith.

Women leading congregational singing was a bit of a gray area. The Passion conferences welcomed Christy Nockels to the stage, although it was clearly stated that she was *not* a pastor. Nockels was singing *with* the conference attendees, not preaching *to* or *over* them. These prepositional differences were enough of a distinction for churches with women songleaders. For others, the line between leading music and leading other forms of liturgy was too blurry, so women were relegated to backup singing. Occasionally, women were tolerated, but antagonistic rhetoric from the likes of Mark Driscoll made it clear that music that could feminize the believer was a non-starter. This ruled out much of the worship music from Vineyard and other Charismatic worship leaders, who reveled in Jesus as the Bridegroom and the worshiper as the Bride. Driscoll ridiculed what he deemed to be "chickified" worship leaders "singing prom songs to Jesus." He advocated for more masculine, intellectual music that would spread Reformed doctrine.

Classifying congregational singing as a conduit to the truth of God elevated songwriting to the status of preaching, which was, for Neo-Reformed thinkers, the purview of men. Unsurprisingly, worship songs written by women plummeted in the early aughts.[27] Not all megachurches producing popular music that landed on the CCM charts promoted strict male-female hierarchies. The fact that worship music was likely created in and for megachurches, however, meant that more music was being written and performed by music pastors, many of whom were white men who preferred rock music—a consistently white, male genre—and gravitated toward working with their white, male friends.

Young, Restless, and Reformed worship leaders were highly influential in the United States, but global Charismatic worship networks were steadily growing domestically and internationally. The success of the megachurch Hillsong was a testament to the power of the top-selling worship band. Hillsong's Australian founder Pastor Brian Houston had a grand vision to influence the world through music, and Hillsong Church became an ad hoc record label, developing talent and launching artists' careers. Under Houston's leadership, Hillsong created anthemic rock that emphasized the prosperous, victorious life available to those who believe. Houston also created a college that attracted students from around the world, particularly the United States, who wanted to learn how to recreate the church's soaring sounds and emotive musical altar calls. Hillsong and the youth-oriented band Hillsong United released worship songs played in congregations across the globe.[28]

Hillsong Church was not the only Charismatic congregation with global ambitions and reach. Spanish- and Portuguese-language worship music also continued to boom during the early 2000s, led by groups like Miel San Marcos, a Guatemalan-based worship band, Dallas-based worship songstress Christine D'Clario, Brazilian-born and Argentinian-based Marcos Brunet, and Brazilian worship leaders like Raquel Kerr Borin and Ana Paula Valadão. Ghanaian worship superstar Sonnie Badu launched "Sonnie Badu Worships" programs in 2008 and held them in Ghana, England, German, Italy, Ireland, Canada, and the United States. Indonesian-born Sidney Mohede converted to Christianity while living in Southern California, where he became a worship leader. Mohede returned to Indonesia in the late 1990s and began ministering at Jakarta Praise Center Youth Ministry, and under his leadership the band True Worshippers released a series of worship albums featuring songs like 2009's "Hosanna (Be Lifted High)," which became a global hit.

At Passion conferences, worshipers raised their hands and shouted to God, but, for the most part, they did as their leaders instructed, and extemporaneous expressions rarely came from attendees. Charismatic worship services, however, were another story. As they offered songs to God, practitioners did not just raise their hands or speak in tongues quietly under their breath. They offered words of prophecy and spoke in tongues from the stage. They brought up sick people for prayers of healing. They exorcized demons. They waged war against the devil by banging the tambourine and waving bedazzled praise flags. Some even brought items representing their sinful past—a Voodoo doll, a ouija board, a pornographic magazine—to destroy at the altar of praise.

CCLI charts showed that songs that emerged from those networks—like Darrell Evans' "Trading My Sorrows," Israel Houghton's "You Are Good," and Hillsong's "My Redeemer Lives"—were in heavy rotation in white evangelical congregations. Common themes across worshiping communities reflected teachings from institutions like Rhema Bible College and Christ for the Nations: spiritual warfare; triumphant victory over sin, sickness, poverty, and death; invocations of the Holy Spirit; the kingship of Jesus, and fervent anticipation of his Second Coming; zealous Zionism. The popularity of Hillsong, Bethel, and others demonstrated how Charismatic and Pentecostal Christians had, for all intents and purposes, won the worship wars.

Singles from charismatic congregations rarely made it on Christian radio in the 2000s, or onto the charts of *CCM*, however, and one reason was format. Pentecostal and Charismatic practitioners preferred protracted worship songs, and radio-length versions of worship-oriented rock music felt, to many, like an imposition on the work of the Holy Spirit. Christian radio also preferred English-language songs, which obscured a growing global network of congregational music in Charismatic and Pentecostal congregations.

Yet, in spite of Piper's theological warnings, Driscoll's disgust, and radio's reticence, the mystical practices and vibrant cosmologies of the Charismatics seeped into even the most vigilant congregations through music. In 2009, Giglio, Tomlin, and their British Charismatic worship colleague Matt Redman created what *Christianity Today* called a "superstar church" in Atlanta. Passion City Church was, in many ways, a permanent, stationary version of the Passion Conference. Giglio's genial renditions of Baptist-inflected Reformed truths abounded, as did the signature Passion Conference music experience. In a far cry from white Baptist services of the past, however, attendees responded to the worship music by lifting their hands, crying, shouting, and even dancing.

More and more churchgoers in the United States followed suit. By 2006, the Pew Forum estimated that 23 percent of American Christians, regardless of their denominational affiliation, had adopted Charismatic practices and beliefs.[29] They lifted their hands and closed their eyes in worship; they cried while they sang; they believed in divine healing and prophetic utterances; some even spoke in tongues.

Passion networks helped expand the reach of Pentecostal music into Baptist and Reformed circles. In 2007, Jesus Culture popularized "How He Loves," a passionate song about the overwhelming love of God reminiscent of medieval mystics like Teresa of Avila. The song's evocation of a "sloppy wet kiss," its emotive plea that God's "love is going deep tonight," along with the almost nine minutes of running time kept it off of most radio stations. The David Crowder Band released a respectable four-minute version and changed "sloppy wet kiss" to "unforeseen kiss," a lyric that Southern Baptist college students could sing without blushing. When Crowder covered "Like a Lion," a song by Daniel Bashta, the son of Charismatic missionaries, the song brought to Passion audiences celebrations of miracles, awakenings, and triumphant declarations that the resurrected God lived in the body of the believer and roared "like a lion." In effect, Crowder and sixsteprecords baptized Pentecostal music.

The "Sleeping Giant" and the "Army"

The conservative white evangelical parents who sang along to Passion songs in church were George W. Bush's core constituents, and his administration worked to exploit the natural affinities between CCM audiences and the Republican Party. The status of CCM as the soundtrack of the GOP seemed secure on the evening of September 2, 2004, when Michael W. Smith was invited to perform "There She Stands" at the 2004 Republican National Convention. "I love this president," he said to a sea of revved-up conservatives in New York City's Madison Square Garden, "and I love this country." Thousands of delegates waved tiny American flags in a darkened stadium as Smith sang about the flag standing as a symbol of hope, "when evil calls itself a martyr."

Not all conservatives, however, recognized what CCM artists brought to the Republican Party. Conservative talk-radio host Glenn Beck complained on air that the Democratic National Convention had "hip" acts like Bruce Springsteen, while the Republicans only had Third Day and Jaci Velasquez. A caller identifying himself as David Carr, drummer for Third Day, called in to assure Beck that the band included "big fans" of his who listened regularly and that they had sold over four million records.[30]

Mark D. Rodgers, staff director for the Senate Republican Conference (and former chief of staff to Republican Senator Rick Santorum), understood what Glenn Beck did not: that CCM stars offered entrance into a vast network of evangelical activists and media makers. Rodgers, a longtime fixture on Capitol Hill, had a well-developed theory of social change, borrowed from James Davison Hunter's notion that Christians ought to be a "faithful presence" in "elite levels of sectors that shape worldview."[31] "Who are the elites of our day?" reasoned Rodgers, "If we are talking about strategically engaging sectors that shape worldview, it felt to me like art and entertainment was a sector that should be a priority."

Beginning in 2001, Rodgers made concerted efforts to create relationships with mainstream entertainers and CCM artists. He attended the GMA Dove

Awards, struck up conversations with many of CCM's leading figures, and began hosting briefings about key political issues. "Politics is downstream of culture," Rodgers noted; "Christian artists play a role with their craft in shaping world view, moral imagination, what we love, and what we hate."

When U2's Bono began approaching American politicians to support debt relief in Africa, Rodgers knew exactly what to do. "The strategic way to reach evangelicals is to recruit evangelicals," Rodgers suggested, "to basically recruit and connect with Christian music artists." Bono was one of the biggest rock stars in the world, and his influence over CCM rockers was pronounced. The Irish band's blend of Christian imagery and outspoken support for organizations like Amnesty International was a model for many CCM artists, who often cited Bono as an artistic and spiritual role model. Youth pastors and Young Life leaders had long used the existential longing in "I Still Haven't Found What I'm Looking For" to prime students for altar calls.

Bono traded on this iconic status within Christian music communities to support the efforts of his nonprofit DATA, an acronym for Debt, AIDS, Trade, Africa. In December of 2002 he appeared before a cross-section of CCM stars curated by journalist Jay Swartzendruber and Charlie Peacock at Peacock's Art House studio. Bono had engaged with some of the world's biggest movie stars and most prominent politicians—people who had much bigger global reach than even the biggest CCM star—but figures like Michael W. Smith or Switchfoot offered the organization a chance to harness the considerable political fervor of CCM audiences and direct it toward debt relief and funding for the AIDS crisis. Bono referred to the assembled group as a "sleeping giant" and urged them to use their platforms to encourage fans to petition their elected officials to "keep America's promise" and provide relief to the beleaguered African continent.[32]

The CCM stars present that day responded with enthusiasm. Peacock, Margaret Becker, Kevin Max, Out of Eden, and many others contributed to Thomas Nelson's 2002 edited volume *The Awake Project: Uniting Against the African AIDS Crisis*, alongside George W. Bush, Bono, and Desmond Tutu. Sparrow Records released *In the Name of Love: Artists United for Africa*, a U2 cover album, and donated a portion of the proceeds to HIV/AIDS relief. A few CCM stars visited the African continent. In 2002, Jars of Clay launched Blood:Water, a nonprofit focused on clean water, sanitation, hygiene, and programs that supported vulnerable people living with HIV/AIDS. Two years after he founded DATA, Bono and Kennedy relative Bobby Shriver created the ONE Campaign, which aimed to end poverty in Africa, and they set their sights on garnering support from some of the most prominent white evangelical leaders. Rick and Kay Warren of Saddleback Church, at that time one of the largest and most influential churches in the nation, became key public spokespersons for the campaign.[33]

When CCM stars appeared on Capitol Hill to urge lawmakers to forgive African debt, elected officials assumed that they represented the thousands of fans who turned out to see them on the festival circuit. Their efforts produced concrete legislative results. With broad bipartisan support, President George W. Bush launched the President's Emergency Plan for AIDS Relief (PEPFAR), and the 108th Congress passed H.R.1298—United States Leadership Against HIV/AIDS, Tuberculosis, and Malaria Act of 2003, which was the beginning of billions of dollars in American aid to the African continent.

When David Crowder Band alumnus Mike Hogan took a job as a regional field director for the ONE Campaign, however, he discovered that evangelical celebrity endorsement did not necessarily translate to widespread grassroots support among evangelicals. Many were worried about how aid dollars were spent, especially when it came to sex education. Others had a hard time focusing on international concerns when the needs of their own youth-group students seemed pressing. In Southern evangelical megachurches in particular, the idea that ONE was not campaigning for individual, Billy Graham–style conversions was a problem. "One mega-church youth pastor said to me that while they were committed to taking care of the poor, unless we were actively preaching the gospel, he had no interest in it," recalled Hogan. In the end, white evangelicals ended up showing little interest in the work. "For every amazing partner from the evangelical world that came aboard to help," Hogan noted, "there were probably 10 or more that wouldn't dream of it."[34]

The lack of widespread interest in DATA or the ONE Campaign was, on one level, puzzling. American missionaries had long idealized providing aid to Africa, and organizations like Compassion International and World Vision successfully garnered decades of support for "needy" children from CCM partnerships. Missionary efforts were usually intertwined with specific articulations of Christian theology, however, and neither DATA nor the ONE Campaign required or promoted evangelical conversion. What's more, Compassion and World Vision were highly individualistic, and the appeal to individual Christians to support poor children abroad fit within their personalized salvation model. It was harder to create an altar-call moment around structural issues like debt relief, and harder still to get conservative evangelicals to rally around helping people suffering from what had been known in many evangelical circles as "gay cancer."

But in cases where their goals were aligned, savvy marketers recognized the buying power of CCM audiences. Mel Gibson, one of the biggest film stars of the aughts, found that CCM support could provide his film, *The Passion of the*

Christ, with an evangelical stamp of approval that obscured its controversial content. In June of 2003, the US Conference of Catholic Bishops and the Anti-Defamation League released an eighteen-page report arguing that the script (and its source material, *The Dolorous Passion of Our Lord Jesus Christ: From the Visions of Anne Catherine Emmerich*) was inaccurate and unscriptural, and portrayed Jews as uniformly negative. The embattled Gibson turned to conservative evangelicals for help.

White evangelicals, on the whole, paid little attention to the ADL or to Catholic bishops, but they loved Gibson's *Braveheart*. And, like him, they felt beleaguered by mainstream media outlets. Gibson showed the film to several hundred evangelical pastors at National Association of Evangelicals president Ted Haggard's church. On September 18, 2003, Gibson screened the film before a group of Nashville-based CCM and country artists. At the screening, Gibson portrayed himself as a victim of spiritual attack.[35] Moved to tears, a CCM artist asked Gibson how the assembled entertainers could assist. "Help me build an army," the star of *Braveheart* told the group.

The war for Gibson's film was waged in part through merchandise. *The Passion of the Christ—Songs (Original Songs Inspired by The Film)* included contributions from Third Day, MercyMe, Steven Curtis Chapman, Kirk Franklin, P.O.D., MxPx, and Scott Stapp from Creed. With the support of CCM artists and other evangelical celebrities and denominational leaders, *The Passion of the Christ* became a mainstay in evangelical Good Friday and Easter services. Megachurches held showings of the film. Smaller churches combined their resources to host *Passion of the Christ* events. CCM fans used film stills set to songs from Third Day, Avalon, Casting Crowns, or Michael W. Smith to create fan art. The CCM army delivered; Gibson's film went on to gross $612.1 million.

Recording Industry Wars and "Monumental Cultural Shifts"

As CCM audiences mobilized themselves to wage war through ticket sales, the business of CCM and the entire recording industry battled for survival. Napster, a file-sharing service that allowed people to download music for free, debuted in 1999. The result was a catastrophe for record sales. And while Napster lost a high-profile court battle with Metallica and the Recording Industry Association of America (RIAA) in 2001 and declared bankruptcy, file sharing ultimately won the hearts and minds of the general public. Sites like KaZaA, LimeWire, and MyNapster appeared in Napster's wake. The

RIAA tried legal action, but found itself suing sympathetic file-sharers, including children like twelve-year-old Brianna LaHara. Few sided with the professionals whose livelihoods were disappearing.[36]

As the RIAA lost in the court of public opinion, labels buckled. Many closed. Others consolidated. By 2004, four major corporations distributed about 71 percent of all music; by 2011, "The Big Four," as they were known, controlled about 88 percent of the market.[37] In 2001, Apple announced the creation of iTunes, which served as a digital library and retail outlet. iTunes began selling all songs for ninety-nine cents, which undermined the marketability of albums, but guaranteed at least some income from the sale of singles. CCM labels responded with mergers and acquisitions of their own. In 2001, Gaylord Entertainment–owned Word Records bought Squint and replaced Steve Taylor as general manager. EMI acquired 50 percent of the West Coast independent label Tooth & Nail.

Mainstream music outlets floundered. Wherehouse Entertainment filed for bankruptcy in 2002. Tower Records declared bankruptcy in 2004. Borders Books and Music held on longer, but liquidated in 2011. Most Sam Goody stores had closed by the end of that year. Christian bookstores, the historic hub of CCM curation and discovery, also crumbled when faced with pressure from file-sharing sites and online retailers like Amazon. Independent stores shuttered around the country. Juggernaut chains like Lifeway, Family Christian Bookstores, and Cokesbury reeled. As the decade wore on, the annual CBA conferences, once attended by thousands in convention centers around the country, held modest gatherings in single ballrooms of Nashville's Opryland Hotel.

The loss of Christian bookstores was catastrophic for CCM, because that was where most evangelical moms bought music. In 2002, the Gospel Music Association published an industry review, which noted that 84 percent of CCM buyers were white, 60 percent were women, 70 percent were married, 67 percent were "homemakers," and 80 percent owned homes.[38] Beckys were still funding the business.

The collapse of CBA bookstores, the longtime cultural hub of white evangelical entertainment, was an incalculable loss for the industry, and it broke the hearts of small independent bookstore owners who saw their business as the Lord's work. When the last of their five Christian bookstores closed in 2017, Mark and Ruth Bingle pleaded, "It would be an honor if our customers would pray for us."[39] Suddenly, CCM was without its most visible gatekeepers. NRB radio stations remained, but without CBA store owners, who had virtually defined what constituted "Christian," the industry lost a significant sense of identity.

Sponsorships, ads, and concert revenues were all growing, and eventually the mainstream music industry adjusted to the new realities of file sharing and streaming.[40] Bandcamp (created in 2007), an online audio-distribution platform, also created new distribution methods for musicians and labels. Profits for CCM, Black Gospel, and Southern Gospel music, however, lagged behind. In 2006, "religious music" made up 5.5 percent of all music sales; just a year later that percentage had dropped to 3.9 percent.[41] *CCM Magazine* founder John Styll, now president of the Gospel Music Association, noted that CCM consumers did not think that "Thou Shalt Not Steal" applied to file sharing. "It's difficult to compete with free," he noted; "It's really a huge problem."

For CCM, file sharing was just one troubling development among many. In 2008 Charlie Peacock took stock in the pages of *CCM Magazine*. "The pattern [of the CCM industry] is an increasingly unsuccessful business model," he argued, "run by people trapped in a system intent on slow, incremental change in the face of monumental cultural shifts."[42] One such shift was a rapidly diversifying American population. CCM had failed to adapt to the country's diversifying listening tastes. CCM produced in the 2000s came mostly from white artists, which was in stark contrast to mainstream charts like the *Billboard Hot 100*, where Black artists and historically Black musical genres like rap and hip hop charted more often than music by white artists.[43]

A notable exception to that rule was hip-hop and spoken-word artist Jason Emmanuel Petty, who performed as Propaganda, and climbed to number fourteen on *Billboard*'s Christian Albums chart. His 2012 single "Precious Puritans" critiqued Reformed pastors for quoting unapologetic slaveholding Puritan theologians like Jonathan Edwards to Black congregants. Propaganda argued that attempts to stymie racism through "colorless rhetoric" was tantamount to erasure. "It might be nice," he said, "not to have to consider race." When white Neo-Calvinist preachers romanticized slaveholding theological voices and "the richness of their revelation," Propaganda argued that such confessions from the pulpit produced in Black listeners "bewilderment and heartbreak." "You know they were chaplains on slave ships, right?" Propaganda asked his listeners, "Would you quote Cortez to Aztecs, even if they theology was good?"

True to their Reformed disposition, Neo-Calvinist white men released a flurry of written responses. Some, like pastor and Reformed Baptist blogger Joe Thorn, argued that it was "brilliant." Others, like firebrand Owen Strachan, complained that talking about Puritan heroes who defended slavery ought to be done with "nuance." Many more supported Strachan's position implicitly by continuing to promote interest in Puritan slaveholders, regardless of the pain that it caused their Black colleagues and congregants. John Piper, after years of promoting Edwards' many virtues, categorized Edward's slaveholding as a mere "blind spot."[44]

For many Black pastors and congregants on the Reformed conference circuit, the response to "Precious Puritans" showed the limits of what Reformed theology could do in white American churches. "A lot of African Americans gravitate toward Reformed theology," noted Rev. Dr. Mika Edmondson, a prominent Black Presbyterian pastor who shared the conference stage with John Piper and wrote for *The Gospel Coalition*, "because it's a theology that promotes a God that is bigger than the oppressor." Edmondson noted that for Black worshipers in white Reformed spaces, the fact that luminaries like Piper embraced the writings of figures like Jonathan Edwards over prolific abolitionists like nineteenth-century Presbyterian George Bourne, was telling. Piper refused to give Edwards up as one of his most treasured teachers, and many white worshipers in Reformed congregations followed his lead.

"Precious Puritans" was mostly ignored on Christian radio; Piper-approved Chris Tomlin's music, however, continued to enjoy a wide audience. Neo-Calvinists were perhaps the most cantankerous opinionators, but they were not the only ones to prefer white, male music. Suburban moms of the 2000s made their tastes clear: Christian music charts of that decade were overwhelmingly white. TobyMac's Gotee Records produced Black pop singers Out of Eden and hip-hop duo GRITS, and marketed them to CCM audiences, but few of those offerings landed on the CCM charts.

In addition to CCM and Christian radio's lack of non-white entertainers and worship leaders, the genre also suffered when digital music trends diversified mainstream music. The model of creating Christian alternatives depended on an agreed-upon canon of "secular" pop music, which was harder to do with so many digital options for listeners. In the 1980s, it was reasonable to assume that most young people listened to Michael Jackson and Madonna, but as popular music diversified and fragmented, the Top 40 was no longer a reliable measure of what young people wanted.

CCM comparison charts were getting harder and harder to make in the twenty-first century, anyway, because fewer young musicians wanted to be on the "Christian alternative" side of them. Charlie Peacock had identified an existential theological and philosophical threat facing CCM: more and more young evangelical singers, songwriters, artists, and entertainers were not satisfied by being famous within evangelical mass-media networks. They wanted to succeed in the general market.

The Southern California rockers Switchfoot were prime examples. Lead singer Jon Foreman felt that "half of who we were was lost" when the band's debut album was marketed only to CCM audiences. Pop star Mandy

Moore was a Switchfoot fan, and the soundtrack to her 2002 film, *A Walk to Remember*, featured several of their songs. Switchfoot ended up signing a mainstream record deal to release *The Beautiful Letdown* in 2003. Their singles were featured on teen soap operas like *One Tree Hill*. The band charted on Top 40 radio, and their music videos climbed the MTV and VH1 charts.

Switchfoot was joined by other bands whose members (or at least some members) were Christian, but whose music was meant for mainstream listeners. As "emo" (short for emotional) music emerged from hardcore and punk scenes into the mainstream, passionate singers like Chris Carrabba, former lead vocalist of Tooth & Nail's Further Seems Forever, brought songs about emotional scars and "Screaming Infidelities" to the number two spot on the *Billboard* 200 as Dashboard Confessional. Fans memorized every word of Dashboard Confessional's earnest personal expressions of triumph and tragedy, and packed venues across the country to sing along.

Switchfoot and Dashboard Confessional's success with mainstream audiences proved that while lyrics about rejecting sex ed in public schools did not typically resonate with general market listeners, songs exploring existential questions like "Meant to Live" or heartbreak like "Rapid Hope Loss" did. They were joined by other bands like Gotee's Relient K, which had mainstream success in the early aughts. Along the way, Matt Thiessen, Relient K's lead singer, voiced frustration with being sold as a "Christian" band. "If I was Jewish and I was writing songs about Judaism, you (wouldn't) sell me only in Jewish bookstores," he told *Billboard* in 2007; "I feel like Christian music gets segregated."[45]

Relient K's desire to distance itself from the marketing category of "Christian rock" was understandable, because the genre's artistic reputation in mainstream circles remained abysmal. "Christian rock is a musical genre," wrote John Jeremiah Sullivan in the pages of *GQ Magazine* in 2004, "the only one I can think of, that has excellence-proofed itself."[46] For the most part, Switchfoot and Relient K remained in the CCM orbit, however, and they were publicly diplomatic about being unwillingly marketed as "Christian."

Others were not as measured. Mute Math was so frustrated with the label of "Christian band" that they sued their record label for marketing them as such.[47] Many other pop rockers like the Fray, Evanescence, One Republic, or the Jonas Brothers ascended in Top 40 radio without CCM networks or the "Christian" label. Meanwhile, musicians with roots in the Christian-rock world, like Damien Jurado and Pedro the Lion, garnered critical acclaim from general market outlets like *Pitchfork*, but as independent artists, not "Christian" ones. Sufjan Stevens landed on *Rolling Stone*'s best of the 2000s list, but certainly not as CCM. Pop singer Katy Hudson grew up listening to

Jennifer Knapp and Jars of Clay and released a CCM album, but ultimately found superstar status in the mainstream as Katy Perry.

For those raised on a strict CCM diet, mainstream bands with ties to evangelicalism like Mumford & Sons—which included Vineyard pastors'-kid-turned-folk-rocker Marcus Mumford—were a welcome change. "The sanitization and kid-friendliness of Christian music seemed to stifle a lot of the emotions and struggles I had as a teenager," recalled one teen in early 2000s Annapolis, Maryland, "I was homeschooled and carpooled ALL the time with families from church for soccer, co-op classes, summer jobs, and over the years I grew to hate the local Christian radio station with a passion—as a teen I was still drawn to mainstream artists who seemed at least somewhat religious (The Fray, Lifehouse, Mumford & Sons) but weren't on Christian radio."

For fans like Anthony, it was exciting to see Christian bands make it in the big time, or when indie bands with Christian-rock roots received critical acclaim, because it signified that they were cool. That kind of sought-after cultural capital was not typically associated with CCM. Identifying "Christianish" bands, therefore, became something of a youth-group pastime. Were-they-or-weren't-they Christian bands were the source of constant conversation. Lifehouse, a band with roots in the Vineyard Church, had the most successful song of 2001 on the US Hot 100 *Billboard* charts with "Hanging by a Moment." The single could be interpreted as a song about romantic love, or, in classic Vineyard fashion, a song about romance between Christ and a believer. Any Creed or Evanescence or The Fray song could be dissected in a similar fashion.

Even mainstream audiences were in on the project. In 2003, satirical news site *The Onion* lampooned the ambiguities around the "Christianish" bands of the early 2000s in a story about a fictional Christian rock band called Pillar of Salt whose bassist "remains oblivious to the fact that he is in a Christian rock band." Brad enjoyed the metal music he was playing, *The Onion* reported, but he was puzzled by the band's stance on purity culture, completely unfamiliar with the band's influences ("Whitecross, Third Day, and Stigmata"), and misinterpreted the band's love songs to Jesus as songs about women. "Jack writes a lot of songs about chicks," the clueless bassist noted of the fictional band's lead writer, " 'Your Love,' 'When You Return,' 'I Confess.' "[48] The fact that *The Onion* audience would get the joke was proof that the "subculture" of white evangelicalism was quite well known to mainstream audiences.

Mainstream-minded young evangelical music makers spelled trouble for the future of CCM in part because they diminished the talent pool of the industry. Ryan Tedder was, like many CCM stars, a pastor's-kid graduate of Oral Roberts University, with the musical talents of many Charismatics who had come before him. In another era, Tedder might have been a Michael W. Smith or Clay Cross. Tedder, however, was not interested in being a "Christian artist." He wrote for pop superstars Beyoncé and Jennifer Lopez. His band OneRepublic ascended to the top of mainstream charts without any stops at True Love Waits rallies along the way.

Bands like The Fray or Mumford & Sons made things like CCM comparison charts confusing. Educating evangelical parents about the alternatives to Pentecostal pastors' kids like the purity-ring-wearing Jonas Brothers seemed like a less critical task than finding Christian alternatives to Britney Spears or Nirvana, and it was confusing to explain why Switchfoot was safe for listeners but Jimmy Eat World or Coldplay should be approached with caution. These contradictions and ambiguities had arguably always been present, but the early aughts put them into high relief when more and more of the institutions that made up the sequestered evangelical world were disappearing.

These monumental cultural shifts were accompanied by shifts in evangelical practices that further undermined the prominence of evangelical music in the twenty-first century. Youth-group attendance just was not what it had been in the early aughts, and neither were church camps, Sunday School, or Vacation Bible Schools—core components of CCM exposure and distribution.[49] Weekly, age-specific church attendance for young people began to lose out to other forms of childhood enrichment favored by suburban, middle-class white evangelicals. Kids' sports leagues competed with churches for after-school activities, weekend games, and summer camps. Evangelical sports organizations like the Fellowship of Christian Athletes thrived in the 2000s, and they did not need members to attend Sunday services or youth group to create a sense of evangelical community.[50]

Sports were perhaps the biggest competition, but they were also joined by a host of extracurricular favorites like academic tutoring, theater classes, language classes, dance classes, or other forms of betterment favored by middle-class parents. Indeed, by the end of the decade, young evangelicals could spend the majority of their adolescent years rarely attending youth group, Sunday School, or Sunday services. Absence from congregational life often translated to a lack of exposure to and appreciation of CCM music.

Evangelical caregivers were also changing a lot about where and how often they worshiped, which further undermined CCM's development networks. Medium-sized churches declined as evangelical churchgoers consolidated in larger and larger megachurches in the 2000s.[51] Aspiring CCM acts of the past had relied on mid-sized congregations for financial support and exposure; with only small or large congregations, new bands did not have the ability to build nation-wide audiences through touring. In addition to undermining CCM development, megachurches embraced rock worship music and invested in their own house bands, which decreased demand for touring talent. The rise of worship bands also decreased demand for "special music" numbers imitating vocal virtuosos like Sandi Patty or Steve Green.

As they migrated to megachurches, evangelicals attended church less often, which meant less exposure to Christian music—worship music or otherwise.[52] Megachurches were often nondenominational, and many suburban white evangelical worshipers disaffiliated from the denominations that they once proudly supported. Parents no longer felt that it was necessary to raise Southern Baptist or Nazarene children, which meant that they were also less likely to ensure that their children attended denominational gatherings, another key distribution hub for CCM acts. Thus, stadium rock became the preferred liturgical music in megachurches, even as CCM entertainment declined. The music of the minivan was increasingly driven by worship bands.

CCM was in decline by every discernable measure. Cam Floria's Seminar in the Rockies, once a major annual confluence of youth-group hopefuls and Christian-college bands, record-label executives, managers, artists, and entertainers, shrunk. It was acquired by the Gospel Music Association, and by 2009, a much smaller Nashville-based version of the event was rebranded as "Immerse." The GMA was also in danger of collapsing, however, and the future of the organization was in doubt.

In 2012, BarlowGirl, CCM superstar purveyors of purity, called it quits and disappeared from the world of abstinence rallies. Carman, architect of CCM's spiritual warfare, found a natural home on Christian television, and while he was still making millions a year, the Champion's music rarely charted or appeared on Christian radio. Amy Grant, matriarch of Christian-pop stardom, was mostly known for doing heartwarming Christmas concerts. Michael W. Smith, patriarch of Christian-pop idolatry, continued doing patriotic worship concerts. Cornerstone, the hub of edgier, quirkier Christian alternative rock, held its last festival in 2012.

In 2012, the "Big Four" record labels consolidated again when Universal Music purchased EMI, placing the CCM industry one step further away from the white evangelical communities that had created the genre. The previous year, Jackie Patillo, a seasoned music-industry veteran who had worked in Southern Gospel, CCM, and Black Gospel, took over an ailing GMA. Patillo was the first woman of color to hold the position, and she understood her task to be, at least in part, to expand the historic white base of Southern Gospel and CCM industries. The GMA was, at that point, on the brink. "Are you sending me there to bury it?" Patillo asked God when she prayed about taking the job, "Or do you mean to resurrect it?"

Losing the "Great Culture War"

Christian radio remained vital by focusing more and more on conservative white suburban moms who still played CCM in the car with their children. Moms listening to the rapidly expanding Salem Media stations were increasingly exposed to conservative political agendas. *CCM Magazine* was purchased by Salem Communications and by 2001 had parted ways with founding editor John Styll over "different views" about the future of *CCM*.[53] In subsequent years, the magazine's editors and reporters were encouraged to present stories that upheld the conservative political aims of the magazine's parent organization. The world may have moved on, but Christian radio listeners still voted for Rebecca St. James as their favorite female artist. Skillet was their favorite band.[54] Evangelical publishers still pumped out advice books like Thomas Nelson's (2004) *The Complex Infrastructure Known as the Female Mind: According to Relient K*, which included "biblical advice for girls of any type to become women of God."

Yet, an uncomfortable question haunted what remained of CCM: if evangelical entertainers were an essential part of the brine creating evangelical pickles, what was there to be done if pickling did not work? If, for example, a youth-group teen listened to Christian "emo" rock bands, and did not come to the conclusion that voting for the Republican Party was the best way to express their faith, did the project fail? A 2011 study showed that evangelical youth-group attendance did not, necessarily, result in adult attendance later on in life. The children of evangelical baby boomers raised with CCM as a "pastoral" presence that guided them through life began to question its efficacy as a form of child-rearing or Christian catechesis.[55]

The notion that teetotalling as well as refraining from social dancing, cursing, "rated R" movies, sex outside heterosexual marriage, or secular music would bring spiritual health and vitality to the believer, the church, and the nation had sustained CCM as an industry for decades, but in the 2000s, rejecting such "worldly" practices no longer seemed like a central part of the faith. Southern Baptist preachers in Missouri began trying to use beer as an evangelism tool in 2007. Christian colleges around the country that once banned "social dancing" held galas on campus. Ray Boltz, whose dramatic "I Pledge Allegiance to the Lamb" had provided conservative activists with fuel for the fire of their frustrations about living through the Clinton years, came out as gay in 2008. Congregations that had banned staff from watching R-rated films screened *The Passion of the Christ* in their sanctuaries. Some, like Mark Driscoll, proudly swore from the pulpit.

The strict holiness teachings about sexual abstinence before life-long heterosexual marriage from True Love Waits also came under fire from evangelicals raised in the brine of CCM. For example, Rachel Held Evans, who had been raised with Christian-bookstore music and material culture, began blogging about how she was reevaluating the theologies and practices she had been taught. Held Evans' blog became a hub for other children of evangelicalism to wrestle with how they had been formed by evangelical mass media. In her *New York Times*–bestselling *Evolving in Monkeytown: How a Girl Who Knew All the Answers Learned to Ask the Questions* (2010), she recalled how "Contemporary Christian Music hum[ed] in the background" of her childhood in conservative evangelicalism. For Held Evans and her many readers, the world that CCM helped to construct was unnecessarily rigid and theologically empty. As an adolescent, Held Evans had been a virginity-pledge-card-carrying, self-professed "poster child for the True Love Waits movement," but as a woman, Held Evans and a growing cohort of disillusioned and disaffected evangelicals eschewed the idea that virginity before heterosexual marriage, or celibacy, were the only ways to live Christianly.

CCM also had notable defectors in the new millennium. Jennifer Knapp moved to Australia in 2002 and announced in 2004 that she was taking a break from music and leaving the world of CCM. In 2009, Knapp revealed that she was starting to write music again, and her CCM fans rejoiced. A year later in 2010, however, Knapp announced that she had been in a relationship with a woman since 2002. She refused to renounce her religion, however, and insisted that being open about her sexuality had deepened her faith. The venues that had once welcomed her as the woman who opened for Audio Adrenaline declined to invite her back. "Pretty much the whole Southeastern United States was out of the question after that," said Knapp.

Knapp, Held Evans, and other disillusioned former CCM artists found fellowship through a network of blogs, social-media platforms, and gatherings. The Wild Goose Festival, which began in 2011, was in many ways modeled after the Greenbelt Festival in the United Kingdom.[56] The gathering represented the "moral minority" of white evangelical liberalism, which had been systematically expunged from CCM as the business grew, consolidated, and coalesced around conservative politics.[57] Together, Wild Goose attendees worshiped and learned from liberal Christian public figures like Jim Wallis, Richard Rohr, Nadia Bolz-Weber, and Brian McLaren, while Sarah Masen, Ashley Cleveland, Derek Webb (formerly of Caedmon's Call), and Jennifer Knapp provided music. The festival was produced on a shoestring budget. Meanwhile, Creation Festivals hosted much larger gatherings with conservative speakers like Louie Giglio and music from TobyMac, Third Day, and Skillet.

As the soundscape of white evangelicalism fractured and lost its financial and cultural footing, public perceptions of white evangelicals' political power also faltered. After enjoying two terms with fellow evangelical George W. Bush in the highest office in the land, white evangelical voters struggled to connect with the 2008 Republican nominee for president, Senator John McCain. McCain campaigned alongside his Charismatic Christian running mate Republican Governor Sarah Palin, but they were an odd couple who never gelled with white evangelical voters. McCain's experienced, bipartisan "maverick" brand of Republicanism chafed against Palin's proudly inexperienced, "pitbull" pitch to the country.

In the runup to the 2008 presidential election, James Dobson was disappointed in McCain and complained to the *New York Times* that he was not much better than the pro-choice Democratic candidate Barack Obama. "They [McCain and Obama] don't give a hoot," said Dobson, "about the family."[58] Conservatives also struggled with how to respond to Obama's optimistic appeal to millennial voters, his engagement with evangelicals interested in issues like poverty or sex trafficking, and his clear evocation of the Christian spirituality and ethic of the Black Church.[59] Obama visited ten Christian colleges during his campaign and made inroads with white evangelicals under the age of thirty, which some took as a sign that the longstanding political conservatism of white evangelicalism could be undone.[60]

Many Democrats believed that the diversifying United States would deliver electoral victories over conservative white Republicans for the foreseeable future. White evangelicals could protest, but they could not overturn the demographic shifts that had put Obama in the White House. It was hard not to interpret at least some part of the decline of CCM as part of a larger loss in cultural territory for the white evangelical networks that created and sustained it.

Several prominent CCM artists did their best to support the Republican National Committee (RNC) during the Obama years. Michael W. Smith endorsed Rick Santorum for president against Barack Obama in 2012. Smith's candidate, however, did not make it through the primaries. When the RNC nominated Latter-day Saint Mitt Romney and Catholic Paul Ryan for the Republican ticket, they gestured toward evangelicals, in part by inviting CCM entertainers like the Katinas and Charismatic music-pastor-turned-American Idol-winner Danny Gokey to perform.

These efforts did not, however, produce an electoral win for the Republicans. Stinging from the loss, the RNC released the "Growth and Opportunity Project," known colloquially as the RNC "autopsy." In it, the

RNC made the case for adopting more inclusive rhetoric and policy that would engage women and non-white voters. The autopsy identified several communities that would be key to resurrecting the Republican Party: "Hispanics, Asian and Pacific Islander Americans, African Americans, Women, and Youth."[61]

Save for the mention of utilizing "church fellowship meetings" to register voters or bolster the party's ground game, however, the report did not mention engaging Christians with specific messaging or policy goals. The Pew Forum noted that Obama lost ground with white evangelicals in 2012 compared to 2008, but within the autopsy those findings did not seem to translate to opportunity.[62] The case for the emerging Democratic majority had become widely accepted as probable fact, even within the RNC.

Like a Lion

CCM activists, however, were determined not to go down without a fight. In 2011, fronted by DC Talk alumnus Michael Tait, the Newsboys released *God's Not Dead*. The lead single covered Daniel Bashta's "Like a Lion" and renamed it "God's Not Dead (Like a Lion)." The retooled title reframed the song as a culture-warring repudiation of Nietzsche's famous claim that "God is dead," rather than a celebration of the miracles of the resurrection.

The video captured evangelical angst about a debased culture and the power of God that would ultimately overcome it. As the video begins, Michael Tait is sitting at a café when he peeks out of the corner of his eye and spots a newspaper declaring "GOD IS MYTH." Scenes flash of unsuspecting cafe patrons being bombarded with messages that God is irrelevant or dead or nonexistent. Slowly, as the song progresses, the band leads everyone to proclaim that while science may have declared that "God is a myth," the truth remained: "God's not dead." The song pitted the living God against a godless mainstream culture.

That year, evangelical filmmakers Pure Flix Productions began filming on *God's Not Dead*, the movie, based on a book written by Nashville-based megachurch pastor Rice Broocks. In the film, a lone white evangelical young man named Josh Wheaton faced off against an "atheistic" philosophy professor who issued an ultimatum to his students: sign a paper declaring that "God is dead" or fail the class. Through the eyes of young Josh Wheaton, white evangelical parents were faced with their worst fear: their children being coerced and manipulated by atheists and leftists.

In the end, happily for Josh Wheaton, the Newsboys saved the day. By the final credits, Wheaton and his friends discovered that a key to living a proud, public Christian life was attending a Newsboys concert. The god of Contemporary Christian Music-fueled activism was not dead. "He's living on the inside," the Newsboys sang as they embarked on a Compassion-sponsored sixty-plus-city tour, "roaring like a lion."

8
#LetUsWorship
The Soundtrack of Evangelical Discontent (2012–2021)

God's Not Dead—the story of the Newsboys and their fans triumphing over university-based atheism—was a surprise hit at the box office. The film cost two million to produce, and when it was released in 2014, it raked in over sixty million dollars. With profits like these, sequels were bound to follow.

The fourth *God's Not Dead* film starred Contemporary Christian Music (CCM) singer-songwriter Francesca Battistelli as a mother whose "individual liberty" to homeschool her children was threatened. Battistelli, an acting novice, was homeschooled as a child and homeschooled her children, so she felt a personal stake in the story. "It wasn't hard to say yes to this franchise," she said, "especially after reading the script and just knowing the content."[1] *God's Not Dead* content typically included lengthy monologues—with swelling stringed accompaniment—highlighting the critical role that devout evangelicals play upholding American values.

In the post-Obama years, white evangelicals proved that they were not dead, as voters or as consumers. The days of CCM artists as powerful "tools of evangelism," however, were mostly in the past. The coalition of media makers, parachurch organizations, conservative white Protestant denominations, and other evangelical institutions was in precipitous decline.

DC Talk and the State of CCM's Evangelicalism

The trajectories of the three members of DC Talk—the youth-group-iest of youth-group bands—tell the tale of the state of CCM in American public life. One path was taken by TobyMac, who remained a CCM industry leader and a much-fêted artist. McKeehan's fans stuck with him over the years as he played Christian music festivals as well as smaller venues like the Favored Women's Conference in Branson, Missouri. McKeehan's songs still exuded the positivity that appealed to Christian radio listeners.

And TobyMac continued to serve as a role model, as did others. For Josh Woods, who grew up in the 1990s in Michigan, artists like TobyMac "shaped my imagination of what faithfulness to God looked like." "I got saved listening to an Amy Grant song on my car stereo," recalled one fan who discovered CCM in the 1980s; "[i]n a single moment, I realized God's love for me and that He gave His only Son as a sacrifice for *me*!"

Through CCM, many a fan developed a close relationship with God, made lifelong friends, entered the ministry, and even found a spouse. Some note how Christian rock "gave Christian kids a pastoral voice encouraging them in their faith."[2] The songs often remained sources of deep emotional and spiritual comfort. When he was in middle school in the 1980s, Matt, a CCM fan, suffered debilitating panic attacks. CCM soothed him when he woke up stricken by anxiety. "I would get my Walkman and put on 'His Love Was Reaching' by David Meece," he wrote. "That song would calm me down, and I'd go back to sleep to the rest of the cassette—I stopped having those panic attacks many years ago, but that song is still a great source of comfort whenever I hear it."

The memory of CCM as a source of positivity and encouragement was perhaps preserved most affectingly in numerous obituaries of fans who came of age in the 1970s, 1980s, and 1990s. Contemporary Christian Music appeared alongside favorite pastimes, family members, and pets. "Butch loved the Lord and loved attending church and listening to Contemporary Christian Music," noted one obituary of a man from Minnesota who died at age sixty-three in 2022. Brian, from Ohio, who died in his fifties, was memorialized as an "avid Contemporary Christian Music follower, especially enjoying TobyMac, Newsboys and Stryper."

The Jesus Music, a film about CCM produced by K-Love, Amy Grant, and Michael W. Smith, presented the kind of "positive and encouraging" take on the industry that fans could expect from a documentary produced by a Christian radio station. Released in 2021, the polished, rosy retrospective told the story of CCM through interviews with some of the biggest Nashville-based names in business. The film's neat narrative showed how Jesus People planted the seeds, Amy Grant and Michael W. Smith grew the business from seedling to maturity, and DC Talk reaped the benefits of CCM in full bloom. Special music maven Sandi Patty and Pentecostal showman Carman, two of the top-selling figures in CCM, received only brief nods. Tooth & Nail rebels barely figured into the story.

Negativity, in *The Jesus Music*, was scant. Interviewees noted that then-deceased Larry Norman was a "difficult person," offered vague criticism of Christian-on-Christian disapproval of rock and roll and divorce, and levied chastisements of racism in CCM. Some hard times were discussed—the tragic death of Toby McKeehan's son, Russ Taff's abusive upbringing, Amy Grant's divorce, tensions within the ranks of DC Talk—but dissenting voices were kept to a minimum. Ray Boltz and Jennifer Knapp were conspicuously absent. Like a good K-Love song, suffering and sorrow were short-lived, and they took a back seat to tale of the triumph of worship music as a worthy successor to CCM.

Those who marketed and sold CCM, however, recognized that the genre was clearly in decline. "The Becky that we have all known and loved for years on CCM radio, she's in her fifties now," noted one marketer from Sony Music's CCM conglomerate Provident Entertainment in 2021; "[o]n Christian radio, the audience has gotten older—they are not getting any younger." Sales diminished as Beckys aged. "The numbers," according to one CCM insider on the condition of anonymity, "are not good for non-worship music."

By the 2020s, CCM—the once-roaring juggernaut of evangelical entertainment—was a shadow of its former self. So was much of the vast web of white evangelical institutions that had upheld the business. Brentwood Benson Music, inheritor of John and Eva Green Benson's 1902 Holiness songbook legacy and owner of the world's largest Christian music-publishing catalog, abruptly closed in 2021. Church choral music in white evangelical circles had been in decline for many years, and even the biggest name in that business could not compete in the arena-rock-driven world of the twenty-first century. Benson Brentwood's closure announcement included a note that the business would live on in a "subscription service to download [worship] videos, charts and other contemporary resources."[3]

Most independent Christian bookstores also closed. In 2015, the largest CBA retailer, Family Christian Bookstores, filed for bankruptcy and shut their last stores in 2017. The once-mighty Southern Baptist chain Lifeway closed their brick-and-mortar stores in 2019, and the Christian Booksellers Association officially collapsed.[4] Even in companies that were seeing increased sales, music was a declining share.[5]

Christian music festivals struggled too. Creation Festival, the largest, canceled their 2018 gathering in Washington state and went on indefinite hiatus in 2020. Creation took over the long-running Ichthus Festival in Kentucky but, after many sputtering starts and stops, announced its demise in 2016. A smaller version of Ichthus relaunched in 2021. The long-running Sonshine Festival, where the Newsboys had recorded their live rendition of "God's Not Dead," went on indefinite hiatus in 2017 due to "financial reasons."

Perhaps the most damning blow for the Creation organization came in 2018 when Harry Thomas, a co-founder of Creation Festival, was convicted of child sexual abuse and assault and sentenced to eighteen years in prison. Thomas died in 2022. The organization moved back to the Agape Campground that year and hosted 50,000–60,000 attendees, a far cry from their multi-site festivals that welcomed upward of 800,000 attendees in the early 2000s.[6] In 2023, the festival's leadership announced "the end of the longstanding, multi-day event historically held at Agape Farm."

Hardcore devotees of the Tooth & Nail catalog still gathered at events like Furnace Fest or Audiofeed. There, Gen X and millennial fans introduce the aesthetics and ideals of Christian hardcore and punk to younger generations. But many of the bands and the fans no longer identified as Christian, to say nothing of "evangelical."[7]

CCM was not an outlier; many white evangelical parachurch organizations have struggled in the twenty-first century. Intervarsity's 2022 Urbana Missions Conference, for example, attracted only a fraction of what it did at its height in 2000. Camp Kanakuk, the Branson-based destination that launched so many CCM acts, became embroiled in a legal battle regarding sexual abuse of campers. Youth Specialties still advertised mass-media events like Billy Graham's "My Hope For America" in 2013, alongside the work of CCM artists, but there were fewer new artists to introduce and smaller youth ministries to serve.

In addition, evangelical denominational affiliation and congregational membership fell, and youth-group attendance fell with them, as the religiously unaffiliated population grew.[8] CCM even fell out of fashion in youth-group culture. According to Mark Ostreicher, director of the Youth Cartel, and one-time president of Youth Specialties, in the early 2000s it became clear that youth ministers had less use for CCM than they did in previous years. "We found that worship music transcended the individual tastes of youth leaders," he recalled; "if you were booking entertainment, you'd have to think about whether you want rock or rap or whatever, but if you were leading worship, everyone would join in and stay engaged."[9]

In order to lead the Gospel Music Association into a sustainable future, Jackie Patillo promoted a "big tent" approach to reaching audiences outside the typical CCM market niche. "He [God] needed a nurturer," Patillo believed, and she set out to nurture the Gospel Music Association (GMA) to health as a trade organization for multi-racial, multi-ethnic expressions of "faith-based music." Patillo partnered with Lipscomb University, a small Christian university in Nashville, and negotiated space to house the organization and host a much more modest GMA Dove Awards. The GMA featured Black Gospel music, and English-, Spanish-, and Portuguese-language worship music, along with the organization's historic base of predominantly white artists and entertainers that would best be classified as Southern Gospel or CCM.

Christian radio stations, the largest of which were affiliated with Salem Media (parent company of The Fish) or Educational Media Foundation (the parent company of K-Love and Air1), were in many ways the last remaining gatekeepers of what constituted "Christian" music. "Faith-based" music, the category usually applied to CCM, gospel, and worship music, continues to consolidate in the United States—Capitol Christian Music's share, for example, grew from 46.3 percent of the market in 2020, to 52.1 percent in 2022.[10]

Savvy Christian radio marketers have stayed afloat and tempered their loss of white suburban moms by courting English-speaking Latinas. Latinx listeners experience music as family units differently than white suburbanites do, noted Alexandria "Alex" Davila, CEO of Adarga Entertainment Group, which specialized in reaching transnational Latinx listeners. At a 2021 Gospel Music Association–sponsored conversation about "faith-based" music, Davila noted that Latinx listeners in the United States and abroad seek music that appeals to multi-generational families and often includes appreciation for indigenous musical forms present in Spanish- and Portuguese-language cultures.

Salem Media made up for the loss of CCM audiences by expanding its conservative political talk-radio offerings. Even on the music side of Salem's business, the pressure to promote Republican talking points was intense, and among some of Salem Media's Christian music employees, Salem's emphasis on conservative politics has caused dismay. "Christian music is like the gateway drug to conservatism," one employee said on condition of anonymity; "I signed on to share music to spread the gospel, not this."

For others, however, emphasizing conservative politics was simply the cost of doing business. Salem's stock price is nowhere near its 2004 height of around thirty dollars per share—indeed, the share price has fallen steadily over the years and sits just under a dollar as of this writing. The "political revenue"—including programming from rightwing firebrands like Dinesh D'Souza and Eric Metaxas—from their talk-radio stations helped to forestall even larger losses.[11] Because much of its financial future was and is tied to the political conservatism of its audience, and the growing conservative arm of Christian radio, the Christian music industry remained reluctant to challenge the dominant beliefs of conservative white evangelicalism.

On Salem and K-Love airwaves, "faith-based" Christian radio existed in the 2020s much as it did in the early 2000s. The primary audience was conservative evangelical mothers "in the car," and Becky-related content still appeared on the airwaves. Rebecca St. James became a wife and mother, rebooted her career as a worship leader, and in 2021 began hosting *Rebecca St. James Friends & Family*, a weekly podcast on marriage and parenting on K-Love's "Access More." Singers like Tauren Wells or Lauren Daigle occasionally crossed over into the mainstream.

While Salem's political offerings included exuberant castigations of Democrats and American liberalism, on The Fish, they stuck to longstanding themes of family safety. When asked why they listened, the Christian radio audience parroted Salem Media's slogan: "It's safe for me and my family to listen to," and "The hosts sometimes add light-hearted humor that's family-friendly." Christian Music Broadcasters, a 600-member industry trade organization, issued advice for broadcasters in September 2022 that echoed the approach from 2002: "Your listener is looking for spiritual encouragement without negativity, without anger, without judgment."

Corporations that cater to conservative white evangelicals like Cracker Barrel still pursued partnerships with CCM greats like Steven Curtis Chapman. Disney World still hosted TobyMac concerts. The Newsboys became a CCM legacy band with rotating casts of singers and musicians from a plethora of well-known groups from the 1990s. Until its demise, Brentwood-Benson continued cranking out patriotic music every Fourth of July. Most winters, Amy Grant and Michael W. Smith sold out nostalgic, Christmas-themed tours. Even as Christian radio celebrated CCM fixtures like TobyMac, however, deserters abound.

Exvangelical Deconstruction

A second path for CCM can be found in the story of Kevin Max, who became a CCM icon as the powerhouse rock vocalist of DC Talk. Later, he would disavow the form of evangelicalism that made him a star. Over the years, he developed more progressive ideas about faith and politics, and he made clear that he no longer belonged in the evangelical world he once reigned over. He announced in 2021 that he identified as an "exvangelical," a neologism that signified an escape from the strict theological and political boundaries of white evangelicalism. Max called himself "Anti-war, Pro-Peace, Anti-Hate, Pro-Love," and an "exvangelical socialist liberal." He renounced many of the conservative white evangelical values set to music in DC Talk's albums and occasionally shared his story on "exvangelical" podcasts. Max, who was long-time friends with Larry Norman, positioned himself as a fellow outsider, a rebel voice out of step with traditional CCM.

Max was just one of many CCM artists—and fans—who eventually rejected the world that raised them. Many grew to see mainstream CCM as "[Baby] Boomer capitulation to commercialized entertainment and religious consumption."[12] For some, the genre amounted to a "gutless," simplistic Christianity. "[CCM] was a priesthood that provided shallow but often intense experiences to its parishioners," reckoned Zach Barton, who came of age during CCM's height. It "encouraged them to spend their money heavily at the altar of 'experience' and, being an industry for profit, took more than it offered."

To those defectors, CCM's conservative political messaging, aimed at young people, seemed like coercive indoctrination. Some felt uncomfortable with the uncritical patriotism present in so many CCM songs. Others saw CCM missionary efforts as a form of colonialism and as an instrument of white supremacy.[13] Many felt hoodwinked by the unending promises that the end of days was near. Carrie Daukas, who grew up going to CCM concerts in Tempe, Arizona, could not support World Vision children when the pitch was given by her favorite musician, because she was a child herself without the means to contribute. "I remembered feeling so much guilt and shame for simply being a child without any income and therefore being unable to do what was being asked of me," she recalled. "This guilt and shame would become the theme of my life throughout my time as an evangelical."

So much of CCM was about regulating teen sexuality, and nowhere were the effects of CCM more evident than in evangelical and exvangelical responses to CCM's promotion of conservative sexual ethics. "The longest-lasting influence [of CCM], I think, was Rebecca St. James' song 'Wait For Me,'" wrote Melody Rowell, who grew up listening to St. James during the height of purity culture in the 1990s and early 2000s; "I even had a journal with her picture on the cover, that was for writing letters to my future husband—which I did—from like 6th grade until I got married at age 30." "Even when I no longer considered myself evangelical," Rowell wrote, "even when my sexual ethics shifted, I still couldn't shake the purity culture that had embedded itself in my brain, and I stayed a virgin until my wedding night." Rowell gave her journal to her new husband. "He was very appreciative of the letters from my older self," she wrote, "but thought the letters from my younger self were . . . nuts—I was obsessed with **not having** sex so that I would be worthy of a Christian husband."

For Nikki Leonti, the road from CCM abstinence icon, to teen parent, to working musician was difficult. But she put her talents to work, did backup singing for the likes of country superstar Carrie Underwood, and was a vocalist on *Glee*, a popular television show about high school choral singers. She also began to write songs for the Disney Channel.

It took Leonti years, however, to realize that, as a child at that time, the adults in her life—and the world of evangelical abstinence celebrity—had failed her. "I was in my thirties before I thought that way," recalled Leonti, "for years I just thought it was all my fault." Determined to imagine a different future for her children, Leonti wrote a song to her daughter, the baby born to her as a teen, about the key that had once signified her sexual purity. "There was a time though that I had hoped to pass this on," she wrote of the object, but also the ideology that formed her childhood, "but she'll never wear something this heavy."

For many LGBTQ+ CCM listeners, these messages were especially fraught. For Lauren McIntyre, who grew up listening to TobyMac and Casting Crowns outside Grand Rapids, Michigan, in the 2010s, CCM's association with evangelical sexual ethics made much of the music unpalatable. "The Newsboys shared an anti-gay video on Facebook shortly after I came out as a lesbian," she recalled; "I was already being mistreated by my church and Christian friends, and to read the homophobic comments on their post just sent me further into a spiral of depression and spiritual trauma. To this day, I will experience physical symptoms of anxiety if I hear one of their songs on the radio."

CCM had significant influence on the young adulthood of singer-songwriter Matthew Blake. Blake, who uses the pronouns they/them, grew up in a conservative Plymouth Brethren congregation, where listening to CCM artists like Amy Grant and Clay Cross was edgy. As a young person, they subscribed to *CCM Magazine* and dreamed of a career in the industry. When it was career day at school, and students were asked what they wanted to be when they grew up, "For me, it was always 'CCM artist.' "

In 2020, Blake began performing songs in drag as Flamy Grant. The response was overwhelming, and they met fans around the country who described the alienation they felt from their communities, but testified to the power that Amy Grant and others had, even after they had left the world of white evangelicalism behind. "If you feel seen," they noted, "that's a big thing to a queer kid in the church." "I sang [Amy Grant's hit] El Shaddai in a drag club and a church," Blake said. In both venues, "People weep."

Some non-white evangelicals raised with CCM as the sound of Christian orthodoxy began looking back on the genre with mixed feelings. Many recalled the fun of concerts and festivals but are now reckoning with what it meant to have their faith shaped profoundly by music of white suburban evangelicalism. "I think a lot of us in the Korean American church are struggling," recalled one CCM listener who came of age in the 1990s, "with how to reconcile our relationship to CCM and worship music and that whole world."

For others, CCM and its cultural accouterments—the youth-group all-nighters, the See You at the Pole gatherings, and the abstinence pledges—served as evocative shorthand for growing up evangelical. Acting out Carman songs and Acquire the Fire battle anthems lived in their memories as oddities—experiences that were not necessarily negative, but silly and strange. "What *was* that?" asked one fan rhetorically; "sometimes I'm just embarrassed by it all." "I've come to learn that CCM is just a machine to gain as much money as possible by cranking out artists who can make money," remarked Emmanuel Fernandez, who grew up in a Spanish-speaking Assembly of God congregation in Bakersfield, California. "But there's no denying the impact those bands I loved made in my life."

Evangelical Re-construction

A third path can be found in the story of Michael Tait, who felt compelled to stand against the exvangelicals. "Morality issues, life issues," he told *The Christian Post* in October of 2021—"you should stand on a certain point, and if you question that, [you] are deconstructing the faith."[14] Like Tait, some former CCM figures became outspoken supporters of what they deemed to be "orthodox" Christianity. After ZOEgirl disbanded in 2006, Alisa Childers and her spouse ended up in a congregation that explored progressive theology, and she went through a period of disillusionment. She escaped by listening to conservative white evangelical apologists like Frank Turek and re-made herself as a public apologist with a sizable YouTube audience. From her new platform, Childers created videos that promote biblical inerrancy and "Christian worldviews" and warn of the dangers of "progressive Christianity" and universalism.

In 2021, Childers posted "CCM and Deconstruction: Why Are So Many Leaving the Faith?" In the video, she interviewed CCM colleagues Jeremy and Adrienne Camp, as well as Skillet's John and Korey Cooper, to explain "why we are seeing so many highly-platformed Christians leaving the faith, and to testify why we still believe." That year, John Cooper self-published *Awake and Alive to Truth: Finding Truth in the Chaos of a Relativistic World*, which promised readers "a journey through some [of] John Cooper's personal stories, the doctrine of original sin, the authority of Scripture [and] the danger of trusting your emotions." For Childers and Cooper, the emotional pull of ideas like universal salvation or metaphorical readings of the Bible were grave threats.

In the heyday of CCM, Childers and Cooper would have been able to sing of the dangers of progressivism in a three-and-a-half-minute song and reach millions. Those days, however, are gone. Instead, Cooper and Childers get their ideas out on social-media platforms and write books arguing against liberalism; Cooper gave a lengthy interview to *Fox News*, warning of the dangers of progressive ideas.

CCM may no longer crank out musical role models for young evangelicals *en masse*, but Michael Tait and the Newsboys appearing in the *God's Not Dead* franchise—along with the *Left Behind* series and a plethora of Hallmark Channel film versions of Christian romance—showed that conservative evangelical media makers were alive and well. The Holiness impulse to shape young white evangelical youths lived on too. The emergence of influencers like Sadie Robertson Huff—who grew upon her family's reality show *Duck Dynasty* and had a role in the *God's Not Dead* franchise—demonstrated how evangelicals continued to view mass media as a promising way to shape young bodies. Robertson Huff became a bestselling author, sought-after conference speaker, and World Vision partner. Robertson Huff posted idyllic photos of her spouse and child, sold Bible-themed workout gear to her Instagram followers, and preached "submissive womanhood" to thousands of fans around the nation.[15]

Robertson Huff was not alone. The attempt to catechize evangelicals through mass media lived on through a host of young evangelical social-media influencers who created aspirational ideals of a prosperous and beautiful life with God. Gabe Poirot, a social-media evangelist who began spreading the good news as a student at televangelist Kenneth Copeland's Bible college, used short videos to encourage his followers to embrace Jesus and anticipate the Second Coming.[16] He also stumped for Republican candidates, posted anti-abortion messages, and encouraged his brethren to flee worldly lusts. These efforts showed that conservative evangelical activism lived on, even when the institutional structures that created and sustained CCM were diminished.

Donald Trump and the Politics of CCM

As in many corners of white evangelical media and activism, the political conservatism of CCM was given a surprising jolt in 2016 by Donald J. Trump. Trump, a gaudy businessman-turned-reality-television-star, proved that CCM and worship music could still energize white evangelicals politically.

In the aftermath of Trump's election, commentators grasped for why evangelicals had embraced a man who cheerfully violated their most precious moral standards. Scholars showed that Trump's triumph among white evangelicals—a reported 81 percent voted for him—was the logical outcome of generations of evangelicals' embrace of militant masculinity, racism, and economic inequality.[17] Trump also displayed a canny understanding of the world of evangelical celebrity. Some political pundits figured that white evangelicals who loved the public piety of George W. Bush would balk at the unrepentant lechery of Trump, but Michael W. Smith, a friend of the Bush family, dutifully worked with "My Faith Votes," an organization chaired by Republican Mike Huckabee to encourage voter turnout among his fan base in 2016.

Smith was not unique. The Trump campaign and subsequent presidency benefitted from ongoing support from CCM artists. Michael Tait endorsed Trump. He and the Newsboys led worship at the White House in 2019. Tait garnered a podium shout-out from the president in 2020. Steven Curtis Chapman happily visited the White House and bonded with Vice President Mike Pence, who was a fan. Trump's status as a political outsider, gaudy aesthetics, and longstanding appreciation for New Jersey hit all the right notes with Carman. In the wake of Trump's surprising 2016 election, he wrote a 2017 novelty ode to "T.R.U.M.P./the biggest political upset you'll ever see."

As it did in many other evangelical institutions, the Trump presidency brought simmering tensions within CCM circles to a boil. Nowhere were these tensions more visible than in the politics of race, gender, and sexuality. For many Black Christians, particularly those who worked in white evangelical spaces like CCM, white evangelical support for Trump was perhaps not entirely surprising, but still a source of anger, frustration, and dismay. Donald Trump was sued by the US Justice Department in 1973 for discriminating against Black tenants, after all, and his relationship to Black Americans did not improve over the subsequent years. The Trump administration launched a crusade against critical race theory (CRT), a branch of legal scholarship that explores, among many things, "the ways in which racial inequality is embedded in structures in ways of which we are very often unaware."[18] Trump helped popularize the term and distort it beyond recognition, while promoting the idea that investigating systemic racism was a threat to the United States. When protesters took to the streets in the wake of the killing of George Floyd, Trump said that, had protestors breached the White House fence, they would "have been greeted with the most vicious dogs, and most ominous weapons."[19]

Rapper, singer, and songwriter Lecrae, onetime darling in white Neo-Reformed circles, found that when he questioned evangelical support for Trump, or spoke out about anti-Black racism during the Trump presidency, his audience dissipated. As early as February 2016, Lecrae openly questioned why anyone would support Trump, and that summer, he supported protests for racial justice. He also wrote a 2016 op ed in *Billboard* in the wake of the deaths of Alton Sterling and Philando Castile, two Black men killed at the hands of police, and the sniper attack on police officers in Dallas, Texas. Lecrae posted videos explaining to his audience the Black Lives Matter movement, an effort "to eradicate white supremacy and build local power to intervene in violence inflicted on Black communities."[20] "We're in the wake of a lot of systemic racism and oppression," he said, "that's happened for years. It's not a long time ago."

As Lecrae delivered what he believed to be a Christian message, he found that he was "met with silence or discord by white evangelicals." In fact, calls to end systemic racism in white evangelical circles were often dismissed as part of a conspiracy to de-Christianize the American population.[21] Lecrae saw shows canceled, and when they were not, they drew much smaller crowds. "My family and I," he recalled, "took a financial hit."[22] "It was precisely rap's social critique that eventually put the conservative evangelical Reformed crowd at odds with Lecrae," recalled Black Reformed pastor Rev. Dr. Mika Edmonson, "When they discovered that his Black art included a Black social critique, they dismissed him out of hand."

Even Kirk Franklin, who had a long and friendly relationship with the predominantly white CCM industry, found the limits of that relationship at the Dove Awards. While accepting an award in 2016 for Best Gospel Artist, Franklin made a direct plea to the audience. "I have a lot of friends in this room," he said, "of many shades and colors that I've walked a life for the last 23 years with—great men and women in the contemporary Christian community." "When police are killed," he said, "we need to say something; when black boys are killed, we need to say something, and when we don't say something, we're saying something." Franklin went on to lead the audience in a prayer for repentance, and his speech was met with a standing ovation. When the Trinity Broadcasting Network (TBN) aired the show, however, that part of Franklin's speech was edited out.

In 2019, Franklin used his Best Gospel Artist acceptance speech to call attention to the death of a Black woman, Atatiana Jefferson, who had been killed by a white police officer. Franklin asked for prayer for Jefferson's family, and the family of the police officer. Again, TBN cut the speech from the broadcast. Franklin announced shortly thereafter that he would boycott anything to do with the GMA or TBN. "For so long, the [musical] terms 'Christian' and 'Gospel' for many are code words for 'white' and 'black,'" he told his audience, "which history may teach us was a setup for this unfortunate place we find ourselves in today." "Not only did they edit my speech," he noted, "they edited the African American experience."

During those years, Toby McKeehan, who had for decades included "ending racism" as a core part of his ministry, did not give full-throated public support to anti-racist protests that sprang up around the nation. McKeehan avoided using the phrase "Black Lives Matter" and instead posted memes on social media noting that Jesus "ended the debate on which lives matter. He died for all," which was much closer to the "All Lives Matter" slogan adopted by critics of anti-racism protests.

The 2017 video for TobyMac's "Love Broke Thru," a song about personal conversion, used images of protests and police, and presented personal prayer as the solution to social unrest. When asked about the imagery by *Billboard*, McKeehan would only say that "we need God to break through and heal our divided nation." When *Billboard* inquired in April of 2017 about the effect of Trumpism or Black Lives Matter on their careers, Amy Grant, Skillet, Crowder, DC Talk, Britt Nicole, and TobyMac either did not respond or declined to speak on the record.[23]

In September of that year, Lecrae, tired of being held up as a "mascot of white evangelicalism," discussed his conscious choice to step back from his close association with white evangelical communities with Dr. Christina Edmondson, co-host of *Truth's Table*, a popular Christian podcast "built by Black women and for Black women." After noting that he had spent much of his career making music known for "placating or trying to make a song that caters to a white audience in any fashion," he was changing course. Lecrae wondered out loud about who he was if he was "not getting pats on the back from John Piper."[24]

Piper issued a response, which was published by *Christianity Today*. In it, Piper argued that the category of white evangelicalism "puts too many whites in bed together," and he tried to end with a hopeful note.[25] But, it was hard not to see that the Young, Restless, and Reformed movement's notion that their theology could transcend any and all social constructs had not overcome the color line in the United States. "When they [Black Christians] find that that message is only confined to doctrines of justification and has nothing to say to our social situation," noted Mika Edmondson, "then by and large, African Americans will say, 'I can't stay in that space.'"

Systemic racism was not the only flashpoint that energized evangelicals during the 2010s. When the Supreme Court guaranteed a constitutional right to same-sex marriage across the United States in 2015, it came as a blow to many within conservative evangelical media circles. The Obama administration added insult to injury by bathing the White House in rainbow lights signifying gay pride. "We've lost the entire culture anyway," said James Dobson. "It's about control of the public schools and it's what happens in universities," he continued; "[i]t's about the economy and it's about business and it's about the military and it's about medicine. It's about everything." After denouncing the Supreme Court's authority and noting that with "the right president, it could be overturned," Franklin Graham issued an invitation to a "Festival of Hope" in Birmingham, Alabama. Attendees heard more of Franklin Graham's "message of hope," along with appearances from the Newsboys, Kirk Franklin, and Michael W. Smith.

White evangelicals' dismay about gender, sex, and identity grew as the binaries between male and female, gay and straight became less distinct in public discourse. Conversations about queerness and pronoun use—and transgender children, in particular—were cause for concern at Focus on the Family. "The growing transgender movement fights against God's design for male and female," the organization warned in 2015. The Trump administration energetically took up Dobson and Graham's line of reasoning and classified diversity training about sexual identity and race discrimination as a danger to the republic.[26]

Jennifer Knapp and industry veteran Nancy VanReece argued in 2019 that excluding "faith rebels" who "are queer, cuss, drink and have sex" from the boundaries of CCM was a mistake; the rebels had something valuable to say, they claimed. They just needed industry gatekeepers and CCM audiences to "hand them a mic."[27] Unsurprisingly, Christian radio playlists continued their practice of platforming only those who publicly presented as straight, clean-spoken models of sobriety.

Those who came out or spoke out about including LGBTQ+ Christians in CCM circles suffered losses of social and financial capital. Knapp noted that venues that had welcomed her as the opening act for Audio Adrenaline closed their doors to her after she came out. Ray Boltz all but disappeared from the Southern Gospel circuit he once frequented. When Dan Haseltine of Jars of Clay questioned opposition to gay marriage in 2014, Christian radio stations reportedly pulled the band's catalog, and some fans deleted Jars of Clay from their streaming playlists.

Figures like Sandi Patty or Michael English, who had publicly admitted to adultery, were eventually allowed back into the fold, but breaking with evangelical teachings about homosexuality was a bridge too far. Once an artist dissented from strict evangelical teachings around sex and sexuality, "they are gone," said one Christian radio marketer on condition of anonymity, "and they can't come back." Amy Grant's fans still showed up for Christmas concerts after she said in 2021 that "gay, straight. It does not matter," but radio marketers expressed skepticism at the thought of a new non-Christmas album enjoying radio airtime.

Grace Semler Baldridge, an independent singer-songwriter who performs as Semler, challenged Christian radio's status as *the* gatekeeper of Christian music. Semler identifies as genderqueer and non-binary, and grew up the child of an Episcopal priest—ostensibly outside the reach of conservative white evangelicalism. But they also grew up listening to TobyMac and Relient K, and as host of a 2020 docu-series *State of Grace*, Semler explored how straight, heteronormative ideals were promoted through CCM. Their 2021 song "TobyMac," told from the perspective of Semler as a teen, explored a truly CCM conundrum: Semler had a crush, but was at a loss when it came to sharing that expression through CCM songs. "Growing up I often had to create mixtapes for girls I was interested in," they recalled, "but the only music I had access to was Christian." "When TobyMac said you consume me," Semler sang of their love interest, "I thought of her of how her eyes see through me."

In 2021, Semler released *Preacher's Kid*, a confessional, impassioned extended play recording about being queer and Christian. They insisted on categorizing it as "Christian music," a market niche once dreaded by entertainers hoping to crossover into the mainstream. "I have a lived Christian experience," they told NPR in an interview; "[m]y faith is deeply important to me." To the surprise of many—including Semler—*Preacher's Kid* shot to the top of the Apple Music charts. The story of an unsigned artist taking the top spot on iTunes was newsworthy, but, to the surprise of no one in the Christian Music industry, Semler's music was not featured on K-Love or Salem radio stations. Semler's story did not appear in *CCM Magazine*.

Semler and *Preacher's Kid* showed, however, that technology was changing how the label of "Christian music" or "CCM" could be applied in the digital age. An artist like Semler, who would have been easily excluded from Christian bookstores and Christian radio in the 1990s, could not be ignored in the 2020s.

The once-neat distinctions between CCM as "spiritual vitamins" for white suburban youths, and so-called secular music as depraved and worldly, were now blurry at best. Mainstream artist Chance the Rapper covered "How Great Is Our God" in 2016, and pop superstar Justin Bieber played a worship set at Coachella, a mainstream music festival, in 2018. Semler charted on iTunes as a Christian artist but was missing from the Dove Awards. Ye, aka Kanye West, a rapper and hip-hop megastar, had the top-selling Christian album of 2020, but his music did not make big impact on Christian radio. Nathan John Feuerstein, a white rapper who performs as NF, won a Dove Award and had the top-selling Christian album on *Billboard*, but he did not identify as a

"Christian artist." Dolly Parton and Carrie Underwood, two of the top-selling women in country music, were nominated for Dove Awards in 2022.

Semler was not the only one to benefit from digital streaming platforms. What counted as "Christian music," as determined by K-Love and The Fish, remained largely male, white, and worship-oriented, but Spotify's Christian artists reflected shifting demographics in the United States and the blurring lines between sacred and secular. John Jin Han, known on Spotify as Han, wrote music for "Asian Americans who feel out of place in white spaces" and garnered almost two hundred thousand subscribers. Sam Rivera, the Portland, Oregon–based son of Salvadoran immigrants, sings songs of love and longing to God and gained over 122,000 followers on YouTube. Black singer-songwriter Antoine Bradford's "Safe," a love song to his wife based on Ephesians 5, would have given Steven Curtis Chapman's "I Will Be Here" a run for its money as a celebration of marital devotion. Han, Rivera, and Bradford drew listeners by the millions on Spotify. Much of their music included classic revivalist themes of sin and salvation and encouraged Christians to overcome struggles with their faith.[28]

TikTok, a short-form video-hosting service that allowed creators to make videos with musical accompaniment, further shifted music taste-making and gatekeeping. As of 2022, TikTok reigned as one of the top social-media platforms for teens.[29] Those short clips began to drive streaming trends. Songs that trend on TikTok—new or old—drove listeners to Spotify or YouTube and were likely to land on the *Billboard* charts. This, of course, drew attention from record labels, and TikTok entered into licensing agreements with the "Big Three." Like many other streaming platforms, TikTok relied on an algorithm to give users the content that they want and then more and more of that content, to keep them engaged.[30]

Viral songs had a distinct advantage when it came to landing music on Christian radio: they were vetted theologically and politically by the market itself and were established by the masses as "safe for the whole family," which decreased the risk for radio. Those in worship-music publishing and radio marketing and artists themselves agreed that no one was sure how viral hits became viral. On Christian radio, such songs gained legendary provenance often attributed to Providence.

TikTok also revived interest in older hits, like Grits' "Ooh Ahh (My Life Be Like) [feat. TobyMac]," which has been featured in 2.5 million TikTok videos, and it paved the way for new artists like Montell Fish. Fish, who began by identifying as a "Christian rapper," turned away from making what he called "aggressively Christian music" and told *Billboard* that he did not want to do either gospel or CCM. Instead, Fish created moody, acoustic-driven soundscapes that racked up listens.[31] What the Becky-driven marketing of Christian radio overlooked, digital streaming platforms like Spotify revealed.

Worship in the Digital Age

Even on Christian radio, streaming changed how songs were discovered and promoted. Some large Christian radio stations mix worship music with artists like Lauren Daigle or TobyMac; at other stations, worship music dominates the playlists.[32] Christian-music marketers distinguished between the Beckys of CCM and a new generation of worship-music listeners by analyzing their buying habits. The "Christian retail, Christian venues, and Christian radio" suburban moms were "lean-back" listeners—they listened to whatever radio curated for them. Worship-music listeners, by contrast, were younger and more diverse, on average, and they were "lean-in" listeners.

Lean-in listeners curated, through digital streaming platforms, their own musical catalogs that include worship music from Christian radio alongside mainstream favorites. Streaming platforms like Spotify, launched in 2011 in the United States, quickly overtook radio in terms of listenership, but also in terms of taste-making. Spotify, along with other streaming juggernauts like Apple Music and YouTube, allowed lovers of CCM and worship music to curate their own listening experiences, and by around 2014, streaming services were driving radio playlists through a strange and mysterious process known as virality.

The music lean-in listeners chose was, for the most part, the stadium-rock-worship music of megachurch evangelicalism. Many theories have been floated to explain why CCM declined and worship thrived, but one explanation was simply financial sustainability. As major record labels acquired intellectual property in the form of worship-music copyrights, they collected sizable licensing fees from Christian Copyright Licensing International (CCLI), which facilitated payment to copyright holders when their music was performed.[33]

Major conglomerates like EMI Christian Music Group offset the financial losses from CCM's decline by signing and promoting more worship partnerships with ministries like Bethel and Jesus Culture, because they offered revenue streams from worshiping communities that entertainers did not: local churches. "CCLI became the conduit of an incredible [financial] resource," observed prolific Vineyard worship leader David Ruis. Thus, as the 2010s progressed, major labels signed more and more worship acts.

For some involved in the worship music industry, CCM's decline was seen as a moral victory. CCM was focused on profits and entertainment, the logic went, and not the Christian's first calling, to worship God. From this perspective, the rise of worship music was about Christian churches bringing musical gatekeeping back under congregational or denominational authority.

Some of worship music's ascent, however, was tied to the rise of Charismatic megachurches. In 2014, Hillsong UNITED finally cracked the code and created a radio-friendly single called "Oceans (Where Feet May Fail)." The ballad's soaring lyrics, "Spirit lead me where my trust is without borders," could have been a metaphor for how far Hillsong itself had come. The Australian Pentecostal megachurch had become an international movement with outposts in the United Kingdom, Ukraine, and the United States. Imitating the Vineyard Church, Hillsong's recipe for creating a growing global network included top-selling popular worship music. To the Vineyard model, Hillsong's Brian Houston added theologies of prosperity and Christian dominion, along with an affinity for American televangelist networks, and a healthy amount of celebrity glamor.

Hillsong NYC maximized the worship music "personality trend" in every way with the ultra-groomed, meticulously styled Carl Lentz, a Southern American preacher who had attended Hillsong College in Australia. As pastor of Hillsong NYC, Lentz presided over what *GQ* magazine dubbed "New York City's hippest megachurch" with professional lighting, polished preaching, and thrilling worship sets. "I started coming to Hillsong [NYC] because of the music," enthused one devotee. "Oh Holy Spirit," attendees sang, lifting their hands in mystical fervor, "burn like a fire, all consuming, consume me." The weekly pop-music extravaganzas attracted a steady stream of celebrity attendees, including pop icon Justin Bieber, A-list film star Chris Pratt, and reality-TV moguls Kylie and Kendall Jenner.

Lentz's star rose alongside fellow well-known, non-denominational Charismatic preachers like Chad Veach in Los Angeles and Judah Smith in Seattle, and together they gave a lot of concerned Pentecostals and Charismatics hope for the future. Even though young people were trending away from Christian affiliation in the United States, the rise of Lentz seemed to suggest that "network Christianity" led by media-savvy Charismatics could possibly reverse that trend.[34] As so-called hypepriests disseminated images of good-looking young people singing pop songs to God, a new future seemed possible for American Christianity.[35]

Living by American celebrity culture, for Lentz, meant dying by it. In 2022, he confessed to an extra-marital affair, and allegations of an abusive, toxic work environment quickly emerged in the wake of the sex scandal. Brian

Houston soon became embroiled in his own controversy and legal troubles sparked by a documentary series chronicling alleged abuse in the famously famous Hillsong Church and college in Australia. Hillsong USA began to collapse.

There were some who wondered if the downfall of Lentz, Houston, and Hillsong would lead to a decline in the model of glossy worship hits dominating the Christian music airwaves. But Bethel, a church in Redding, California, and Jesus Culture, a revivalist youth organization that had spun off from Bethel, continued to create hit after hit. In the music of these Charismatic powerhouses, Satan was sent to hell, the Spirit of God was loosed over the earth, and the believer experienced healing of the soul and body. As was the case with Hillsong (and Vineyard before that), Bethel and Jesus Culture operated as congregations, but also as a record label, development team, and platform.

They were joined on the Christian radio airwaves by Elevation Worship, another worship collective housed at Elevation Church, a Southern Baptist congregation pastored by Steven Furtick in Charlotte, North Carolina. Furtick was a Southern Baptist on paper; in the pulpit, however, he was a fiery figure with a fervor to rival even the most exuberant Pentecostal. Elevation Worship songs included plenty of classic Baptist altar calls ("O Come to the Altar"), but they were typically Pentecostal, too. Elevation music emphasized the kingship of Jesus ("There Is a King"), the triumphant Christian life ("Already Won"), and the generational blessings of God available to the believer ("The Blessing"). The music of Elevation Church mirrored the style of its pastor, and in their many live recordings, the Elevation Worship team had all of the classic stadium worship elements: flashing lights, a polished backing band, and expertly styled worship leaders.

Maverick City, a worship collective founded in Atlanta, Georgia, by Tony Brown and Jonathan Jay, expressed a "desire to look at the marginalized people in the CCM and the gospel world, and bring those voices to the center." Jay had been raised in a Black church as a child and listened to Kirk Franklin and the Winans, but at age eleven, his parents began attending a white congregation, where he was introduced to MercyMe and Chris Tomlin. The music of Maverick City reflected that background. It was an intentional mashup of white stadium-rock and Black Gospel music chords and vocal runs. "In the Christian music space," noted Maverick City member Norman Gyamfi, "Christian music generally denotes 'white' music, and Gospel simply means Black, until you have the founding of Maverick City Music."[36] In its many social-media videos, Maverick City presented an idyllic vision of an interracial worshiping community. Black, white, Latinx, and Asian worshipers sang songs of praise, often in the round.

Unlike other worship collectives, Maverick City had no congregational affiliation. Maverick City's parachurch status allowed it to embody ideals that were rare in congregational life. The theological wrangling, administration, and structures of power that reveal embedded racial hierarchies within congregations and denominations were seemingly stripped away, and the sounds of multi-racial, young, beautiful people remained.

The Christian lifestyle magazine *Relevant* called Maverick City "a leap forward for Church Music—an evolutionary step forward that the whole genre has been waiting for without realizing it," but not everyone appreciated how the sounds and lyrical content of Maverick City aligned with historically white worship music like Elevation. Some, noting the lengthy history of white appropriation of Black music, had questions about the project. Chandler Moore, one of the most prominent worship leaders in Maverick City, addressed his critics on social media in 2022. "[People] think I'm not 'black' or 'Pentecostal' or 'gospel' because of the restraint I have in the music I release, but you're not gonna hear a lot of that (unless you really study our music), because of the restraint I have to have for the audience I'm assigned to," he wrote, concluding that "the more broad your audience becomes, the more restraint is needed."[37]

For Moore, his "assignment" meant reaching audiences outside the Black Pentecostalism of his youth, and giving up signature practices for the sake of audience breadth was an acceptable trade. For others, compromise and "restraint" for the sake of "broad" audiences seemed like a betrayal of Moore's Black church roots. Frustrated commenters argued that Moore's comments were selling out to a conservative white market and "and a slap in the face to the Black church."[38]

COVID-19 and #LetUsWorship

Because worship lyrics did not include on-the-nose political exhortations once popular in CCM, some mistakenly believed that worship music stood apart from white evangelical politics. The COVID-19 pandemic, however, demonstrated otherwise. In the spring of 2020, the United States shut down most aspects of public life—including church attendance—because of the COVID-19 virus.[39] The virus, a respiratory illness that threatened the lives of millions, was thought to spread especially quickly through singing, which meant that for months, churches were also encouraged to refrain from communal singing.

Worship music produced by large, tech-driven Charismatic megachurches benefitted, counterintuitively, from the COVID-19 pandemic. While they could not welcome the masses to worship in auditoriums, they had sophisticated technological and financial resources to change course and create high-production-value music and preaching online. In many ways, COVID-19 sped up a phenomenon already underway in evangelical worship.

As evangelical congregations chafed under COVID-19 regulations, Elevation Worship and Maverick City released live worship songs that found global audiences. The comforting, beautifully shot worship experiences provided the devout with credible substitutes for the megachurch worship experiences they were missing. At-home worshipers enjoyed skillfully shot closeups of enthusiastic worshipers, without the pain, frustration, and potential for infection of real, live people. Christ for the Nations alumna Kari Jobe and her husband Cody Carnes co-wrote "The Blessing," a musical version of Numbers 6:24–26, with Elevation Church's Steven Furtick, and the song went viral. Denominations, congregations, schools, and parachurch organizations around the world created digital, multi-language versions of the song that carried blessings through the internet when in-person worship was impossible.

In many ways, the music of Elevation Church, Hillsong, Bethel, Jesus Culture, and Maverick City seemed like a gift to worshiping communities during difficult times. Of course, for those pastoring smaller congregations with fewer resources, the COVID-19 pandemic was devastating, and the musical sensations of Maverick City did little to slow their losses. The high production value of large-scale Charismatic worship gatherings was impossible to replicate in smaller settings. Accompaniment aides for small and medium-sized congregations were marketed to smaller churches, but American evangelical worshipers favored the entire stadium experience: big crowds, virtuosic performances, smoke machines, and flashy lights.

And they were willing to pay for it. The glossy, stadium-rock sounds of modern worship flourished as protective pandemic measures lifted. CCM stadium tours were few and far between, but Maverick City, Elevation, Kari Jobe, and others played stadiums and other large venues, with ticket prices that varied, but sold for up to $200 per worshiper. Indeed, while jangly guitars and blue-eyed soul soloists were few and far between on mainstream *Billboard* charts, white male rock guitarists ruled on K-Love, Way-FM, and The Fish. In 2021, Fender, one of the largest guitar companies in the United States, estimated that one out of every three guitars sold—around $600 million dollars of product—was sold to churches for praise-and-worship music.[40]

As the worship market grew in the United States, it consolidated. As of 2023, the Top 25 worship-music songs reported through CCLI and other worship music charts were made by worship leaders associated with only a handful of megachurches including Bethel, Hillsong, Elevation, and Passion.[41] These few music makers created the music for a majority of American Protestant congregations using CCLI, large and small.

The worship-music industry was an undeniably profitable business, and American-centric, white-majority, English-language-favoring Christian radio stations promoted only a fraction of its transnational reach. For example, African American worship leader William McDowell had an international audience for his gospel-inflected worship leading. According to McDowell, while listening to Saddleback Church's Rick Warren, the Holy Spirit called him to found a congregation. McDowell's ministry drew attendees in Ghana and Guyana as well as in Orlando, Florida. Guatemalan worship group Miel San Marcos, American-born Spanish-language worship star Christine D'Clario, and Brazilians Marcos Brunet, Raquel Kerr Borin, Ana Paula Valadão, and Diante do Trono continued to lead worship transnationally alongside newcomers like Lucas Conslie. In many cases, their followings far outstripped those of their English-language American counterparts, and their international reach was greater than even the biggest household names of CCM.

These transnational Charismatic worship celebrities had no real need for Christian radio as a launching pad. Streaming platforms had given them a workaround. Their radio-unfriendly impulses—lengthy, multilingual songs that included long breaks for speaking in tongues, altar calls, and sermons—racked up views by the billions on digital platforms. In 2019, for example, Jesus Image Church, based in an Orlando, Florida, suburb, released "Yeshua," their version of a dance anthem, written by Gui Brazil, a Christian DJ living in Portugal. Jesus Image's repetitive, nineteen-minute-long song, retooled as a dramatic paean by pastor Michael Koulianos, captured the end-times, Zionistic fervor typical of Charismatic Christianity. Jesus Image did not have to add a catchy verse or edit out any of the flag dancing and interpretive ballet to accumulate over sixty-three million views on YouTube (and counting). Two years later, when Lucas Conslie and Marcos Brunet recorded a twenty-seven-minute-long bilingual version at the Upper Room, a Charismatic ministry in Dallas, they had no trouble acquiring 3.2 million views. As of 2022, the song has yet to make inroads on Christian radio.

Sinach's "Way Maker" offers a striking example of how global worship music has circumvented US-based radio gatekeepers. It also demonstrates the enduring pattern of white evangelical appropriation of Black music in the United

States. Long before it hit the radio, Way Maker was an international sensation. Les Moir from Integrity Music met Osinachi Kalu Okoro Egbu, a megachurch worship leader from Nigeria known professionally as Sinach, in 2014, but her prodigious talents did not come to the attention of American worshiping audiences until the Pentecostals of Alexandria recorded Sinach's 2015 worship anthem "Way Maker," in 2016. Michael W. Smith's daughter Anna saw their eleven-minute-plus rendition, which had gone viral on YouTube (as of 2023, the video had 35 million views). Anna introduced "Way Maker" to her father, who produced a sleek, four-minute version that was ideal for Christian radio. Smith's version shot to the top of the CCLI worship charts in 2019, and worship rockers Leeland covered "Way Maker." The two white men's versions became definitive in most stateside congregations. Sinach, meanwhile, formalized a licensing agreement with Integrity that year.

"Way Maker" also shows the continued power and pliability of worship music as a force in American public life. On the surface, the lyrics of worship music are distinct from CCM, in part because they do not contain within them overt political directives. Most worship songs, after all, do not encourage the listener to celebrate American patriotism or refrain from "secular" music or oppose abortion or avoid sex outside of marriage. But worship songs can become political anthems. "Way Maker" was used at racial-justice protests against police violence. But it was also used at pro-Trump rallies. And "Way Maker" became a defiant hymn for churches refusing to comply with COVID-19 meeting restrictions.

When it came to harnessing the political fervor of the COVID-19 era, few outstripped one-time volunteer Bethel worship leader Sean Feucht. Feucht was not much of a songwriter, and his voice was nondescript. He was ambitious, though, and, what he lacked in musical talent, he made up for in self-promotion and political activism. Feucht came in third place in a 2020 primary bid to serve as a Republican congressman in California, but he quickly regrouped and became a staunch supporter of Donald Trump.

Living in the largely Democratic state of California, Feucht saw opportunity when the state adopted strict measures banning in-person gatherings to combat the coronavirus. Feucht styled himself as a "worship-protestor" who resisted health restrictions related to the COVID-19 pandemic. He began marketing his gatherings in California and then began "Let Us Worship" events flouting COVID-19 restrictions around the country.

On the Let Us Worship Tour, Feucht decried Black Lives Matter protests as a "riot." He courted liberal ire by targeting progressive cities like Portland, Oregon, where far-right activists like Tusitala "Tiny" Toese of the Proud Boys served as self-appointed crowd control.[42] Feucht also created "Hold the

Line," an organization with a broad mission to engage "with the church and young people across the country" to "take a stand for what is right." "Right," according to Hold the Line, included anti-abortion, religious liberty, free speech, and limited government.

On October 25, 2020, Feucht went to the US Capitol with a guitar and a mission to bring Hold the Line to Washington, DC. "REVIVAL OR BUST," he told his social-media followers, and an estimated thirty-five thousand showed up to express their patriotism and frustration with life in America. One way of looking at Feucht's gathering was that it was a kind of "B-Team" Washington DC rally for evangelicals. A month earlier, the "A-Team" had assembled at the Lincoln Memorial, where Vice President Mike Pence greeted Billy Graham's son Franklin, Harvest Christian Fellowship pastor Greg Laurie, and worship leader Michael W. Smith. Feucht's meeting was smaller, and attendees included newly elected, conservative Senator Josh Hawley from Missouri, and Jentezen Franklin, a Charismatic televangelist from Gainesville, Georgia, with a Zionist ministry aimed at "Helping Fulfill Biblical Prophecy in the Holy Land."

Another way to look at Feucht, however, was that he represented a different variety of evangelical activism. Feucht's apocalyptic vision of the United States won the support of Don Finto, who prayed anointing prayers over then-candidate Feucht in 2020. Feucht framed his opposition to COVID-19 restrictions as a form of rebellion and branded his work as part of the legacy of the Jesus movement. His long, blonde hair and beachside services, coupled with groovy, retro fonts that retooled the artwork of the Jesus movement, certainly felt familiar to white boomer Charismatics. Feucht gained the approval of Greg Laurie, an early Jesus-movement figure who had risen to become a megachurch-pastoring, Trump-supporting Southern California institution. Laurie's 2018 book *Jesus Revolution: How God Transformed an Unlikely Generation and How He Can Do It Again* (released as a film in 2023 by Lionsgate) included his reflections on the hippie revivals of his youth.

Billy Graham had understood that music was formative, and his white evangelical coalition respected CCM as a tool for evangelism, but for Charismatics, praise-and-worship music was much more than a tool. For Sean Feucht and his fellow worship leaders, praise-and-worship meetings were about accessing power from an "enthroned, Godly King."[43] The act of praising and worshiping, in other words, gave the worshiper power from God and established the Kingdom of God on earth, in this case, at the United States Capitol.

Feucht was one among many Charismatic worship leaders who provided Donald Trump with robust and sustained support throughout his presidency.

As a celebrity himself, Trump understood how to garner media attention and harness it for his purposes, and throughout his presidency, the White House enjoyed highly visible support from well-known worship leaders and televangelists.

Trump ran an unconventional and counterintuitive campaign, particularly when it came to engaging with white evangelicals, the longstanding base of the Republican Party. When Trump put together an "evangelical advisory board," he included the usual suspects in white evangelical political activism, but he also widened the category of "evangelical" to include Pentecostal and Charismatic celebrities like Tony Suarez and Rodney Howard-Browne. They, in turn, showered him with praise and prayers.

Trump went further than any previous president to welcome Charismatics and Pentecostals. Pentecostal televangelist Oral Roberts once met with John F. Kennedy, as well as Richard Nixon and Jimmy Carter. And in 1985, Ronald Reagan gave a very friendly interview to Charismatic Baptist media mogul Pat Robertson. But as a whole, Pentecostals were not part of the inner circle of evangelical politics.[44] Billy Graham, the Southern Baptist, had the most public access to the highest office in the land. Trump, by contrast, rolled out the red carpet for Pentecostal and Charismatic celebrities.

Though Trump was by no means devout, he accepted their prayers for anointing and submitted himself to their rituals of prayer. He attended their praise-and-worship services. He especially relished Pentecostal prophecies comparing him to David, the ancient warrior-king of Israel, or when Pentecostal preacher Lance Wallnau called Trump a "modern-day Cyrus," a Persian king chosen by the Lord to "navigate in chaos."

Rather than appealing primarily to the Billy Graham–esque respectable Baptist networks, Trump latched onto Charismatic media magnates like Paula White-Cain, who shared candidate Trump's showy aesthetic and scandalous personal history. As Trump's so-called personal pastor, she stumped for Trump on digital platforms and on television. White-Cain also brought Pentecostals and Charismatic celebrities into Trump's orbit. On the campaign trail, White-Cain accompanied him to elaborate public prayer sessions where prominent Pentecostal and Charismatic leaders anointed Trump for the work of the presidency in 2016.

The Trump campaign made sure to stop at megachurch congregations in so-called battleground states, like Darrell and Belinda Scott's New Spirit Revival Center in Cleveland, Ohio, and the International Church of Las Vegas in Nevada, where candidate Trump received divine anointing and prophetic blessings. Charismatic pastor Jeremiah Johnson prophesied that Trump, then a longshot candidate, would win, and his prophecy included a play on Trump's name and the preferred instrument of Pentecostal predictions about the end of time. "Trump," he said, "shall become My trumpet to the American people."

While in office, the Trump administration invited worship leaders to the office for "faith briefings." In December of 2019, the White House posted a picture of the president surrounded by a crowd of worship leaders. Present that day were Hillsong's Brian Houston, Sean Feucht, Kari Jobe, and Cody Carnes. The worship leaders prayed for their president and the White House made sure to post a video of Jobe and Carnes speaking rapturously about "what God is doing in our White House."[45]

Celebrity and flamboyant aesthetics were one thing that Charismatic and Pentecostal worship leaders shared in common with the president, but that was not the full extent of their relationship. Trump loved public spectacle as much as Pentecostals and Charismatics. He held rallies around the country that resembled revivals.

Trump, the self-professed deal maker, also gave Pentecostals and Charismatics a lot of what they wanted in terms of public policy. Trump moved the US Embassy in Israel from Tel Aviv to Jerusalem, which was, to many, a fulfillment of God's plan for the end of time. Charismatics, especially white Charismatics, had long been preoccupied with Israel. Moving the US Embassy, they believed, put the United States on the right side of divine history. The move also fed the perception that Donald Trump was less a president than a potentate—a ruler of truly biblical proportions.[46] Trump also appointed Amy Coney Barrett to the Supreme Court, widely seen as an effort to give white evangelicals what was their most prized public-policy change, and the subject of so many CCM songs: the capacity to overturn *Roe v. Wade.*

Trump publicly supported conspiracy theories, many of which enjoyed wide circulation in Charismatic and Pentecostal circles. The most prominent conspiracy promoted by Trump during his presidency was QAnon, which first appeared in 2017 on an internet forum called 4chan. Like all viral internet phenomena, QAnon had many varieties, but the central story could be the premise to a Frank Peretti novel: "the world is controlled by a secret cabal of Satan-worshiping pedophiles who are abducting, abusing, and ritualistically murdering children by the thousands."[47] QAnon took off in evangelical circles, and many Charismatics and Pentecostals, long accustomed to stories about spiritual warfare and children in danger, dove into the narrative.

QAnon, however, was only one among many stories swirling in Charismatic and Pentecostal circles during the Trump presidency. As always, they sought to interpret current events prophetic biblical texts. Established Pentecostal and Charismatic media personalities like *Charisma Magazine* speculated about the end of time, as did new media operations like *Elijah List* and thousands of YouTube and TikTok prophets who wove together internet conspiracies, Donald Trump's pronouncements about the world, and their interpretations of the books of Revelation, Isaiah, Ezekiel, and more.

Trump's engagement with Charismatic evangelicalism was smart, politically. The denominations that created so much of CCM—Baptists and Nazarenes and Methodists—declined sharply in the 2020s. Much of that loss is due to a rise in the so-called nones, people who claim no religious affiliation. But these denominational structures have also been supplanted by non-denominational congregations that are institutionally unaffiliated, and practically Pentecostalized in their worship, and tied together by worship music that is untethered from the worshiping communities that created it.

During his reelection campaign, Trump received enthusiastic support from the likes of Feucht, who prayed for Trump and for King Jesus to reign in the United States, and Michael Tait, who prayed over Trump with Paula White-Cain at a campaign rally in Florida. In the weeks leading up to the 2020 presidential election, Kim Walker Smith of Jesus Culture released "Worth the Fight," the theme song for *The Trump I Know*, a 2020 film that aimed to show the president was an advocate for women. The song used language of light and dark, good and evil, and naturally put the Trump administration in the camp of light and goodness. "This is gonna take an army," she sang. Charismatic prophets did their part and declared in the pages of *Charisma Magazine* that God had given them divine insight into the fact that Trump would win a second term.

In spite of his appeals to and support from Charismatic and Pentecostal celebrities, Trump was not reelected in 2020. In the days following his loss, Trump received robust support from an unofficial cabinet of Charismatic and Pentecostal media makers. Trump's pastor Paula White-Cain dispatched "angels in Africa" to come to Trump's aid. Pillow entrepreneur and Charismatic devotee Mike Lindell visited the White House to strategize. The so-called apostles and prophets of C. Peter Wagner's independent Charismatic church growth networks rallied around Trump, whom they saw as God's anointed leader.

Trump's Charismatic faithful came out in force to defend him. The devil had deceived the world, they said, and stolen the election from its rightful winner, Donald J. Trump. "Put on the full armor of God," they advised one another as they approached the seat of American democracy, "so that you can take your stand against the devil's schemes." Prophecies abounded; Trump had not lost, was the gist. He would be president in 2021.

Disgruntled American citizens from across the nation gathered at the United States Capitol on January 5, 2021, for a two-day "Jericho March," to protest the recent presidential election of Democrat Joe Biden and pray that Vice President Mike Pence and members of Congress would overturn the 2020 election results. There, participants reenacted the story of Joshua and the Israelites, who marched around the Canaanite city of Jericho seven times, blew shofars, and watched as the city walls crumbled.[48] Some wore t-shirts that claimed that Donald Trump's presidency was, in actuality, a cosmic battle between good and evil.

It sounded like something that Carman himself might have scripted. The Capitol protestors included a variety of religious practices and practitioners, to be sure, but the Charismatics were out in full force. Extemporaneous prayers abounded; prophecies were spoken. That day, a small group of protesters danced in front of a small platform just outside the Capitol building. Bundled up to ward off the weather, they waved hankies, clapped their hands, held the Stars and Stripes, and blew shofars. The stadium-rock-worship music of the Newsboys blared from a speaker, the CCM anthem of their discontent. "My God's not dead," they sang defiantly, "He's surely alive."[49]

Epilogue

Blow the Trumpet in Zion

On January 6, 2021, Jericho Marchers again brought shofars to the US Capitol. Participants blew their instruments to tear down the walls of a supposedly corrupt election process and reinstate Donald J. Trump as the rightful president of the United States. Along with the musical accompaniment, Charismatics like Mike Lindell, Joshua Feuerstein, and Paula White-Cain spoke at the Jericho March. Some of the Jericho marchers joined insurrectionists who overtook the US Capitol, which the official Jericho March organization would go on to denounce.

Shofar blowing and Jericho Marching were not the only Charismatic sights or sounds observable during the attack on the American Capitol. Prophets prophesied. Flag dancers danced. A Buffalo-festooned Jake Angeli, aka the "Q-anon Shaman," led extemporaneous prayer to which his compatriots responded with closed eyes, raised hands, and "amens" and "yes, Lords."[1]

In spite of the exuberant horn blowing, flag waving, and spiritual intercession, however, the Jericho March did not result in another term in office for Donald Trump. A few of the prophets apologized for their mistaken predictions. But many more just tweaked the message a bit to account for a Biden presidency and continued prognostications about the end of days.

In fact, Trump's loss energized the faithful. Nowhere were the fumes of Trump's 2020 loss more potent than on the ReAwaken Tour, an eclectic series of gatherings held mostly at Pentecostal and Charismatic congregations around the United States that were part revival meeting, part political rally, and part carnival. At ReAwaken events, the faithful sway to the worship music (Sean Feucht has appeared on the tour) and listen to speeches by QAnon conspiracy theorists, election deniers, hellfire-and-brimstone preachers, and anti-vaccine activists. Trump allies like former White House national security advisor Michael Flynn gather alongside Charismatic prophets like Amanda Grace, known for her exuberant appropriations of Jewish practices like shofar blowing.

Unlike the comparatively staid revival meetings held by Franklin Graham under the umbrella of his father Billy Graham's organization, ReAwaken tours were raucous. They were also surprisingly ecumenical. In addition to

Pentecostal and Charismatic prophets and prophetesses, journalist Sam Kestenbaum has observed that meetings serve a "diverse market," bound together by the apocalyptic, conspiratorial rhetoric. "There are multi-level marketers, crypto traders, naturopathic bodybuilders, telepaths, and metaphysical entrepreneurs," notes Kestenbaum, "The overarching mood is Charismatic, but the ReAwaken tent appears big enough to welcome Catholics, Jews, New Agers, Mennonites and curiosity-seekers of numerous persuasions and backgrounds."

Many consider themselves to be waging a holy war, at the cusp of the Second Coming. Worship anthems like Bethel Church's "Raise a Hallelujah" arm them for the fight. "My weapon," they sing, "is a melody." The musical war of the ReAwaken tour reflected a vision of the nation common among predominately—although not exclusively—white Charismatics in the United States. Trump-backed Republican Doug Mastriano, an acolyte of Wagner's New Apostolic Reformation (NAR) teachings, ran for governor in Pennsylvania, and he used Steven Curtis Chapman's "The Great Adventure" as his theme song on the campaign trail. Mastriano's campaign often featured NAR preacher Lance Wallnau, who envisioned the United States as a "promised nation for his [Jesus'] inheritance," and promoted the "Seven Mountain" approach to bringing the nation under the dominion of Jesus. Mastriano rejected the label of "Christian Nationalism," but he firmly supported the idea that the separation of church and state was a "myth," and that the United States was and ought to always be a Christian nation. Meanwhile, in true Charismatic style, his wife Rebbie Stewart gushed about the couple's love of Israel.

Mastriano lost, but others, like Charismatic Colorado Congresswoman Lauren Boebert, a frequent collaborator with Sean Feucht, won. Boebert also believes that the separation of church and state is "junk" and embraces the notion that the nation ought to be "Christian." The United States is important, in this construction of the world, but not unique. "There have been two nations created for God's glory," Boebert argued, "Israel and the United States of America."

This Charismatic nationalism kicked into high gear when the Supreme Court overturned *Roe v. Wade* on June 24, 2022. Conservatives around the country rejoiced, and none with more abandon than worship leaders like Sean Feucht and Kim Walker Smith. Feucht led worship outside the US Supreme Court in response. He recalled attending The Call DC, where he heard exhortations against *Roe v. Wade*. "It was really like I felt like I got the heart of God for this issue," he said, "and I began to pray ever since I was 17 years old." That battle was, in Feucht's mind, won in June of 2022. "We're going to give

Him praise," he said to *Fox News Digital*, "because only He could do something like this in our generation." Walker Smith, who is affiliated with Jesus Culture, expressed the jubilation that the CCM and worship-music communities felt after decades singing protest songs against access to abortion. "What a day to be alive!!" Walker posted on her official social-media accounts, "PRAISE GOD!! Goodbye Roe v. Wade!!"

Pentecostal and Charismatic worship leaders like Feucht, Walker-Smith, and Kari Jobe—once a group with a brand too "fanatical" for the Pentecostal Church of the Nazarene—are now at the vanguard of conservative white evangelical activism in the United States. Through their recorded music and traveling worship gatherings, their influence transcends denominational boundaries. Congregations that have little historic connection to Pentecostals or Charismatics now reverberate with an apostolic, prophetic, wonder-working, dominion-seeking, Zionistic, apocalyptic cosmology ushered in through their songs.

These practitioners are difficult to categorize. Observers use a variety of terms to parse out the different strands: Renewalists, Pentecostals, Charismatics and Neo-Charismatics, denominational Charismatics, and independent Charismatics. The revivalist practices that bind them, and the music they share, however, make one thing clear: traveling through songs and revivalist rituals, Pentecostal and Charismatic ideas are both potent and durable. Americans may be worshiping less often and leaving denominations at historic rates, but Charismatics have never been beholden to denominational affiliation. Indeed, Charismatic and Pentecostal beliefs and practices—like belief in prophecy, divine healing, and the idea that God anoints leaders like Donald Trump—are no longer fringe. They may very well represent the future of evangelical identity.[2]

Charismatic visions of the United States certainly seem to be on the rise. During the heyday of CCM, American exceptionalism was an important part of the music. Sandi Patty's ode to the nation as "the lantern of hope from the harbor still shines," for instance, rested on the idea that the United States was God's special nation. But for many Charismatics and Pentecostals, so deeply formed by premillennial dispensational teachings about the end of time, there is only *one* chosen nation in this world.[3] God has granted the United States a role to play in order to usher in the Second Coming of Christ, and that role is to support God's chosen nation of Israel. In this conception of history, democracy may come or go, but as long as the United States supports the Holy Land, it will experience God's favor and blessings.

This type of nationalism is not built on Cold War formulations of American exceptionalism. Pentecostal and Charismatic nationalisms are quite portable.

Any and all nations can and should support the nation of Israel, the logic goes. The blowing of shofars is a call to spiritual war that can be found in Australia, Brazil, South Africa, Guatemala, Canada, and the United States, and distributed on social-media platforms like YouTube and TikTok.

Pentecostal and Charismatic ideas about spiritual warfare and physical warfare intersected in believers' support for Donald Trump in the United States. The *evangélicos* of Brazil did the same for their president, Jair Bolsonaro. Charismatic evangelicals in the United States and *evangélicos* in Brazil are distinct, but many of their political and musical tastes overlap. Jair Bolsonaro, known in some circles as the "Trump of the Tropics," shared the former American president's populism. He also shared Trump's popularity among *evangélicos*, the majority of whom, regardless of denominational affiliation, have adopted Charismatic worship practices.

Like Trump, Bolsonaro's *evangélico* supporters reveled in the president's opposition to abortion. They showered praise on the president and prayed for spiritual warfare on his behalf. They also shared a propensity for large-scale revival meetings featuring praise-and-worship music. In 2020, Bolsonaro attended The Send Brazil, a gathering that included a reported 141,000 young people that hoped to "turn to Jesus and send out missionaries." Michael Koulianos from Jesus Image was there, along with Dante Bowe from Maverick City, and Steffany Gretzinger, an alumna of Bethel Music.

When he visited the United States in 2022, Bolsonaro visited Lagoinha Church in Orlando, Florida, which is pastored by André Valadão, a Rhema Bible College and Christ for the Nations alumnus and brother of Ana Paula Valadão. As polls showed Bolsonaro trailing behind his leftist opponent, ex-president Luiz Inácio Lula da Silva, he doubled down on the *evangélico* vote.

When Valadão's father, Márcio Valadão, celebrated his fiftieth year in ministry in the summer of 2022, the Bolsonaros went to Lagoinha Church to celebrate him. Jair Bolsonaro is Catholic, but the First Lady of Brazil—the much-loved, telegenic Michelle Bolsonaro—grew up listening to Ana Paula Valadão's band Diante do Trono and watching the ministry on television. In the heat of a reelection campaign, First Lady Bolsonaro praised Ana Paula Valadão as her "spiritual mother." Michelle Bolsonaro went on to depict her husband's campaign as a war between good and evil. Before they left Lagoinha Church, the Bolsonaros knelt as the church prayed over the couple, and over the "Christian nation" of Brazil, and against the demonic ideologies and spiritual battles that threatened their country. Shofars blew along with applause as the congregation said the final "amen."

In the weeks leading up to the election, Ana Paula Valadão enthusiastically encouraged her followers on social media to vote. Michelle Bolsonaro shared a video of Valadão dressed in yellow and green, the colors of the Brazilian flag, singing patriotic music to a crowd that was waving and saluting Brazilian flags. As Sandi Patty had done in front of Lady Liberty in 1986, Valadão stood before her fellow citizens and sang about taking possession of the inheritance God had for her people. The song, "Brasil," took 2 Chronicles 7:14 and applied it to Valadão's homeland. When the First Lady voted for her husband on October 30, 2022, she posted a picture of herself wearing a t-shirt bearing the Israeli flag. "*Que as bençãos do nosso Deus estejam sobre o Brasil e sobre Israel*," she captioned her photo; "May God's blessings be upon Brazil and Israel."

Like his populist counterpart in the United States, however, Jair Bolsonaro lost a close reelection campaign. Ana Paula Valadão expressed dismay and posted prayers for unity, but some of her followers planned to take to the streets. Others called for military intervention. Jair Bolsonaro refused to concede, but in the end, he traveled back to Orlando, Florida, when his successor was installed in office.

On January 8, 2023, two years and two days after the failed insurrection at the United States Capitol, Bolsonaro's supporters overwhelmed Brazil's Presidential Palace, Congress, and Supreme Court. Many protestors prayed as they gathered outside the gleaming, white, modernist dome of Brasilia's Complexo Cultural da República. Video footage from that day captured a lone figure, standing amid flag wavers and passersby and police, blowing a shofar to the sky, declaring spiritual war.

These global songs of worship and warfare would probably surprise the "business-priests" of the twentieth century, like John T. Benson and Jarrell McCracken, who envisioned the American marketplace as an altar of praise over which they could preside. They positioned themselves as gatekeepers who guarded the boundaries of white, middle-class Christianity in the United States and promoted the gospel through media and marketing.

Their species is now endangered. The white Holiness and Baptist denominations that birthed such figures and fueled CCM are now dwindling. The altar is now transnational. The networks that propel worship music are often opaque; many of the creators of worship music are affiliated to international Charismatic media networks who need neither denominations nor established evangelical organizations to promote their work. The distribution networks of pious Christian bookstore owners are now agnostic online retailers and algorithms. Becky no longer rules.

While there is no doubt that the white Holiness revivals that kickstarted the Benson Company are fewer and further between than they were decades ago, a surprisingly old-school revival occurred on February 8, 2023, at Asbury University in Wilmore, Kentucky, the home of the 1970 Ichthus Festival.

After a typical chapel service, the predominately white student body sang and prayed for hours and then days on end, and came to the altar in Asbury Chapel, much like generations of Holiness and Welseyan revivalists had done before them.

Word of the revival meeting spread quickly on social media, and the gathering garnered international attention. Thousands of people travelled to the small town to see it. Millions more watched live video footage online. A few other Christian colleges saw their own complementary revival meetings.

Opinions about the "authenticity" of the revival abounded. As critics and proponents weighed in, a surprising consensus emerged among white Protestant observers. Most found the youth of the worshipers and the relative simplicity of the services to be refreshing. Kari Jobe traveled to Wilmore and posted a video of the gathering to her social-media account. Progressive author and activist Shane Claiborne spoke warmly of the revival. Trump-supporting firebrand Greg Locke visited, and he shared his experiences with *Charisma News*. But, notably, no well-known worship leader or preacher took the stage at Asbury. On February 24, Asbury University closed the worship space to the public, and the outpouring, as the university calls it, is now memorialized on the university's website. There, testimonies of altar calls are gathered through a website submission form, where they reside alongside stories from previous generations of Wesleyan Holiness revivalists.

For those familiar with the business of worship, the Asbury Revival was notable because of how its low production value subverted the powerful forces of the worship market. Public performances of songs in church, sung from memory without lyric projection, are not beholden to the business of worship: the licensing and copyrights, the ticket sales and merchandise. Some worship leaders took note. "I don't know if those young adults were fully aware of what they were doing," noted one seasoned worship music writer, "it was revolutionary."

The revolution, so far, has not been spread widely. The scope of this small revolution was limited. Many of the songs sung at the outpouring were greatest hits of the worship business such as the 2001 hit "Here I Am to Worship." The community singing them—Christian college students with the means and opportunity to attend a private Christian university—knew them, most likely, because they had some exposure to the evangelical soundscape of the megachurch. And, while the low-fi, low-key meeting was compared favorably to the tech-driven glamor of megachurch services, the only reason people could weigh in on the meeting at all was because streaming platforms allowed world-wide exposure.

As was the case in the world of CCM, there are some critics of the business of Christian worship. Some argue that the dominance of stadium-rock-style worship on Christian radio homogenizes Christian worship and sets an unattainable standard for struggling medium or small congregations. Others are critical of how worship "hits" turn over faster and faster to meet consumer demand. Some claim that the high production value of worship music discourages the thing that it purports to encourage: congregational singing.

By most measures, however, the worship industry remains strong, built on a century of marketing know-how. The market, however, is an unwieldy and unpredictable ministry partner. If the history of CCM teaches anything, it is that those who think they can harness it for their own ends are often unprepared for the influence that consumers and markets and technological interventions have over commercialized religion.

Indeed, now that algorithms have taken the place of most white evangelical gatekeepers, the market itself is shrouded in a kind of tech-driven mystery; the people and communities behind the billions of streams are hidden. But, if CCLI charts reveal anything, the worship industry still shapes and is shaped by the culture and demographics of megachurches. Small-scale efforts have been launched to re-establish theological boundaries around worship music, but congregations like Bethel, Hillsong, Elevation, and Passion continue to curate the songs shaping untold numbers of worshipers around the world, as does Maverick City. As megachurches have consolidated worshipers, they have gotten considerably more diverse. Megachurches remain predominately white, suburban, and middle-class, but whereas 21 percent of megachurches were multiracial in 2000, 58 percent were in 2020.[4]

For those with the means to participate in person, there are seemingly endless ways to consume this form of Christian worship. In the spring of 2023, Elevation Worship announced its fifteenth studio project, along with an arena tour scheduled for the summer and fall. On the Elevation Nights tour, worshipers were promised praise with the band and a chance to hear from preacher Steven Furtick, who as of 2023 was no longer tied to the Southern Baptist Convention. "Join us," the group announced on Instagram, "for a night of worship + a WORD." T-shirts and sweatshirts were for sale in the "shop" section of Elevation Worship's website. Live performance tracks were sold in the "resources" section. The "Official Platinum" worship experience, purchased through Ticketmaster, was priced at around $165.30 per ticket.

Notes

Introduction

1. Daniel Ramírez demonstrates in *Migrating Faith: Pentecostalism in the United States and Mexico in the Twentieth Century* how Pentecostal hymnody carried ideologies in Pentecostal migrant communities in the United States and Mexico. (Chapel Hill: University of North Carolina Press, 2015).
2. Eileen Luhr's *Witnessing Suburbia: Conservatives and Christian Youth Culture* (Berkeley: University of California Press, 2009) and Heather Hendershot's *Shaking the World for Jesus: Media and Conservative Evangelical Culture* (Chicago: University of Chicago Press, 2010) explore CCM as part of a broad network of late twentieth-century evangelical media.
3. Ritual theorist Catherine Bell argues that rituals and ritualized acts are "strategic power relationships—schemes that hierarchize, integrate, define, or obscure." In the ritual of revival, power is created and managed through the relationship among preachers, music leaders, and attendees. Catherine Bell, *Ritual Theory, Ritual Practice* (New York: Oxford University Press, 1992), 216; this ritual was developed in the late 1700s and early 1800s, Leah Payne, *Gender and Pentecostal Revivalism* (New York: Palgrave Macmillan, 2015).
4. Daniel Vaca, *Evangelicals Incorporated: Books and the Business of Religion in America* (Cambridge, MA: Harvard University Press, 2019), 230. Sociologist Max Weber argued in the early twentieth century that predominantly Protestant nations like the United States had a distinct relationship with capitalism; this book explores how the American marketplace formed—and was formed by—predominately white evangelicals over time through the industry of CCM. Max Weber, *The Protestant Ethic and the Spirit of Capitalism* (New York: Taylor & Francis, 2013).
5. Stacy L. Smith, Katherine Pieper, Karla Hernandez, and Sam Wheeler, "Inclusion in the Recording Studio? Gender and Race/Ethnicity of Artists, Songwriters and Producers across 1,100 Popular Songs," *USC Annenberg Inclusion Initiative*, January 2023, https://assets.uscannenberg.org/docs/aii-inclusion-recording-studio-jan2023.pdf.
6. Works exploring how Black Gospel music influenced American culture include: Zach Mills, *The Last Blues Preacher: Reverend Clay Evans, Black Lives, and the Faith That Woke the Nation* (Minneapolis, MN: Fortress Press, 2018); Reiland Rabaka, *Civil Rights Music: The Soundtracks of the Civil Rights Movement* (New York: Lexington Books, 2016); Andrew Billingsley, *Mighty Like a River: The Black Church and Social Reform* (New York: Oxford University Press, 1999).
7. See for example Andrew Mall, *God Rock, Inc.: The Business of Niche Music* (Los Angeles: University of California Press, 2020); Jay R. Howard and John M. Streck, *Apostles of Rock: The Splintered World of Contemporary Christian Music* (Lexington: University Press of Kentucky, 2015); David W. Stowe, *No Sympathy for the Devil: Christian Pop Music and the Transformation of American Evangelicalism* (Chapel Hill: University of North Carolina Press, 2011); Shawn David Young, *Gray Sabbath: Jesus People USA, the Evangelical*

Left, and the Evolution of Christian Rock (New York: Columbia University Press, 2015). Randall J. Stephens' *The Devil's Music: How Christians Inspired, Condemned, and Embraced Rock'n'Roll* (Cambridge, MA: Harvard University Press, 2018), by contrast, explores the Holiness and Pentecostal roots of rock and roll.

Chapter 1

1. Ritual theorist Catherine Bell argues that rituals and ritualized acts are "strategic power relationships—schemes that hierarchize, integrate, define, or obscure." In the ritual of revival, power is created and managed through the relationship among preachers, music leaders, and attendees. Catherine Bell, *Ritual Theory, Ritual Practice* (New York: Oxford University Press, 1992), 216. This ritual was developed in the late 1700s and early 1800s; Leah Payne, *Gender and Pentecostal Revivalism* (New York: Palgrave Macmillan, 2015).
2. Other influences include Oberlin perfectionism, Keswick "higher life" proponents, Quakers, Mennonites, Catholics, and divine healing movements. Leah Payne, "Bobs and the 'Character of Our Citizenship': Early Pentecostals, Women, and Public Life in the United States of America," *Nova Religio: The Journal of Alternative and Emergent Religions* 23, no. 2 (2019): 42–63; Keri Day, *Azusa Street Reimagined: A Radical Vision of Religious and Democratic Belonging* (Stanford, CA: Stanford University Press, 2022), 7.
3. David D. Daniels III, "'Until the Power of the Lord Comes Down': African American Pentecostal Spirituality and Tarrying," in *Contemporary Spiritualities: Social and Religious Contexts*, ed. Clive Erricker (London: Continuum, 2001), 175; Sherry S. DuPree, *African-American Holiness Pentecostal Movement: An Annotated Bibliography* (New York: Garland Publishing, Inc., 1996), 479.
4. Reformers popularized congregational singing in the early modern era, and typesetting and printing-press innovations of this era popularized hymnals in Protestant circles in Europe and the New World. See: Margaret Aston, *Broken Idols of the English Reformation* (New York: Cambridge University Press, 2016), 21. Jon Solomon, *Ben-Hur: The Original Blockbuster* (Edinburgh: Edinburgh University Press, 2016), 210; Colleen McDowell, "Victorian Bibles," in *Religion and American Cultures: An Encyclopedia of Traditions, Diversity, and Popular Expressions*, vol. 1, ed. Gary Laderman and Luis León (Santa Barbara, CA, 2003), 429–431.
5. John T. Benson Jr., *A History of the Pentecostal Mission, 1898–1915* (Nashville, TN: Trevecca Press, 1977), 115.
6. Ibid., 44.
7. Matthew Avery Sutton traces the ascent of apocalyptic thinking in the United States in: *American Apocalypse: A History of Modern Evangelicalism* (Cambridge, MA: Harvard University Press, 2014).
8. G. F. Taylor, "Song Books," *The Pentecostal Holiness Advocate* 7, no. 28 (November 1923): 15.
9. Darren E. Grem, *The Blessings of Business: How Corporations Shaped Conservative Christianity* (New York: Oxford University Press, 2016), 19–22.
10. C. H. Morris, "God's Kingdom Is at Hand," *Jewel Songs* #18 (Nashville, TN: Pentecostal Mission Publishing Company, 1910); *North American Foreign Missions, 1810–1914: Theology, Theory, and Policy*, ed. Wilbert R. Shenk (Grand Rapids, MI: William B. Eerdmans, 2004).

11. James R. Goff, *Close Harmony: A History of Southern Gospel* (Chapel Hill: University of North Carolina Press, 2002), 17.
12. Donald H. Akenson, *Exporting the Rapture: John Nelson Darby and the Victorian Conquest of North-American Evangelicalism* (New York: Oxford University Press, 2018); George Marsden, *Fundamentalism and American Culture* (New York: Oxford University Press, 2006), 271; Alison Collis Greene, *No Depression in Heaven: The Great Depression, the New Deal, and the Transformation of Religion in the Delta* (New York: Oxford University Press, 2016), 61.
13. *The Scofield Reference Bible: King James Version* (New York: Oxford University Press, 1917), iv.
14. H. C. Morrison, "The World War in Prophecy; the Downfall of the Kaiser, and the End of the Dispensation," *Living Waters* 37, no. 9 (March 1918): 7; "Letters on the Apocalypse," *Living Waters* 37, no. 9 (March 1918): 8.
15. Harriet E. Jones, "The King's Call," #D1, *Living Water Songs*, vol. 2, John T. Benson Music Company, 1908.
16. Charles H. Lippy, *Do Real Men Pray? Images of the Christian Man and Male Spirituality in White Protestant America*, 1st ed. (Knoxville: University of Tennessee Press, 2005), 81; Gail Bederman, *Manliness and Civilization: A Cultural History of Gender and Race in the United States, 1880–1917*, Women in Culture and Society (Chicago: University of Chicago Press, 1995), 17; Payne, *Gender and Pentecostal Revivalism*.
17. "Old Time Religion," #223, *The Revival No. 3: Suitable for All Kinds of Religious Meetings*, Charles D. Tillman, 1899. For an exploration of white Southern nostalgia, see: James C. Cobb, *Away Down South: A History of Southern Identity* (New York: Oxford University Press, 2005); Tara McPherson, *Reconstructing Dixie: Race, Gender, and Nostalgia in the Imagined South* (Durham, NC: Duke University Press, 2003); Robert Darden, *People Get Ready! A New History of Black Gospel Music* (New York: Bloomsbury Academic, 2004), 122–123; ragtime, for example, was first published by white composer W. H. Krell. See: K. J. Greene, "Copyright, Culture & (and) Black Music: A Legacy of Unequal Protection," *Hastings Communications and Entertainment Law Journal* 21, no. 1 (1998): 357. White gospel music media innovators like Homer Rodeheaver, who published "Rodheaver's Negro Spirituals," therefore, were part of this larger form of cultural appropriation.
18. Chris Armstrong, "'Wrestling Jacob': The Central Struggle and Emotional Scripts of Camp Meeting Holiness Hymnody," in *Singing the Lord's Song in a Strange Land: Hymnody in the History of North American Protestantism*, ed. Edith Blumhofer and Mark A. Noll (Tuscaloosa: University of Alabama Press, 2004), 171–195.
19. Colleen McDannell, *Material Christianity: Religion and Popular Culture in America* (New Haven, CT: Yale University Press, 1995), 84; Todd M. Brenneman, *Homespun Gospel: The Triumph of Sentimentality in Contemporary American Evangelicalism* (New York: Oxford University Press, 2014), 94; M. B. Williams and Charles D. Tillman, "My Mother's Bible," #75, *The Revival No. 2: Suitable for All Kinds of Religious Meetings*, Charles D. Tillman, 1899.
20. Robert N. Bellah and Phillip E. Hammond, *Varieties of Civil Religion* (Eugene, OR: Wipf & Stock Publishers, 2013); music was an important part of instantiating the theology of the Lost Cause in the American South during the early twentieth century. See: Arthur Remillard, *Southern Civil Religions: Imagining the Good Society in the Post-Reconstruction Era* (Athens: University of Georgia Press, 2011), 84; Goff, *Close Harmony*, 35.

21. Ernest Hurst Cherrington, *The Anti-Saloon League Year Book 1923* (Westerville, OH: The Anti Saloon League of America Publishers, 1923), 292; Ernest Hurst Cherrington, *The Anti-Saloon League Year Book 1930* (Westerville, OH: The Anti Saloon League of America Publishers, 1930), 195.
22. Vivian A. Drake, "Behold the Hands Stretched Out for Aid," #44, *Garden of Spices: A Choice Collection for Revival Meetings, Missionary Meetings, Rescue Work, Church and Sunday School* (Indianapolis, IN: Grace Publishing Co., 1900).
23. Carolyn DeSwarte Gifford, "Temperance Songs and Hymns," in *Religions of the United States in Practice*, vol. 1, ed. Alisa Clapp-Itnyre and Julie Melnyk (Princeton, NJ: Princeton University Press, 2001), 159 (158–170).
24. Joseph F. Kett, "Adolescence and Youth in Nineteenth-Century America," *The Journal of Interdisciplinary History* 2, no. 2 (Autumn 1971): 283–298; Nancy Lesko, *Act Your Age! A Cultural Construction of Adolescence* (London: Routledge, 2012), 50; Sara Moslener, *Virgin Nation: Sexual Purity and American Adolescence* (New York: Oxford University Press, 2015), 16–47.
25. The concept of purity in American adolescence had racial and classed overtones. Sara Moslener explores the concept of social purity and its intersection with temperance work in *Virgin Nation*, 17.
26. DeSwarte Gifford, "Temperance Songs and Hymns," 159; Brian Roberts, *Blackface Nation: Race, Reform, and Identity in American Popular Music, 1812–1925* (Chicago: University of Chicago Press, 2017), 153.
27. Michael Jacobs, "Co-opting Christian Chorales: Songs of the Ku Klux Klan," *American Music* 28, no. 3 (2010): 368–377. https://doi.org/10.5406/americanmusic.28.3.0368.
28. Marsden, *Fundamentalism and American Culture*, 185.
29. Alex MacDougall, email correspondence, April 20, 2021.
30. Benson, *A History of the Pentecostal Mission*, 94; see for example Methodist songbooks promoting temperance advertised in the Southern Baptist *Baptist and Reflector* 10, no. 31 (June 30, 1877): 446; Randall J. Stephens, *The Devil's Music: How Christians Inspired, Condemned, and Embraced Rock 'n' Roll* (Cambridge, MA: Harvard University Press, 2018), 32.
31. Tona J. Hangen, *Redeeming the Dial: Radio, Religion, and Popular Culture in America* (Chapel Hill: University of North Carolina Press, 2001), 21–22.
32. Aimee Semple McPherson, "The Cathedral of the Air," *The Bridal Call Foursquare* 8, no. 2 (June 1924): 4.
33. Aimee Semple McPherson, "Be a Radio Missionary! Through Providing One 'KFSG Radio Day' You May," *The Bridal Call Foursquare* 9, no. 10 (March 1926): 2.
34. William Robert Glass, *Strangers in Zion: Fundamentalists in the South, 1900–1950* (Atlanta, GA: Mercer University Press, 2001), 25.
35. Carolyn L. Kitch, *The Girl on the Magazine Cover: The Origins of Visual Stereotypes in American Mass Media* (Chapel Hill: University of North Carolina Press, 2001), 4.
36. Margaret A. Lowe, *Looking Good: College Women and Body Image, 1875–1930*, Gender Relations in the American Experience (Baltimore, MD: Johns Hopkins University Press, 2003), 113.
37. DuPree, *African-American Holiness Pentecostal Movement*, 414. While most historians trace the origins of the Pentecostal movement to the interracial revivals led by William Seymour in Los Angeles, historian Iain MacRobert has shown that the movement quickly fractured; see: Iain MacRobert, *The Black Roots and White Racism of Early Pentecostalism in the USA* (London: Palgrave Macmillan, 1988); Aimee Semple McPherson's Los

Angeles–based ministry marked a shift in white Pentecostals aligning with white, middle-class culture (Payne, *Gender and Pentecostal Revivalism*).

38. Karen Sternheimer, *Celebrity Culture and the American Dream: Stardom and Social Mobility* (New York: Routledge, 2011), 2–3.
39. Eric Weisbard, *Top 40 Democracy: The Rival Mainstreams of American Music* (Chicago: University of Chicago Press, 2014), 8.
40. Grant Wacker, *America's Pastor: Billy Graham and the Shaping of a Nation* (Cambridge, MA: Harvard University Press, 2014), 8.
41. Hangen, *Redeeming the Dial*, 145.
42. The proof of this mobilization is in the regulation of it by the federal government, which sought to restrict political propaganda from religious broadcasters. Their efforts were rebuffed by ideologues like Christian-fascist Gerald Winrod. Hangen, *Redeeming the Dial*, 125.
43. Bob Lochte, *Christian Radio: The Growth of a Mainstream Broadcasting Force* (Jefferson, NC: McFarland & Company, Inc., 2006), 32.
44. Hangen, *Redeeming the Dial*, 33.
45. Jesse Walker, *Rebels on the Air: An Alternative History of Radio in America* (New York: New York University Press, 2001), 30.
46. Matthew Avery Sutton, *Aimee Semple McPherson and the Resurrection of Christian America* (Cambridge, MA: Harvard University Press, 2007), 82.
47. Hangen, *Redeeming the Dial*, 120.
48. Definitions of evangelicalism are legion. David W. Bebbington's *Evangelicalism in Modern Britain: A History from the 1730s to the 1980s* (New York: Routledge, 1989) analyzed evangelical identity as conversionism (a call to repentance from sin and conversion to the evangelical gospel), activism (the expression of the gospel in an effort to convert the world), biblicism (a belief in authority of Christian scriptures as the source for all truth), and crucicentrism (an emphasis on the atoning work of the cross of Christ). In Bebbington, Mark A. Noll, and George M. Marsden's 2020 edited volume *Evangelicals: Who They Have Been, Are Now, and Could Be*, global ambassador for the World Evangelical Alliance Brian C. Stiller updates this list with one key addition, which reflects evangelical adoption of Charismatic practices and beliefs: "trusting in the empowering work of the Holy Spirit." Molly Worthen's *Apostles of Reason: The Crisis of Authority in American Evangelicalism* (New York: Oxford University Press, 2013) tackles the question of evangelicalism by exploring evangelicalism as a set of questions about Jesus, faith, reason, and authority. Daniel Vaca's *Evangelicals Incorporated: Books and the Business of Religion in America* (Cambridge, MA: Harvard University Press, 2019) explores evangelicalism through book publishing, and Vaca's work analyzes evangelicalism as a commercial religion, defined by capitalism, markets, and marketing culture; this study builds on Vaca's work with the intersecting and often overlapping music business.
49. The production and consumption of conservative white Protestant music, eventually known as CCM, remained geographically dominant on the West Coast and the American South for over a century. See: John Lindenbaum, "The Production of Contemporary Christian Music: A Geographical Perspective," in *Sound, Society, and the Geography of Popular Music*, ed. Ola Johansson and Thomas L. Bell (Farnham, UK: Ashgate Publishing, 2012), 286–287; Darren Dochuk, *From Bible Belt to Sunbelt: Plain-Folk Religion, Grassroots Politics, and the Rise of Evangelical Conservatism* (New York: W. W. Norton, 2010).

Chapter 2

1. Mark Clark-Bates, "Like Texas, Word Records Is Big, Big, Big," *Billboard Magazine*, September 21, 1963, 13, 16.
2. Jarrell McCracken, "The Game of Life," A-side #1, *The Game of Life*, Word Records, 1951, LP.
3. Richard James Burgess, *The History of Music Production* (New York: Oxford University Press, 2014), 59.
4. Thom Granger, telephone conversation with author, July 2, 2018; Charlie Peacock, telephone conversation with author, December 2, 2018.
5. Frank Boggs, *Frank Boggs Sings for You!*, Word Records, 1956, LP.
6. Don Cusic, *The Sound of Light: A History of Gospel Music* (Bowling Green, KY: Bowling Green State University Press, 1990), 138.
7. R. E. Winsett, "Jesus Is Coming Soon," 1942, #84, *Abiding Faith*, R. E. Winsett Publisher, 1947.
8. Dottie Rambo, "The Church Triumphant," *Dottie Rambo and the Imperials*, Heart Warming Records, 1956, vinyl LP.
9. Bob Lochte, *Christian Radio: The Growth of a Mainstream Broadcasting Force* (Jefferson, NC: McFarland & Company, Inc., 2006), 24.
10. Vaca, *Evangelicals Incorporated*, 18.
11. David P. King, "Preaching Good News to the Poor: Billy Graham and Evangelical Humanitarianism," in *American Pilgrim*, ed. Andrew Finstuen, Grant Wacker, and Anne Blue Wills (New York: Oxford University Press, 2017), 126.
12. Billy Graham, Billy Graham Evangelistic Association, "Billy Graham's 1957 New York Crusade Sermon at Yankee Stadium," *YouTube* video, 50:32, July 21, 2017, https://www.youtube.com/watch?v=1aZoqIwHsdM.
13. Billy Graham, *The Hour of Decision*, "Christianity vs. Communism," radio broadcast, February 4, 1951; Billy Graham, *The Hour of Decision*, "Christianity—the Answer to Communism," radio broadcast, August 9, 1953; Billy Graham, *The Hour of Decision*, "Communist Tactics," radio broadcast, May 18, 1958; Billy Graham, *The Hour of Decision*, "Christ or Communism for the World," radio broadcast, August 10, 1958; Billy Graham, *The Hour of Decision*, "Communism vs. God's Law," radio broadcast, May 14, 1961; Billy Graham, *The Hour of Decision*, "How to Combat Communism," radio broadcast, October 29, 1961; Billy Graham, *The Hour of Decision*, "The Soviet Threat to Life on Earth," radio broadcast, September 3, 1961; Billy Graham, *The Hour of Decision*, "Why Communism Is Gaining," radio broadcast, November 17, 1963.
14. Grant Wacker, *America's Pastor: Billy Graham and the Shaping of a Nation* (Cambridge, MA: Harvard University Press, 2014), 147; Billy Graham, *The Hour of Decision*, "My New Year's Resolution," television broadcast, 12:30, March 6, 2012. https://billygraham.org/video/hour-of-decision-1953/; Billy Graham, *The Hour of Decision*, "Hour of Decision Christmas Program," television broadcast, 14:38, December 7, 2015. https://billygraham.org/video/the-hour-of-decision-christmas-tv-program-1952-2/. Richard M. Gamble, *A Fiery Gospel: The Battle Hymn of the Republic and the Road to Righteous War* (Ithaca, NY: Cornell University Press, 2019), 172–174, 196–197.
15. W. Sands Fox, "God Bless Our Boys," #167, *New Songs of Pentecost No. 3*, Hall Mack Co., 1918.
16. Gamble, *A Fiery Gospel*, 198.

17. Billy Graham, *The Hour of Decision*, "How Communist Imperialism," radio broadcast, January 12, 1958, 30:30.
18. Sarah E. Chinn, *Inventing Modern Adolescence: The Children of Immigrants in Turn-of-the-Century America* (New Brunswick, NJ: Rutgers University Press, 2009), 4; Thomas Hine, *The Rise and Fall of the American Teenager* (New York: HarperCollins, 2000), 3.
19. Kristin Kobes Du Mez, *Jesus and John Wayne: How White Evangelicals Corrupted a Faith and Fractured a Nation* (New York: Liveright, 2020), 11.
20. Billy Graham, "Billy Graham Answers Teenagers' Questions," 1962, on *Billy Graham Answers Teenagers' Questions*, Billy Graham Evangelistic Association, 1962, EP, 45 RPM.
21. In addition to his work with World Wide Pictures, Carmichael was musical director for Lucille Ball's television comedy *I Love Lucy* in the 1950s, wrote arrangements for legendary pop and jazz artists like Nat King Cole and Rosemary Clooney, and scored the 1958 science fiction film *The Blob* with Burt Bacharach.
22. Russ Cheatham, *Bad Boy of Gospel Music: The Calvin Newton Story* (Jackson: University Press of Mississippi, 2010), 124. Carmichael produced *Rhapsody in Sacred Music*, an orchestral gospel album on a small Los Angeles record label in 1958, and he scored twenty films for the Graham organization.
23. Hangen, *Redeeming the Dial*, 147.
24. Eugene Poole, "A Texan Sees 'Mr. Texas,'" *The King's Business* 42, no. 11 (November 1951): 31.
25. "Religion: First Christian Western," *Time Magazine*, October 8, 1951, accessed October 12, 2020, http://content.time.com/time/magazine/article/0,9171,859412,00.html.
26. Dorothy Parker, "Rock 'n' Roll Is . . . Worse than a Narcotic," *The Pentecostal Evangel* no. 2263 (September 22, 1957): 17.
27. Denis Jonnes, *Cold War American Literature and the Rise of Youth Culture: Children of Empire* (New York: Taylor & Francis, 2014), 6.
28. A. J. Duncan, "My Experience: 123 Hours of Fasting and Prayer," *Church of God Evangel* 50, no. 16 (June 1959): 7–9. Pentecostals often danced in church settings, referring to this as "dancing in the spirit," but denigrated "social dancing" that was not worship.
29. Randall J. Stephens, *The Devil's Music: How Christians Inspired, Condemned, and Embraced Rock 'n' Roll* (Cambridge, MA: Harvard University Press, 2018).
30. Recent examples include: Cusic, *The Sound of Light*; Robert Darden, *People Get Ready! A New History of Black Gospel Music* (New York: Bloomsbury Academic, 2004); Jay R. Howard and John M. Streck, *Apostles of Rock: The Splintered World of Contemporary Christian Music* (Lexington: University Press of Kentucky, 1999); Stephens, *The Devil's Music*; David Ware Stowe, *No Sympathy for the Devil: Christian Pop Music and the Transformation of American Evangelicalism* (Chapel Hill: University of North Carolina Press, 2011).
31. Mitchell K. Hall, *The Emergence of Rock and Roll: Music and the Rise of American Youth Culture*, Critical Moments in American History (New York: Routledge, 2014), 14, 16, 48, 50, 53; Richard A. Peterson, *Creating Country Music: Fabricating Authenticity* (Chicago: University of Chicago Press, 1997), 41.
32. "Great Balls of Fire" was probably a reference to the Spirit's presence in the form of fire on the heads of the Apostles in Acts 2. Mickey Vallee, *Rancid Aphrodisiac: Subjectivity, Desire, and Rock 'n' Roll* (London: Bloomsbury Publishing, 2014), 80.
33. Stephens, *The Devil's Music*, 28.
34. Phil Kerr, "Music in Evangelism: The Power of Music," *The Foursquare Magazine* 30, no. 4 (April 1975): 17.

35. Stephens, *The Devil's Music*, 47.
36. Bennie Triplett, "On the Spot: A Forum on the Problems of Modern Living," *Church of God Evangel* 48, no. 40 (December 1957): 6–7.
37. Jack Hamilton argues that rock and roll was coded as Black and white until the 1960s, when the genre of "rock" became known as a more serious, sophisticated genre, which was then coded as racially white in: Jack Hamilton, *Just Around Midnight: Rock and Roll and the Racial Imagination* (Cambridge, MA: Harvard University Press, 2016). See also: Glenn C. Altschuler, *All Shook Up: How Rock 'n' Roll Changed America* (Oxford University Press, 2003), 5–6; Michael T. Bertrand, *Race, Rock, and Elvis* (University of Illinois Press, 2000), 7–8.
38. Stephens, *The Devil's Music*, 17.
39. A. Harold Cole, "Christian Maturity," Addresses: Pastor's Conference WMU Convention, St. Louis, MO, 1961, 7–9.
40. A. M. Long, "How to Reach and Hold Our Young People for the Church," *The Pentecostal Holiness Advocate* 42, no. 32 (December 1957): 5; "Our Thriving Sunday Schools," *The Pentecostal Evangel* no. 2238 (March 1957): 8; R. Paul Caudil, "Behold His Glory: 1959 Address to the Southern Baptists Convention," Lecture, Southern Baptist Convention, 1959; Roy F. Smee, "Home Missions," *Herald of Holiness* 47, no. 36 (November 1958): 14.
41. Thom Granger, telephone conversation with author, August 26, 2020.
42. Hall, *The Emergence of Rock and Roll*, 14, 16, 48, 50, 53; Peterson, *Creating Country Music*, 41.
43. Aaron A. Fox, *Real Country: Music and Language in Working-Class Culture* (Durham, NC: Duke University Press, 2004), 258.
44. Arlene M. Sánchez-Walsh explores the relationship between Presley and gospel music, especially his appropriation of Black Pentecostal music of the Church of God in Christ in *Pentecostals in America* (New York: Columbia University Press, 2018), 55.
45. Lochte, *Christian Radio*, 24.
46. Jesse Walker, *Rebels on the Air: An Alternative History of Radio in America* (New York: New York University Press, 2001), 57–58. DJs exposed listeners to established and emerging genres such as rhythm and blues, country, rock and roll, jazz, pop music, novelty songs, and gospel. Recording executives quickly figured out that the key to getting their artists on the air was by developing a good relationship with popular DJs. Many of those relationships were transactional in nature, and DJs lost credibility as arbiters of quality music as stories of "pay for play" schemes surfaced in the press. Jim Cox, *American Radio Networks: A History* (Jefferson, NC: MacFarland, 2009), 182; Walker, *Rebels on the Air*, 59. Midwestern radio-chain owner Todd Storz is credited with revolutionizing song-driven radio by creating Top 40 radio programming. Based on the idea that jukebox patrons chose to repeat a small number of their favorite tunes rather than listen to each and every song available on the jukebox menu, Storz introduced listeners to the biggest-selling and most requested songs in distinct formats (e.g., rock and roll, country, rhythm and blues). Eric Weisbard, *Top 40 Democracy: The Rival Mainstreams of American Music* (Chicago: University of Chicago Press, 2014), 5.
47. Ken Garner, "Radio Format," in *Continuum Encyclopedia of Popular Music of the World*, vol. 1: *Media, Industry and Society*, ed. John Shepherd (London: Continuum, 2003), 461. Critics denounced Top 40 format radio as "pandering or deferring" to popular taste, which is a point of considerable tension among DJs, musicians, and scholars of popular music. For a discussion of the logics of and tensions within pop music formats, as well

as the federal-communications policies that expanded the profitability of Top 40 radio, see: Weisbard, *Top 40 Democracy*, 4–6; Walker, *Rebels on the Air*, 59.

48. Cox, *American Radio Networks*, 173.
49. "RADIO," *The Pentecostal Evangel* no. 2271 (November 1957): 10–11.
50. Altschuler, *All Shook Up*, 4; Joel Dinerstein, *The Origins of Cool in Postwar America* (Chicago: University of Chicago Press, 2018), 7. Dr. Stacy L. Smith, Dr. Katherine Pieper, Karla Hernandez, and Sam Wheeler, "Inclusion in the Recording Studio? Gender and Race/Ethnicity of Artists, Songwriters and Producers across 1,100 Popular Songs," *USC Annenberg Inclusion Initiative*, January 2023, https://assets.uscannenberg.org/docs/aii-inclusion-recording-studio-jan2023.pdf.
51. "Thou shalt not bow the knee to 'Elvis' (Presley) or 'Frankie' (Sinatra) or 'The Beatles,'" wrote Reverent Clayton E. Davis in 1964, "God alone is worthy of thy worship." Clayton E. Davis, "Ten Commandments for Teenagers," *Bridegroom's Messenger* 53, no. 3 (December 1964): 10; George Beverly Shea as told to Fred Bauer, "They Gave Me the Melody," *Herald of Holiness* 55, no. 23 (July 1966): 6–8; "Foursquare Minister Wins Nat'l Hymn-Writing Contest," *The Foursquare Magazine* 36, no. 1 (January 1963): 10; "George Beverley Shea," *The Pentecostal Evangel* no. 2507 (May 1962): 30.
52. Donald McGavran, *Understanding Church Growth* (Grand Rapids, MI: Wm. B. Eerdmans Publishing Co., 1970), 166. McGavran rejected H. Richard Niebuhr's influential philosophy of mission of "philanthropy, education, medicine, famine relief, evangelism, and world friendship," because he reasoned that "doing many good things in addition to evangelism" obscured the "essential task of mission," which was "discipling the peoples of the earth." Rather than giving priority to philanthropy or education, McGavran reasoned, Christians ought to be first teaching the peoples of the world the traditional evangelical doctrine in the most efficient way possible. Donald McGavran, "My Pilgrimage in Mission," *International Bulletin of Missionary Research* no. 2 (April 1985): 54. McGavran, *Understanding Church Growth*, 166.
53. Willy Wilkerson, *The Golden Age of Advertising: The 60s* (Cologne, Germany: Taschen, 2005).
54. The national wealth of the United States increased from $575 billion in 1945 to over $1,700 billion in 1958; the average wealth per American inhabitant increased from $4,100 to $9,800 in the same time period; Raymond Goldsmith, *National Wealth of the United States in the Postwar Period* (Princeton, NJ: Princeton University Press, 2015), 3–4). While the United States economy had tumultuous years in the early 1960s, the overall economy grew considerably in this period. See: James Tobin and George L. Perry, eds., *Economic Events, Ideas, and Policies: The 1960s and After* (Washington, DC: Brookings Institution Press, 2010). Lizabeth Cohen explores how the earning power of white, middle-class men increased most from postwar economic growth, and white, middle-class women—particularly those in growing American suburbs—became the primary consumers in this new material culture. See: *A Consumers' Republic: The Politics of Mass Consumption in Postwar America* (New York: Knopf Doubleday Publishing Group, 2008), 212–227.
55. Mark H. Senter, *When God Shows Up: A History of Protestant Youth Ministry in America* (New York: Baker Publishing Group, 2010), 311.
56. Derric Johnson, telephone conversation with author, September 10, 2020.
57. Roy argues that the reason why "the folk revival [of the mid-twentieth century] was so white revolves around three factors: the continuing legacy of commercial racial categories, the failure of the New Left to control music through a cultural infrastructure as effectively as had the old left, and the cultural momentum of an understanding of folk music as the

music of the 'other' at a time when blacks were trying to enter a system that white middle-class youth were rejecting." W. G. Roy, "Aesthetic Identity, Race, and American Folk Music," *Qualitative Sociology* 25 (2002): 459–469.

58. Gillian Mitchell, *The North American Folk Music Revival: Nation and Identity in the United States and Canada, 1945–1980* (London: Ashgate, 2007), 130; Lawrence J. Epstein, *Political Folk Music in America from Its Origins to Bob Dylan* (Jefferson, NC: McFarland & Company, 2010).
59. Sarah Hill, "'This Is My Country': American Popular Music and Political Engagement in '1968,'" in *Music and Protest in 1968* (New York: Cambridge University Press, 2013), 46–63.
60. Brad Schreiber, *Music Is Power: Popular Songs, Social Justice, and the Will to Change* (New Brunswick, NJ: Rutgers University Press, 2019), 43.
61. Geoffrey Beaumont, *A 20th Century Folk Mass: For One or More Cantors and Congregation* (London: Josef Weinberger, 1956).
62. Cam Floria, "Sing a Happy Song!," 1963, on *Cam Floria and the Continentals*, Word Records, 1963, vinyl LP stereo.
63. Cusic, *The Sound of Light*, 131.
64. Daniel Sack, *Moral Re-armament: The Reinventions of an American Religious Movement* (New York: Palgrave Macmillan, 2009), 177.
65. P. Colwell, "You Can't Live Crooked and Think Straight," 1965, Track #A6 on *Up With People!*, Pace Records, 1965, vinyl LP stereo.
66. John D. Clarke, "Sing Out South Director Inez Thurston Dies at 88," *Richmond Times-Dispatch* (Richmond, VA), February 23, 2009.
67. Bob Oldenburg, "Music in Youth Ministry," Lecture, Southwestern Baptist Theological Seminary Fort Worth, Texas, 1978.
68. Billy Ray Hearn in Charlie Peacock, *At the Crossroads: An Insider's Look at the Past, Present, and the Future of Contemporary Christian Music* (Nashville, TN: Broadman & Holman, 1999), 56.
69. Bob Oldenburg, "Good News," *The Good News: A Folk Musical* (Nashville, TN: Broadman Press, 1967), 15–16.
70. Ibid., 7.
71. Ibid.
72. Ibid., 83.
73. Will Bishop, "'We're Gonna Change This Land': An Oral History Commemorating the Fiftieth Anniversary of Good News: A Christian Folk-Musical," *Artistic Theologian* 5 (2017): 72; Clifton J. Allen, ed., *Annual to the Southern Baptist Convention, 1969* (Nashville, TN: Executive Committee of the Southern Baptist Convention, 1969), 1, 162.
74. Ralph Carmichael and Kurt Kaiser, "We're On Our Way," 1971, Track #A1 on *Natural High*, Light Records, 1971, vinyl LP.
75. Will Bishop, "Christian Youth Musicals: 1967–1975" (New Orleans, LA: New Orleans Baptist Theological Seminary, 2015), 77.
76. Clark-Bates, "Like Texas, Word Records Is Big, Big, Big," 13, 16.
77. "Benson Forms New Book Arm," *Billboard Magazine* (August 1969): 70.
78. Clark-Bates, "Like Texas, Word Records Is Big, Big, Big," 13, 16.
79. Derric Johnson, telephone conversation with author, September 10, 2020. Southern Baptist music minister Roger Breland carried on the collegiate vocal ensemble tradition with his co-ed choral group Truth (an acronym for "Trust, Receive, Unchangeable, True Happiness [in Jesus]").

80. "Their Best Record Is a Safety Record," *Ebony* 23, no. 10 (August 1968): 30.
81. Thurlow Spurr, *In God We Trust*, Tempo Impact Records, 1970, vinyl LP.

Chapter 3

1. Gregory Alan Thornbury, *Why Should the Devil Have All the Good Music? Larry Norman and the Perils of Christian Rock* (New York: Crown Publishing Group, 2018), 51–52.
2. Ibid.
3. John Maiden explores these Anglophone media networks in *Age of the Spirit: Charismatic Renewal, the Anglo-World, and Global Christianity* (Oxford: Oxford University Press, 2023).
4. Michael S. Matthews, "'Rock' Worship," *Princeton Alumni Weekly* 69 (1968): 5.
5. "Hope for America's Hopeless Youth," *The Pentecostal Evangel* no. 2790 (October 29, 1967): 23–26.
6. David Wilkerson, "The Inside Story of Youth's Search for Reality," *The Pentecostal Evangel* no. 2811 (March 24, 1968): 28.
7. Ibid.
8. David Wilkerson, Ted Wise, and Steve Heefner, "Reverend Wilkerson Debates Preachers About Drugs," Bay Area Television Archive, December 7, 1967, https://diva.sfsu.edu/collections/sfbatv/bundles/220932?fbclid=IwAR1msc6mnzd1nDT_CnVuHpMLWl26R4QaF7HKcVzMbyQFFxf7jzieabgfxSE.
9. Journalist Thom Granger notes that by the late 1960s, the West Coast (and Southern California in particular) was the heart of the American rock scene. "When Rock and Roll started, everything was on the East Coast—some out of Chicago, some out of the deep South—but it all shifted. It all came West and by the mid to late 60s, the recording business was moving—with a few exceptions—through the 70s, 80s, and 90s was all headquartered on the West Coast." Thom Granger, telephone conversation with author, August 26, 2020. See also: W. J. Rorabaugh, *American Hippies* (New York: Cambridge University Press, 2015).
10. Larry Eskridge, *God's Forever Family: The Jesus People Movement in America* (New York: Oxford University Press, 2013), 2.
11. Billy Graham, "The Marks of the Jesus Movement," *Christianity Today*, November 5, 1971, 4–5.
12. Eskridge, *God's Forever Family*, 167–168; Gillian Mitchell, *The North American Folk Music Revival: Nation and Identity in the United States and Canada, 1945–1980* (Farnham, UK: Ashgate Publishing, Ltd., 2007), 68.
13. Larry Norman, "No More LSD For Me," B-side #5, *Street Level*, One Way Records, 1970, LP.
14. Chuck Girard and Fred Field, "Since I Opened Up the Door," B-side #3, *Feel the Love*, Good News Records, 1977, LP.
15. Randy Stonehill, "Thank You," A-side #5, *Born Twice*, One Way Records, 1971, LP.
16. Thom Granger, telephone conversation with author, July 2, 2018.
17. Marsha Stevens, "For Those Tears I Died," B-side #5, *Come to the Waters,* Maranatha Music, 1971, LP.
18. Keith Green, Randy Stonehill, and Todd Fishkind, "Your Love Broke Through," B-side #1, *For Him Who Has Ears to Hear*, Sparrow Records, 1977, LP; Gerardo Martí explores the "power-surrender" characteristics of Charismatic and Pentecostal worship in: "Maranatha (O Lord, Come): The Power–Surrender Dynamic of Pentecostal Worship," *Liturgy* 33, no. 3 (2018): 20–28.

19. Annie Herring, "He Loves Me," B-side #h, **with footnotes*, Myrrh Records, 1974, LP.
20. Keith Green and Melody Green, "No One Believes in Me Anymore," B-side #2, *For Him Who Has Ears to Hear*, Sparrow Records, 1977, LP.
21. While premillennial dispensationalism flourished in white Pentecostal and evangelical communities, Frederick Ware discusses the distinct relationship among Black Pentecostals, Black theology, and premillennialism in: "On the Compatibility/Incompatibility of Pentecostal Premillennialism with Black Liberation Theology," in *Afro-Pentecostalism: Black Pentecostal and Charismatic Christianity in History and Culture*, ed. Amos Yong and Estrelda Y. Alexander, Religion, Race, and Ethnicity Series (New York: New York University Press, 2011), 191–208.
22. Larry Norman, "I Wish We'd All Been Ready," B-side #4, *Upon This Rock*, Capitol Records, 1969, LP.
23. Alpus Lefevre, Kim Venable, Mylon Lefevre, Auburn Burrell, Dean Daughtry, "The Old Gospel Ship," A-side #1, *Mylon "We Believe"*, Cotillion Records, 1970, LP.
24. Hal Lindsey, *Late Great Planet Earth* (Grand Rapids, MI: Zondervan, 1970), 8.
25. Ibid., 15.
26. Ibid., 62.
27. Ibid., 70, 94.
28. Ibid., 18.
29. Ray Walters, "Paperback Talk," *The New York Times*, April 6, 1980, section T, page 7.
30. Larry Norman, "I Wish We'd All Been Ready," B-side #4, *Upon This Rock*, Capitol Records, 1969, LP.
31. Annie Herring, "He Is Coming," C-side #C3, *To The Bride*, Myrrh Records, 1975, LP.
32. Randy Matthews, "He Is Coming," B-side #3, *Son of Dust*, Myrrh Records, 1973, LP.
33. Tommy Coomes and Tom Stipe, "The Cossack Song," A-side #4, *Feel the Love*, Good News Records, 1977, LP.
34. Jesse Cosio, "Yahweh," A-side #4, *Feel the Love*, Good News Records, 1977, LP.
35. Merla Watson's "Jehovah Jireh" was the best-known song of this name. Other artists like Gary Ingersoll also used the phrase in folk-rock songs with the same title. Gary Ingersoll, "Jehovah Jireh" A-side #3, *White Dove*, Creative Sound, 1978, LP; John Maiden explores the influence of Merv and Merla Watson over charismatic communities in the United Kingdom, as well as the United States and Canada in *Age of the Spirit*, 59.
36. Lester Ruth and Lim Swee Hong discuss how the Latter Rain movement created modern "praise and worship," in *A History of Contemporary Praise and Worship: Understanding the Ideas that Reshaped the Protestant Church* (Grand Rapids, MI: Baker Publishing Group, 2021), 13–14; John Weaver analyzes the influence of British Israelism on the Latter Rain movement in *The New Apostolic Reformation: History of a Modern Charismatic Movement* (Jefferson, NC: McFarland & Company, Inc., 2016), 25 and Christopher J. Richmann outlines the Latter Rain articulation of British Israelism in *Living in Bible Times: F. F. Bosworth and the Pentecostal Pursuit of the Supernatural* (Eugene, OR: Pickwick Publications, 2020), 182.
37. Conservative evangelical and former Youth for Christ evangelist Lowell Lytle was a notable exception to this rule. In the late 1960s, he created musical ensembles to play Top 40 hits to youth in middle and high schools at school assemblies during the school day. Then, at night, he invited students to an evening concert wherein he gave students a standard revivalist altar call. Lytle's organization toured the country and claimed thousands of

conversions per year, but his methods were not widely accepted in American evangelical circles. See: Eskridge, *God's Forever Family*, 214.

38. Thom Granger, telephone conversation with author, July 2, 2018.
39. Eskridge, *God's Forever Family*, 216.
40. Charles Taylor argues that the post-WWII era, an ethic of authenticity begins to influence popular culture in *A Secular Age* (Cambridge, MA: Harvard University Press, 2007), 475.
41. Chuck Girard and Fred Field, "Little Country Church," A-side #4, *Love Song*, Good News Records, 1971, LP.
42. Chuck Butler, "Ballad of the Lukewarm," B-side #3, Maranatha! Records, 1972.
43. Bob Gersztyn, *Encyclopedia of Contemporary Christian Music: Pop, Rock, and Worship*, ed. Don Cusic (Santa Barbara, CA: ABC-CLIO, LLC, 2009), 182.
44. Andrew Mall, *God Rock, Inc.: The Business of Niche Music* (Los Angeles: University of California Press, 2020), 32.
45. "The Jesus Revolution," *Time Magazine*, June 21, 1971, 1; "Is God Dead?," *Time Magazine*, April 8, 1966.
46. Teri Ann Sramek, respondent, *The CCM Survey*, January 26, 2021.
47. Amy Collier Artman, *The Miracle Lady: Kathryn Kuhlman and the Transformation of Charismatic Christianity* (Grand Rapids, MI: Wm. B. Eerdmans Publishing Company, 2019), 96–97.
48. "The Jesus Revolution," 1.
49. Graham, "The Marks of the Jesus Movement," 4–5.
50. John Joseph Thompson, *Raised by Wolves: The Story of Christian Rock and Roll* (Toronto, Canada: ECW Press, 2000), 36.
51. Edward B. Fiske, "A 'Religious Woodstock' Draws 75,000," *New York Times*, June 16, 1972, 1.
52. John G. Turner, *Bill Bright and Campus Crusade for Christ: The Renewal of Evangelicalism in Postwar America* (Chapel Hill: University of North Carolina Press, 2009), 144.
53. Eskridge, *God's Forever Family*, 174.
54. Ibid.; "The Jesus Revolution," 1.
55. Aaron Griffith, *God's Law and Order* (Cambridge, MA: Harvard University Press, 2020), 135.
56. Eskridge, *God's Forever Family*, 174.
57. Evangelical support for the notion of America as a divinely ordained nation with a special plan from God was increasing in popularity in the 1970s. See for example: Peter Marshall and David Manuel, *The Light and the Glory* (Ada, MI: Revell, 1977).
58. P. F. Sloan, "Eve of Destruction," A-side #1, *Eve of Destruction*, Dunhill Records, 1965, LP.
59. Barry McGuire, "Don't Blame God," A-side #1, Myrrh Records, 1974, LP; Barry McGuire, "II Chronicles 7:14," A-side #1, Myrrh Records, 1974, LP.
60. David Meece, "Come Home, America," A-side #2, Myrrh Records, 1976, LP.
61. Jesse Cosio, "Yahweh," A-side #4, *Feel the Love*, Good News Records, 1977, LP; "Favorites #8," Singspiration Music of the Zondervan Corporation Publishing House, 1975.
62. Paul Baker, "Setting the Good Word to Modern Music," *Billboard Magazine*, July 28, 1979, R-4, R-12, R-18.
63. "Word Spreads Sacred Music's Message: Now It Plans to Build a Jesus Rock Label with a Mod Sound," *Billboard Magazine*, August 19, 1972, T-4.
64. Robert Darden, "Hearn, Billy Ray," in *Encyclopedia of American Gospel Music*, ed. W. K. McNeil (New York: Routledge Press, 2005), 182. Not all labels followed suit. Chuck Smith's Calvary Chapel founded Maranatha! Music in 1971 to create popular music with Christian

messages, but as early as 1974, the label had begun to create "praise and worship" music made specifically for liturgical settings.

65. Baker, "Setting the Good Word to Modern Music," R-4, R-12, R-18.
66. Ibid. Cornerstone Music Festival, sponsored by Jesus People USA, is a potential exception to this rule. Shawn Young explores the eclectic origins of the movement that do include Assemblies of God and Methodist influences in *Gray Sabbath: Jesus People USA, Evangelical Left, and the Evolution of Christian Rock* (New York: Columbia University Press, 2015), 30.
67. Rustin Lloyd, "The Politics of the Righteous: A Religious and Political History of Conservative Neo-evangelicals in Central Florida" (MA thesis, University of Central Florida, 2013), 30.
68. "Jesus '75: The Spirit Lives On," *Christianity Today*, September 12, 1975, https://www.christianitytoday.com/ct/1975/september-12/jesus-75-spirit-lives-on.html.
69. Paul Baker, "Religious Radio: Ain't What It Used to Be," *Billboard Magazine*, July 28, 1979, R-28, R-43, R-45.
70. Ibid.
71. "Word Spreads Sacred Music's Message," T-4. *Billboard* noted that some old-school gospel music like The Gaither Trio was able to get placement over Jesus rock, to the frustration of many record-label executives. Ron Tepper, "Retail Witnesses Financial & Distribution Challenges," *Billboard Magazine*, July 28, 1979, R-20, R-46, R-48-, R-49.
72. Daniel Vaca, *Evangelicals Incorporated: Books and the Business of Religion in America* (Cambridge, MA: Harvard University Press, 2019), 137.
73. The "generation gap" between adolescents and adults became a popular frame for understanding youth and popular culture in the 1960s. See: Sarah E. Chinn, *Inventing Modern Adolescence: The Children of Immigrants in Turn-of-the-Century America* (New Brunswick, NJ: Rutgers University Press, 2009), 168.
74. Kurt Kaiser, "Evie," album back cover, *Evie*, Word Records, 1974, LP; Emily Suzanne Johnson, "Marabel Morgan Defines 'The Total Woman,'" in *This Is Our Message: Women's Leadership in the New Christian Right* (New York: Oxford University Press, 2019; online edition, Oxford Academic, December 23, 2021).
75. Steve Potratz, video conference conversation with author, January 6, 2021.
76. Ibid.
77. Baker, "Setting the Good Word to Modern Music,"R-4, R-12, R-18. Radio stations anxious to create advertising sales argued that religious consumers bought more music and other media than their secular counterparts. One claimed that they were more passionate and engaged and shared as an example a story about a company that advertised mobile homes on the radio and soon sold out due to an influx of radio customers. Baker, "Religious Radio," R-28, R-43, R-45; Larry Norman, "Why Don't You Look Into Jesus," A-side #1, *Only Visiting This Planet*, Verve Records, 1972, LP.
78. Tepper, "Retail Witnesses Financial and Distribution Challenges," R-20; Heather Hendershot explores the role that suburbs played in establishing evangelical mass media in: *Shaking the World for Jesus: Media and Conservative Evangelical Culture* (Chicago: University of Chicago Press, 2010), 153.
79. David Paulson, "Nashville Recognizes Christian Music with New Historical Marker," *The Tennessean*, June 25, 2019, https://www.tennessean.com/story/entertainment/music/2019/07/25/nashville-music-row-christian-music-historical-marker-amy-grant-michael-w-smith-koinonia-coffeehouse/1734353001/.
80. Bill Williams, "Gospel Pubs in Drive for Rights," *Billboard*, October 23, 1971, 1, 72.

81. Paulson, "Nashville Recognizes Christian Music with New Historical Marker."
82. John Styll, telephone conversation with author, August 3, 2018.
83. Thom Granger, telephone conversation with author, July 2, 2018.

Chapter 4

1. Scott M. Marshall, *Bob Dylan: A Spiritual Life* (New York: Post Hill Press, 2021), 36.
2. Sally Hinkle, "Musical Conversion: from Pop to Praising the Lord," *Billboard Magazine*, July 28, 1979, R-18, R-41; Gerry Wood, "A Joyful Noise Rises to New Heights," *Billboard Magazine*, July 28, 1979, R-3, R-18; Tepper, "Retail Witnesses Financial and Distribution Challenges," R-20, R-46, R-48-, R-49.
3. In the late 1970s, Black Gospel and Catholic record labels had their own means of production and distribution (there were also small Mormon and Jewish industries). Tepper, "Retail Witnesses Financial and Distribution Challenges," R-49; Pearl Williams-Jones, "Black Gospel Blends Social Change and Ethnic Roots," *Billboard Magazine*, July 28, 1979, R-12, R-16.
4. Anna Sobczynski, "The Christian Bookstore: New Beat for Record Buyers," *Billboard Magazine*, October 3, 1981, G-12.
5. See: Tepper, "Retail Witnesses Financial and Distribution Challenges," R-48-, R-49; Joshua Clark Davis, *From Head Shops to Whole Foods: The Rise and Fall of Activist Entrepreneurs* (New York: Columbia University Press, 2017), 64.
6. Baker, "Religious Radio," R-28, R-43, R-45. Estimates of radio advertising sales numbers varied widely, but all industry insiders agreed that the medium was on the rise. Stephen Traiman, "Financial Picture Brightens with Contemporary Trends," *Billboard Magazine*, July 28, 1979, R-24, R-41.
7. Sophie Bjork-James, *The Divine Institution: White Evangelicalism's Politics of the Family* (New Brunswick, NJ: Rutgers University Press, 2021).
8. Moslener, *Virgin Nation*, 80; Heather Murray, "Perspectives Daily," *Perspectives on History*, October 2, 2020, https://www.historians.org/publications-and-directories/perspectives-on-history/october-2020.
9. James Dobson, *Preparing for Adolescence* (Glendale, CA: Regal Books, 1978), 10; Hilde Løvdal Stephens, *Family Matters: James Dobson and Focus on the Family's Crusade for the Christian Home* (Tuscaloosa: University of Alabama Press, 2019), 18; Kate Bowler, *Blessed: A History of the American Prosperity Gospel* (New York: Oxford University Press, 2018).
10. Don Cusic, "Amy Grant," in *Encyclopedia of Contemporary Christian Music: Pop, Rock, and Worship* (Santa Barbara, CA: ABC-CLIO, 2010), 227.
11. Jim and Tammy Faye Bakker, *PTL Club*, "Amy Grant," aired November 18, 1981, PTL.
12. Amy Grant, Doris Nichols, and Roy Nichols, *Amy Grant's Heart-to-Heart Bible Stories* (Orlando, FL: Sweet Publishing, 1985).
13. *Possibilities Magazine* 5, 1987; Daniel Silliman, *Reading Evangelicals: How Christian Fiction Shaped a Culture and a Faith* (Grand Rapids, MI, Eerdmans, 2021).
14. *27th GRAMMY Awards*, "Amy Grant accepts the GRAMMY for Best Gospel Performance, Female," aired February 26, 1985, CBS, accessed December 2, 2020, https://www.grammy.com/videos/27th-annual-grammy-awards-best-gospel-performance-female.
15. "Michael W. Smith: Straight Talk About Real Problems," *CCM Magazine*, November 1987, 29.

16. Edward Morris, "Gospel Labels Downplaying Religious Role," *Billboard Magazine*, April 10, 1982, 4, 66.
17. Don Cusic, *Encyclopedia of Contemporary Christian Music: Pop, Rock, and Worship* (Santa Barbara, CA: ABC-CLIO, 2010), 70; Tim Lawrence, *Love Saves the Day: A History of American Dance Music Culture, 1970–1979* (Durham, NC: Duke University Press, 2004), 389–390.
18. Ancil Davis, "Corporate Sponsorship," *Billboard Magazine*, April 26, 1988, C-2, C-7.
19. Bob Darden, "The Word Story: Historic Agreement Helps Reshape Marketing Map for Future Growth," *Billboard Magazine* 97, no. 42, October 19, 1985, G-5.
20. Michael Goldberg, "Amy Grant Wants to Put God on the Charts," *Rolling Stone* no. 449, June 6, 1985, 9–10.
21. Steve Rabey, "Crossover: Christian Singer Appeals to Fans of Secular Pop Music," *Christianity Today*, November 8, 1985, 62; Jimmy Swaggart and Robert Lamb, *Religious Rock 'N' Roll, a Wolf in Sheep's Clothing* (Baton, Rouge, LA: Jimmy Swaggart Ministries, 1987), 75.
22. Tim Dillinger, "The Liberation of Leslie Phillips," *God's Music Is My Life* (blog), July 2, 2021, https://godsmusicismylife.substack.com/p/the-liberation-of-leslie-phillips; Jeffrey Overstreet and Sam Phillips, "A Conversation with Sam Phillips," *Image* no. 60 (2009), https://imagejournal.org/article/conversation-sam-phillips.
23. Edward Morris, "Amy Grant," *Billboard Magazine*, March 17, 1984, 38; John Fischer, "Where the Fingers Don't Touch," *CCM Magazine* 10, no. 5, November 1987, 46.
24. Tyler Huckabee, "Amy Grant Was the Soundtrack to Our Home-Schooled Teenage Lives," *Religion News Service*, December 19, 2019, https://religionnews.com/2019/12/19/amy-grant-was-the-soundtrack-to-our-homeschooled-teenage-lives/.
25. Lester Ruth and Lim Swee Hong, *A History of Contemporary Praise and Worship: Understanding the Ideas That Reshaped the Protestant Church* (Grand Rapids, MI: Baker Publishing Group, 2021).
26. Brent Lamb and John Rosasco, "Household of Faith," B-Side #3, *For God and God Alone*, Sparrow Records, 1986, vinyl.
27. *The Family Revolution*, Billy Graham, Copps Coliseum, Hamilton, Ontario, 1988; *Marriage and the Home*, Billy Graham, Hemisfair Crusade, San Antonio, TX, August 4, 1968.
28. Edward Sears Morgan, *Visible Saints: The History of a Puritan Idea* (Ithaca, NY: Cornell University Press, 1965), 4. Ronald Reagan, "A Vision for America," *The American Presidency Project*, accessed November 23, 2021, https://www.presidency.ucsb.edu/documents/election-eve-address-vision-for-america.
29. Stephen D. O'Leary, *Arguing the Apocalypse: A Theory of Millennial Rhetoric* (New York: Oxford University Press, 1998), 180; Annelise Anderson, "Ronald Reagan and American Exceptionalism," in *American Exceptionalism in a New Era*, ed. Thomas W. Gilligan (Stanford, CA: Hoover Institution Press, 2017), 143–149.
30. Tim Dillinger, "I Don't Wanna Be a Soldier: Teri DeSario Heeds The Call," *God's Music Is My Life*, Substack, May 25, 2021.
31. Jeff Godwin, *The Devil's Disciples: The Truth about Rock Music* (Chino, CA: Chick Publications, 1986); Jeff Godwin, *Dancing with Demons: The Music's Real Master* (Chino, CA: Chick Publications, 1988).
32. Bryan E. Robinson, Bobbie H. Rowland, and Mick Coleman, "Taking Action for Latchkey Children and Their Families," *Family Relations* (1986): 473–478; Jody W. Zylke, "Among Latchkey Children Problems: Insufficient Day-Care Facilities, Data on Possible Harm,"

JAMA 260, no. 23 (1988): 3399–3400; Mark Leiren Young, "Confessions of a Latchkey Kid," *Working Mother* 9, no. 9 (1986): 102; Stephens, *Family Matters*, 58.

33. Kyle Riismandell, "'Say You Love Satan': Teens and Popular Occulture in 1980s America," in *Growing Up America: Youth and Politics Since 1945*, ed. Susan Eckelmann Berghel, Sara Fieldston, and Paul M. Renfro (Athens: University of Georgia Press, 2019), 211–227; John Kenneth Muir, *Horror Films of the 1980s* (Jefferson, NC: McFarland, Incorporated, Publishers, 2010), 576; Sarah A. Hughes, "American Monsters: Tabloid Media and the Satanic Panic, 1970–2000," *Journal of American Studies* 51, no. 3 (2007): 691–719; Jeffrey S. Victor, *Satanic Panic: The Creation of a Contemporary Legend* (Chicago: Open Court Press), 1993; Mary de Young, *The Day Care Ritual Abuse Moral Panic* (London: McFarland, Incorporated Publishers), 2004.
34. "Backwards Masking Bill Proposed in California," *CCM Magazine*, June 1982, 35.
35. See for example: Michael W. Smith's "Be Strong and Courageous," and Steven Curtis Chapman's "When You Are a Soldier," or John Michael Talbot's 1990 "The Battle Belongs to the Lord."
36. Marcus Moberg, *Christian Metal: History, Ideology, Scene*, Bloomsbury Studies in Religion and Popular Music (New York: Bloomsbury Academic, 2015), 3.
37. Julie Bawden Davis, "Appetite for Destruction: Do Teens Crave More than the Music?," *Orange Coast Magazine* 15, no. 11 (November 1989): 148–151; Ronald Enroth, "Rock Music: The Cult/Occult Connection," *The Fundamentalist Journal* 5, no. 2 (February 1986): 18–19.
38. Lynn Van Matre, "Contemporary Christian Sound Making Itself Heard in a Big Way," *Chicago Tribune*, April 14, 1985, accessed December 19, 2020, https://www.chicagotribune.com/news/ct-xpm-1985-04-14-8501210775-story.html.
39. Michael Sweet, interview with author, February 8, 2023.
40. Van Matre, "Contemporary Christian Sound Making Itself Heard in a Big Way," https://www.chicagotribune.com/news/ct-xpm-1985-04-14-8501210775-story.html.
41. Ibid.
42. Francis Schaeffer, *Art and the Bible* (IVP Press, 2006), 17–19.
43. Charlie Peacock, interviewed by author, July 13, 2022.
44. Leah Payne and Dara Delgado, "Carman, Beloved by '90s Evangelical Kids, Was a Pentecostal Showman at Heart," *Religion News Service*, February 2021, www.religionnews.com/2021/02/23/carman-beloved-by-90s-evangelical-kids-was-a-pentecostal-showman-at-heart/.
45. Peretti's small-town America setting is deliberately generic, but fans speculate that Peretti, who was raised in Seattle, Washington, was inspired to create Ashton by Ashland, Oregon, home of Southern Oregon University and home to a thriving New Age community. Silliman, *Reading Evangelicals*.
46. Frank Peretti, *This Present Darkness* (Wheaton, IL: Crossway Books, 2003), back matter.
47. Susan Sontag, *Against Interpretation and Other Essays* (New York: Picador, 1990), 275–292.
48. Emily Zink Kirchner, respondent, *The CCM Survey*, January 27, 2021.
49. Robyn Frazer, "A Contemporary Christian Musical," *CCM Magazine*, August 1987, 10.
50. Norman Melnick, "Colson Is Spellbinding as He Helps Push for Bay Area Religious Station," *The San Francisco Examiner*, May 25, 1982.
51. Bob Lochte, *Christian Radio: The Growth of a Mainstream Broadcasting Force* (Jefferson, NC: McFarland & Company, Inc., 2006), 11–12, 79–97.

52. Dale Coulter, "Neocharismatic Christianity and the Rise of the New Apostolic Reformation," *Firebrand Magazine*, January 18, 2021, https://firebrandmag.com/articles/neocharismatic-christianity-and-the-rise-of-the-new-apostolic-reformation.
53. Adam Perez, "Sounding God's Enthronement: The Early History and Theology of Integrity's Hosanna! Music," in *Essays on the History of Contemporary Praise and Worship*, ed. Lester Ruth (Eugene, OR: Pickwick Publications, 2020), 76.
54. Mark H. Senter, *When God Shows Up: A History of Protestant Youth Ministry in America* (Grand Rapids, MI: United States: Baker Publishing Group, 2010), 306.
55. Jennifer Lynn Stoever, *The Sonic Color Line: Race and the Cultural Politics of Listening* (New York: New York University Press, 2016), 7–8.
56. "Christian Rap Adds More New Artists to Its Roster," *CCM Magazine*, October 1990, 8.
57. Gary J. Hinchman, "Christian Artists: Today's Prophets?," *CCM Magazine*, August 1987, 19; Al Menconi, "Christian Music: Soul Food?," *CCM Magazine*, November 1987, 26.
58. Bob Darden, "Gospel Lectern," *Billboard Magazine* 102, no. 10 (1990): 31.
59. "Taking a Stand," *CCM Magazine*, November 1987, 10.
60. Lisa Guest, "Artists Get Involved in 'Just Say No' Campaign," *CCM Magazine*, June 1987, 23;: Katherine Beckett, *Making Crime Pay: Law and Order in Contemporary American Politics* (New York: Oxford University Press, 1999), 167; David Seay, "Faith and [Body] Works," *CCM Magazine*, December 1985, 26–30.
61. Michael Card, "Lullaby for the Unborn," #12, *Sleep Sound in Jesus*, Sparrow Records, 1989, CD.
62. "Americans Against Abortion: A Petition for Life," *CCM Magazine* 8, no. 6 (1986): 37.
63. Darden, "Gospel Lectern," 31.
64. John Fischer, "When Christianity Pays," *CCM Magazine*, December 1985, 46.
65. Darden, "Gospel Lectern," 59.
66. Van Matre, "Contemporary Christian Sound Making Itself Heard in a Big Way," https://www.chicagotribune.com/news/ct-xpm-1985-04-14-8501210775-story.html.
67. Andrew Mall, *God Rock, Inc.: The Business of Niche Music* (Los Angeles: University of California Press, 2020), 212.
68. *The 700 Club*, "Amy Grant," aired 1991, CBN, accessed December 20, 2020, https://www.youtube.com/watch?v=kPVhWozHuOQ.
69. Bob Darden, "Happy Days Are Here Again: For Expansion-Minded Major Labels," *Billboard Magazine* G-3.

Chapter 5

1. "Narrow Is the Road," *Forefront Records*, 1994, VHS.
2. Steven P. Miller, *The Age of Evangelicalism: America's Born-Again Years* (New York: Oxford University Press, 2014).
3. Gene Edward Veith, "This Present (and Future) Peretti," *World Magazine*, October 25, 1997, https://wng.org/articles/this-present-and-future-peretti-1617340698.
4. Joshua Harris, interview with author, September 7, 2022.
5. Stay-at-home mothering reached historic lows in the 1990s: D'Vera Cohn, Gretchen Livingston, and Wendy Wang, "After Decades of Decline, a Rise in Stay-at-Home Mothers," *Pew Research Center*, April 8, 2014, http://pewresearch.org/social-trends/2014/04/08/after-decades-of-decline-a-rise-in-stay-at-home-mothers/; Stephens, *Family Matters*, 71–72.

6. April Hefner and Gregory Rumberg, "Buying into Family Values," *CCM Magazine*, May 1997, 51–53.
7. Steve Camp, "107 Theses," accessed February 23, 2022, http://www.wphafm.org/107Theses.htm.
8. Matthew Paul Turner, interview with author, August 3, 2022.
9. "50 Years of Christian Bookselling," C-Span, accessed January 13, 2022, https://www.c-span.org/video/?150470-1/50-years-christian-bookselling.
10. Patti Gibbons, interview with author, November 3, 2021.
11. Christian Smith, Melinda Lundquist Denton, Robert Faris, and Mark Regnerus, "Mapping American Adolescent Religious Participation," *Journal for the Scientific Study of Religion* 41, no. 4 (2002): 597–612.
12. Charlie Peacock, *At the Crossroads* (Nashville, TN: Broadman & Holman Publishing Group, 1999), 110.
13. Peacock, *At the Crossroads*, 14–15.
14. William D. Romanowski, "Where's the Gospel? Amy Grant's Latest Album Has Thrown the Contemporary Christian Music Industry into a First-Rate Identity Crisis," *Christianity Today*, December 8, 1997, 44–45.
15. Lynn Garrett and Jana Riess, "Smooth Selling for CBA in Atlanta," *Publisher's Weekly*, July 23, 2001, https://www.publishersweekly.com/pw/print/20010723/31725-smooth-selling-for-cba-in-atlanta.html.
16. "50 Years of Christian Bookselling," C-Span, accessed January 13, 2022, https://www.c-span.org/video/?150470-1/50-years-christian-bookselling.
17. George H. W. Bush, "State of the Union," *New York Times*, January 29, 1992, section A, page 16.
18. Pat Buchanan, "Culture War Speech: Address to the Republican National Convention (17 August 1992)," *Voices of Democracy Project*, https://voicesofdemocracy.umd.edu/buchanan-culture-war-speech-speech-text/.
19. Chip Berlet, "Clinton, Conspiracism, and the Continuing Culture War," *The Public Eye* 13, no. 1 (1999): 17.
20. *CCM Magazine* editor April Hefner and journalist Greg Rumburg noted that finding CCM artists willing to go on the record as Democrats was difficult in the 1990s. April Hefner and Greg Rumburg, interview with author, July 10, 2022. Lani George, "Vote the Rock," *CCM Magazine*, December 1996, 6.
21. Alex MacDougall, email correspondence, April 20, 2021.
22. Frank Perretti, interview with author, September 18, 2018.
23. Joan Wallach Scott, "The Campaign against Political Correctness," *Change: The Magazine of Higher Learning* 23, no. 6 (1991): 30–43; John K. Wilson, *The Myth of Political Correctness: The Conservative Attack on Higher Education* (Chapel Hill, NC: Duke University Press, 1995), 1–2.
24. Michael Card, "Heal Our Land (Song for the National Day of Prayer)," A-side #1, *Heal Our Land (Song for the National Day of Prayer)*, Sparrow Records, 1993, cassette.
25. *Let Us Pray: The National Day of Prayer Album*, Sparrow Records, 1997, CD. Strong sales prompted Sparrow to release a follow-up, *If My People Pray*, in 1999.
26. Carman, "America Again," A-side #12, *Let Us Pray: The National Day of Prayer Album*, Sparrow Records, 1993, CD.
27. Carman, "America Again," #10, *The Standard*, Sparrow Records, 1993, CD.
28. Moslener, *Virgin Nation*, 97.

29. Kristin Kobes Du Mez, *Jesus and John Wayne: How White Evangelicals Corrupted a Faith and Fractured a Nation* (New York: Liveright, 2020), 150–172.
30. Sigrid Cordell, "Loving in Plain Sight: Amish Romance Novels as Evangelical Gothic," *Journal of Amish and Plain Anabaptist Studies* 1, no. 2 (2013): 1–16.
31. Mandy McMichael, *Miss America's God: Faith and Identity in America's Oldest Pageant* (Waco, TX: Baylor University Press, 2019), 98.
32. "Sandi Patty: The Inspirational Balladeer and the Great Divorce," *Cross Rhythms Magazine*, June 1, 1993, https://www.crossrhythms.co.uk/articles/music/Sandi_Patti_The_inspirational_balladeer_and_the_great_divorce/38124/p1/.
33. Matthew Paul Turner, *Hear No Evil: My Story of Innocence, Music, and the Holy Ghost* (New York: Convergent Books, 2010), 191.
34. Wendy Murray Zoba, "Popular Culture: Take a Little Time Out," *Christianity Today*, February 2, 2000, https://www.christianitytoday.com/ct/2000/february7/34.86.html.
35. Anonymous respondent, *The CCM Survey*, January 27, 2021.
36. Sally C. Clarke, "Advance Report of Final Divorce Statistics, 1989 and 1990," *Monthly Vital Statistics Report From the Centers for Disease Control and Prevention* 43, no. 9 (supplement, March 22, 1995): 1–2.
37. James Dobson, *Dr. Dobson Answers Your Questions: Raising Children* (Carol Stream, IL: Living Books, 1992), back cover. See also: James Dobson, *Home with a Heart* (Carol Stream, IL: Living Books, 1999); James Dobson, *Love Must Be Tough* (Carol Stream, IL: Living Books, 1996).
38. Al Menconi, "Rock Music: Why Do Teens Listen?," *Herald of Holiness* 84, no. 9 (1995): 33.
39. "Godly Self Esteem Song Recommendations," *CCM Magazine*, August 1992, 37.
40. Krist Novoselic, *Of Grunge and Government: Let's Fix This Broken Democracy!* (Brooklyn, NY: Akashic Books, 2017), 15.
41. Al Menconi, "Media Update," *The Church Advocate*, 1991, 2; Robert Lewis, *Raising a Modern-Day Knight: A Father's Role in Guiding His Son to Authentic Manhood* (Carol Springs, IL: Tyndale House Publishers, 1997), 14.
42. "What's Up with Today's Entertainment? Separating Trash from Treasure," *Focus on the Family*, 1999, https://www.focusonthefamily.com/parenting/making-wise-entertainment-choices.
43. Moslener, *Virgin Nation*, 97.
44. DC Talk Video Press Kit, *ForeFront Records*, 1992, VHS.
45. Ibid.
46. Lauren R. Kerby explores how white evangelicals are shaped by tours of Washington DC in: *Saving History: How White Evangelicals Tour the Nation's Capital and Redeem a Christian America*, Where Religion Lives (Chapel Hill: University of North Carolina Press), 2020.
47. John Zipperer, "True Love Waits Now a Worldwide Effort," *Christianity Today*, July 18, 1994, accessed February 23, https://www.christianitytoday.com/ct/1994/july18/4t8058.html.
48. Shayne Lee, *T. D. Jakes: America's New Preacher* (New York: NYU Press, 2007).
49. Michael Omi and Howard Winant, "Race and the 'New Democrats,'" in *Civil Rights Since 1787: A Reader on the Black Struggle* (New York: NYU Press, 2000), 814.
50. Jerry Fallwell, Sr., "Ministers and Marches," March 21, 1965, 8.
51. DC Talk, *Narrow Is the Road*, ForeFront Records, 1994, VHS; Mika Edmondson, *The Power of Unearned Suffering: The Roots and Implications of Martin Luther King, Jr.'s Theodicy* (Lanham, MD: Lexington Books, 2016), 175.
52. Justin Hartpence, respondent, *The CCM Survey*, April 19, 2021.

53. Dan Haseltine, "Interlinc Interview with Jars of Clay, Atlanta Fest 2000," *Interlinc*, 2000.
54. Dan Haseltine, "A Christian Experience in the Bars and Clubs of America," email, 2022.
55. Brad Moist, "Dominate '98," *Labeled: "The Stories, Rumors and Legends of Tooth & Nail Records,"* podcast, April 17, 2019.
56. James Hunter, "Heavenly Creatures," *Spin Magazine*, January 1997, 37.
57. Anonymous respondent, *The CCM Survey*, January 27, 2021; Eric Boehlert, "Holyrock and Rollers," *Rolling Stone*, October 3, 1996, 23–24.
58. Brandon Ebel, "Who Is Brandon Ebel?," *Labeled: "The Stories, Rumors and Legends of Tooth & Nail Records,"* podcast, November 28, 2018.
59. Justin Ruddy, *The CCM Survey*, January 27, 2021.
60. Nathan Myrick, "Todd and Becky: Authenticity, Dissent, and Gender in Christian Punk and Metal," in *Christian Punk: Identity and Performance*, ed. Ibrahim Abraham (London: Bloomsbury Academic, 2020), 119–136.
61. Amy D. McDowell, *Gender and Society* 31, no. 2 (April 2017): 223–244.
62. Jonathan Dunn, "Tooth & Nail Kids," *Labeled: "The Stories, Rumors & Legends of Tooth & Nail Records,"* podcast, May 30, 2019.
63. Bob Briner, *Roaring Lambs: A Gentle Plan to Radically Change Your World* (Grand Rapids, MI: Zondervan Press, 1993), 45.
64. Press Release, "Steve Taylor Announces Launch of Squint Entertainment," Word Entertainment Firms, September 18, 1997.
65. Steve Taylor, "Steve Taylor Press Conference at Cornerstone 2003," *The Phantom Tollbooth*, July 4, 2003, http://www.tollbooth.org/2003/features/staylor.html.
66. http://www.christianitytoday.com/music/interviews/2006/switchfoot-1106.html; https://www.xrhythms.co.uk/music/two-decades-music/3430/.
67. "Rock Music Sales Decline in 1998," *CMJ New Music Report* 58, no. 3 (April 12, 1999): 1.

Chapter 6

1. Danielle Kimmey Torrez, interview with author, February 2, 2022.
2. Barry Alfonso, "Jaci Velasquez," *The Billboard Guide to Contemporary Christian Music* (New York: Billboard Books, 2002), 102.
3. Alisa Valdes-Rodriguez, "A Higher Authority Is at Work," *Los Angeles Times*, February 6, 2000, 8–9.
4. Alfonso, "Jaci Velasquez," 103.
5. Trennis Henderson, "Christian Musicians Team Up to Promote True Love Waits," *Baptist Press*, March 20, 1998, https://www.baptistpress.com/resource-library/news/christian-musicians-team-up-to-promote-true-love-waits.
6. Ryan Lytton, respondent, *The CCM Survey*, January 26, 2021.
7. Stephens, *Family Matters*, https://search.ebscohost.com/login.aspx?direct=true&db=e000xna&AN=2339144&scope=site.
8. Jessica Simpson with Kevin Carr O'Leary, *Open Book* (New York: Dey Street Books, 2020), 77.
9. Kay S. Hymowitz, "Tweens: Ten Going on Sixteen," *City Journal*, Autumn 1998, https://www.city-journal.org/html/tweens-ten-going-sixteen-11842.html.
10. Wendy Lee Nentwig, "Promise Keepers," *CCM Magazine*, October 2000, 28.

11. Franklin, for his part, credited the success of his music, especially his 1997 hit "Stomp," to the fact that it was successful on mainstream radio, not to CCM embracing Black Gospel music. Andrew Erwin and Jon Erwin, *The Jesus Music*, 2021, Kingdom Story Company and K-Love Films, 2021, 108 minutes.
12. Rev. Dr. Daniel Prieto, former head of Foursquare Hispanic Ministries, conversation with author, July 12, 2022; Daniel Ramírez, *Migrating Faith: Pentecostalism in the United States and Mexico in the Twentieth Century* (Chapel Hill: University of North Carolina Press, 2015), 24.
13. Dr. João B. Chaves, conversation with author, July 12, 2022; see also João B. Chaves, *Migrational Religion: Context and Creativity in the Latinx Diaspora* (Waco, TX: Baylor University Press, 2021).
14. Monique Marie Ingalls, *Singing the Congregation: How Contemporary Worship Music Forms Evangelical Community* (New York: Oxford University Press, 2018), 146.
15. See, for example, Paul J. Palma, *Grassroots Pentecostalism in Brazil and the United States: Migrations, Missions, and Mobility* (New York: Springer International Publishing, 2022); Jacob Olupona and Regina Gemignani, *African Immigrant Religions in America* (New York: NYU Press, 2007; Chaves, *Migrational Religion.*
16. Kate Bowler and Wen Reagan, "Bigger, Better, Louder: The Prosperity Gospel's Impact on Contemporary Christian Worship," *Religion and American Culture* 24, no. 2 (2014): 186–230.
17. Yvette Garcia, "Revivalism and Restorationism: The Brownsville Revival and Its Leaders' Paradoxical Defense" (PhD diss., Baylor University, 2022); Gabriel Raeburn, "Preaching Prosperity: Pentecostals and the Transformation of American Evangelicalism, 1946–1988," *Publicly Accessible Penn Dissertations* (2022), https://repository.upenn.edu/edissertations/5449.
18. Leah Payne, "The Trump Shall Sound: Politics, Pentecostals, and the Shofar at the Capitol Riots," *Political Theology Network*, September 2021.
19. Adam Perez explores how Jack Hayford's depiction of Jesus as King was enacted through theater and song in: "All Hail King Jesus: The *International Worship Symposium* and the Making of Praise and Worship History, 1977–1989" (PhD diss., Duke Divinity School, 2021).
20. Jeff Clark, "Praise and Worship Music Is Extending Its Reach," *Billboard*, December 5, 1998, 118.
21. Gerardo Martí and Mark T. Mulder, *The Glass Church: Robert H. Schuller, the Crystal Cathedral, and the Strain of Megachurch Ministry* (New Brunswick, NJ: Rutgers University Press, 2020).
22. Rebecca Sodergren, "Is Profit a Problem in Christian Music?," *Pittsburgh Post-Gazette*, February 13, 2000, https://old.post-gazette.com/magazine/20000213christian3.
23. Nathan Myrick, "Todd and Becky: Authenticity, Dissent, and Gender in Christian Punk and Metal," in *Christian Punk: Identity and Performance*, ed. Ibrahim Abraham (London: Bloomsbury Academic, 2020), 119–136.
24. Chris Hauser, interview by author, September 17, 2021.
25. Jennifer Files, "Taking Christian Music to the Masses via the Internet," *Dallas Morning News*, July 31, 1999, https://www.sun-sentinel.com/news/fl-xpm-1999-07-31-9907300671-story.html.

26. Mark Jenkins, "Creed's True Calling: Band Says It's About Rock, Not Religion," *The Washington Post*, Tuesday, September 28, 1999, page C01, https://www.washingtonpost.com/wp-srv/WPcap/1999-09/28/010r-092899-idx.html.
27. Bethany Erickson, respondent, *The CCM Survey*, January 27, 2021.
28. Jane H. Hong, "In Search of a History of Asian American Evangelicals," *Religion Compass* 13, no. 11 (2019): 1–9.
29. "New Division Unites Word Gospel, Myrrh," *Billboard Magazine*, July 18, 1998, 6, 85.
30. Joseph Bottum, "Awakening at Littleton," *First Things*, August 1999, https://www.firstthings.com/article/1999/08/002-awakening-at-littleton.
31. Hanna Rosin, "Columbine Miracle: A Matter of Belief: The Last Words of Littleton Victim Cassie Bernall Test a Survivor's Faith—and Charity," *The Washington Post*, October 14, 1999, C01.
32. Virginia Culver, "Sunday Event Offended Some," *Denver Post*, April 29, 1999, accessed January 24, 2022, https://extras.denverpost.com/news/shot0429h.htm.
33. Chrissy Remsberg, "Reclaiming America Empowers Students to Witness," *The Liberty Champion*, September 7, 1999, 3.
34. Alissa Wilkinson, "After Columbine, Martyrdom Became a Powerful Fantasy for Christian Teenagers," *Vox*, April 17, 2019, https://www.vox.com/culture/2017/4/20/15369442/columbine-anniversary-cassie-bernall-rachel-scott-martyrdom.
35. Cindy, respondent, *The CCM Survey*, January 27, 2021.
36. Michael W. Smith with Gary Thomas, *This Is Your Time: Make Every Moment Count* (Nashville, TN: Thomas Nelson, 2000), 73.
37. "Lou Engle: Answering TheCall in DC," *CBN*, December 10, 2022: https://www2.cbn.com/article/not-selected/lou-engle-answering-thecall-dc.

Chapter 7

1. Todd Hertz, "Was September 11th the Beginning of the End?," *Christianity Today*, September 17, 2001, https://www.christianitytoday.com/ct/2001/septemberweb-only/9-17-34.0.html; Jonathan Vincent, "*Left Behind* in America: The Army of One at the End of History," in *Reframing 9/11: Film, Popular Culture and the "War on Terror"*, ed. J. Birkenstein, A. Froula, and K. Randell (London: Bloomsbury Academic), 45–56.
2. Jerry Jenkins, "'Left Behind' Author Jerry Jenkins on God and September 11," *CNN*, October 3, 2001, http://www.cnn.com/2001/COMMUNITY/10/03/jenkins/.
3. Roger S. Nam, "'Go Sell Your Oil and Pay Your Debt!' Economic Life in Ancient Israel," *The Bible and Interpretation*, May 2014, https://bibleinterp.arizona.edu/articles/2014/05/nam388027.
4. For explorations of white evangelical fear and politics in the twentieth century, see: Jason C. Bivins, *Religion of Fear: The Politics of Horror in Conservative Evangelicalism* (New York: Oxford University Press, 2008); Anthea Butler, *White Evangelical Racism: The Politics of Morality in America* (Chapel Hill: University of North Carolina Press, 2021); John Fea, *Believe Me: The Evangelical Road to Donald Trump* (Grand Rapids, MI: Eerdmans, 2018).
5. Christiane Amanpour, Julie O'Neill, and Taylor Gandossy, "Teen Christians Campaign against Pop Culture," *CNN*, August 23, 2007, http://edition.cnn.com/2007/US/08/22/

gw.teen.christians/; Alan Reid, *Raising the Bar: Ministry to Youth in the New Millenium* (Grand Rapids, MI: Kregel Academic, 2004), 137.

6. Ron Luce, *Battle Cry for a Generation: The Fight to Save America's Youth* (Colorado Springs, CO: Cook Communications Ministries, 2005), 30.
7. Rebecca St. James, *Wait for Me Journal* (Nashville, TN: Thomas Nelson, 2002), 2.
8. Rebecca St. James and Lynda Hunter Bjorklund, *SHE: Safe, Healthy, Empowered: The Woman You're Made To Be* (Carol Stream, IL: Tyndale House Publishers, 2004), 7, 29.
9. Sarah Hampson, "No Sex Please: I'm Not Britney," *The Globe and Mail*, July 16, 2005, https://www.theglobeandmail.com/arts/no-sex-please-im-not-britney/article18241016/.
10. Tony Cummings, "Out of Eden: Keeping Their Clothes On," *Cross Rhythms*, February 25, 2004, https://www.crossrhythms.co.uk/articles/music/Out_of_Eden_Keeping_their_clothes_on/8999/p1/; C. J. Gardner, *Making Chastity Sexy: The Rhetoric of Evangelical Abstinence Campaigns* (Berkeley: University of California Press, 2011).
11. Cummings, "Out of Eden."
12. Laura Johston, "ZOEgirl Puts Morals Before Popularity," *Baptist Press*, October 29, 2001, https://www.baptistpress.com/resource-library/news/zoegirl-puts-morals-before-popularity/.
13. "BarlowGirl Biography," *Yahoo Music*, December 17, 2005, http://music.yahoo.com/ar-310014-bio—Barlowgirl.
14. Jill Serjeant, "Purity Rings Enter World of Sex, Drugs, Rock'n'Roll," *Reuters*, September 12, 2008, https://www.reuters.com/article/us-purityrings/purity-rings-enter-world-of-sex-drugs-rockn-roll-idINN1130986320080912.
15. J. E. Rosenbaum, B. Weathersbee, "True Love Waits: Do Southern Baptists? Premarital Sexual Behavior among Newly Married Southern Baptist Sunday School Students," *Journal of Religious Health* 52, no. 1 (March 2013): 263–275, https://doi.org/10.1007/s10943-010-9445-5. Epub 2011 Jan 28. PMID: 21274632; PMCID: PMC3156853.
16. Erin Roach, "'True Love Waits' Advocate Announces Engagement," *The Courier*, January 20, 2011, https://baptistcourier.com/2011/01/true-love-waits-advocate-announces-engagement/.
17. "Jaci Velasquez: When God Rescripts Your Life," *Life Today with Sheila Walsh*, November 18, 2020, https://www.youtube.com/watch?v=8uGHOrX8z3w.
18. Laura Jenkins, interview with author, May 5, 2022.
19. Matthew Turner, "Oh the Joy of 'Flying,' " *CCM Magazine*, October 2002, 38–39.
20. Sara Groves, interview with author, July 12, 2022.
21. Market research data from 2023 demonstrates Swift's sustained appeal to white, suburban millennials remains strong. Tomás Mier, "Most Devoted Swifties Are Suburban, Millennial, and White, New Survey Finds," *Rolling Stone*, March 13, 2023, https://www.rollingstone.com/music/music-news/majority-america-loves-taylor-swift-1234696362/.
22. David Starling and John Piper, "A Conversation with John Piper," *The Briefing*, October 27, 2011, http://thebriefing.com.au/2011/10/a-conversation-with-john-piper/; Caleb Maskell, interview with the author, February 6, 2023.
23. John Piper, "Is It Ok to Use Musical Instruments in Worship?," July 10, 2009, https://www.desiringgod.org/interviews/is-it-okay-to-use-musical-instruments-in-worship.
24. Justin Taylor, "Reformed Praise," *The Gospel Coalition*, October 29, 2006, https://www.thegospelcoalition.org/blogs/justin-taylor/reformed-praise/.

25. Maren Haynes Marchesini, "'A Heterosexual Male Backlash': Punk Rock Christianity and Missional Living at Mars Hill Church," in *Christian Punk: Identity and Performance*, ed. Ibrahim Abraham (London: Bloomsbury Academic, 2020), 101–118.
26. Rev. Dr. Mika Edmondson, interview with author, September 27, 2022. For a broader discussion of hip-hop and Black Christian involvement in the Neo-Calvinist movement, see: Erika D. Gault, *Networking the Black Church: Digital Black Christians and Hip Hop* (New York: NYU Press, 2022), 41–106.
27. Anneli Loepp Thiessen, "'Boy's Club': A Gender-Based Analysis of the CCLI Top 25 lists from 1988–2018," *Journal of Contemporary Ministry* no. 6 (2022): 65–89.
28. Dr. Tanya Riches, interview with author, March 3, 2022.
29. "Spirit and Power—A 10-Country Survey of Pentecostals," *Pew Research Center*, October 5, 2006, https://pewresearch.org/religion/2006/10/05/spirit-and-power/.
30. Glenn Beck, "The Archives: August 24, 2004," *The Glenn Beck Program*, August 24, 2004, https://web.archive.org/web/20060316084828/http://www.glennbeck.com/archives/08-24-04.shtml.
31. Mark Rodgers, interview with author, July 29, 2022.
32. Casey Baldwin, "Bono, Christian Artists Meet Here to Map Out African AIDS Strategy," *Nashville Post*, July 29, 2003, https://www.nashvillepost.com/home/bono-christian-artists-meet-here-to-map-out-african-aids-strategy/article_2a95ca64-71f5-52ab-baf5-a5e5dc8f7389.html.
33. Jill Sergeant, "US Evangelicals Strive to Change Attitudes on AIDS," *Reuters*, November 28, 2007, https://www.reuters.com/article/us-aids-evangelicals/u-s-evangelicals-strive-to-change-attitudes-on-aids-idUSN2751659320071128; "Hillary Clinton Pays a Call on Rick Warren's Conference on HIV/AIDS," *Baptist News Global*, December 5, 2007, https://baptistnews.com/article/hillaryclintonpaysacallonrickwarrensconferenceonhivaids/#.YsiYALnMLDI.
34. Mike Hogan, email correspondence, April 6, 2023.
35. ADL Press Release, "ADL's Statement on Mel Gibson's 'The Passion,'" June 24, 2003. This also refers to a statement on June 17 by the Catholic scholars in the group, www.adl.org/presrele/mise_00/4275_00.asp. See also Abraham H. Foxman, "Gibson's Passion," *New York Sun*, August 4, 2003.
36. "12-Year-Old Settles Music Swap Lawsuit," *CNN*, February 18, 2004, accessed August 26, 2022, https://www.cnn.com/2003/TECH/internet/09/09/music.swap.settlement/#:~:text=LOS%20ANGELES%2C%20California%20(CNN),their%20lawsuits%20with%20the%20association.
37. "Sony and BMG Merger Backed by EU," *BBC News*, July 19, 2004, http://news.bbc.co.uk/2/hi/business/3908405.stm; "The Nielsen Company & Billboard's 2011 Music Industry Report," January 1, 2012, https://www.businesswire.com/news/home/20120105005547/en/Nielsen-Company-Billboard%E2%80%99s-2011-Music-Industry-Report.
38. MRI Spring 2002, *Contemporary Christian/Gospel Music Industry* review 2001–2002.
39. Pamela Hale Burns, "Lighthouse Christian Stores to Close Last Remaining Shop," December 21, 2009, https://www.dailynews.com/2009/12/21/lighthouse-christian-stores-to-close-last-remaining-shop/.
40. Paul Toscano, "Highest Grossing Concert Tours of 2008," *MSNBC*, February 3, 2008, https://www.cnbc.com/2009/02/03/Highest-Grossing-Concert-Tours-of-2008.html; Felix Oberholzer-Gee and Koleman Strumpf, "File Sharing and Copyright," in *Innovation Policy and the Economy* 10, no. 1 (2010): 19–55.

41. Cynthia Yeldell, "Gospel Music Looks to Internet as Savior for Shrinking Sales," *Nashville Business Journal*, April 27, 2008, https://www.bizjournals.com/nashville/stories/2008/04/28/story7.html.
42. Charlie Peacock, "Charlie Peacock Predicts the Future of Christian Music," *CCM Magazine*, April 1, 2008, https://www.ccmmagazine.com/features/charlie-peacock-predicts-the-future-of-christian-music/.
43. Marc Lafrance, Casey Scheibling, Lori Burns, and Jean Durr, "Race, Gender, and the *Billboard Top 40* Charts between 1997 and 2007," *Popular Music and Society* 41 (2017): 1–17; Bradley Onishi traces how racial demographic changes have energized white evangelicals in historic hubs of CCM like Orange County in *Preparing for War: The Extremist History of White Christian Nationalism* (Minneapolis, MN: Broadleaf Books, 2023), 202–203.
44. Joe Thorn, "Precious Puritans (Pt. 2)," blog, September 25, 2012; https://joethorn.squarespace.com/blog/2012/09/25/precious-puritans-pt-2; Owen Strachan, "Reflecting on Propaganda's Fiery 'Precious Puritans' Rap Song," *Patheos*, September 26, 2012, https://www.patheos.com/blogs/thoughtlife/2012/09/reflecting-on-propagandas-fiery-precious-puritans-rap-song/; John Piper, "Slavery and Jonathan Edwards," *Desiring God*, July 26, 2013, https://www.desiringgod.org/interviews/slavery-and-jonathan-edwards.
45. "Relient K Draws Fans in Christian, Mainstream Markets," *Billboard Magazine*, February 9, 2007, https://www.reuters.com/article/us-relient/relient-k-draws-fans-in-christian-mainstream-markets-idUSN0946170420070210.
46. John Jeremiah Sullivan, "Upon This Rock," *GQ Magazine*, January 24, 2004, https://www.gq.com/story/rock-music-jesus.
47. Mark Joseph, "How to Fix CCM," *Christianity Today*, September 5, 2006, https://www.christianitytoday.com/ct/2006/septemberweb-only/howtofixccm.html.
48. "Bassist Unaware Rock Band Christian," *The Onion*, May 28, 2003, https://www.theonion.com/bassist-unaware-rock-band-christian-1819566943.
49. The Barna Institute, "The State of Vacation Bible School," *Barna Research Release*, July 9, 2013, https://www.barna.com/research/the-state-of-vacation-bible-school/#.UfhGxI2siSp.
50. Dr. Paul Putz, interview with author, April 4, 2022; Paul Emory Putz, "God, Country, and Big-Time Sports: American Protestants and the Creation of 'Sportianity'" (PhD diss., Baylor University, 2018).
51. Warren Bird and Scott Thumma, "Megachurch 2020 The Changing Reality in America's Largest Churches," *The Hartford for Religion Research*, http://hirr.hartsem.edu/megachurch/2020_Megachurch_Report.pdf.
52. "In U.S., Decline of Christianity Continues at Rapid Pace," *Pew Research Center*, October 17, 2019, https://www.pewresearch.org/religion/2019/10/17/in-u-s-decline-of-christianity-continues-at-rapid-pace.
53. Kathryn Darden, "Founder of *CCM Magazine* John Styll Resigns," *GMA Journal*, April 24, 2001, https://www.christianactivities.com/founder-of-ccm-magazine-john-styll-resigns/.
54. "2006 Readers' Choice Christian Music Awards," *Christianity Today*, January 1, 2007, https://www.christianitytoday.com/ct/2007/januaryweb-only/2006readerschoice.html.
55. Brandon Vaidyanathan, "Religious Resources or Differential Returns? Early Religious Socialization and Declining Attendance in Emerging Adulthood," *Journal for the Scientific Study of Religion* 50, no. 2 (2011): 366–387, http://www.jstor.org/stable/41307081; John

Lindenbaum, "The Pastoral Role of Contemporary Christian Music: The Spiritualization of Everyday Life in a Suburban Evangelical Megachurch," *Social & Cultural Geography* 13, no. 1 (February 2012): 69–88.
56. Stephen Knight, interview with author, March 8, 2023.
57. David R. Swartz, *Moral Minority: The Evangelical Left in an Age of Conservatism* (Philadelphia: University of Pennsylvania Press), 2012; Stephen Knight, interview with author, March 8, 2023.
58. Larry Rhoter, "Evangelical Leader Attacks Obama on Religious Views," June 25, 2008, https://www.nytimes.com/2008/06/25/us/politics/25dobson.html.
59. "Running on Faith," *The Pew Forum*, July 10, 2008, https://www.pewresearch.org/religion/2008/07/10/running-on-faith; Michael Wear, *Reclaiming Hope* (Nashville, TN: Thomas Nelson Publishers, 2018), 13.
60. "A Post-election Look at Religious Voters in the 2008 Election," *Pew Research Center*, December 8, 2008, https://www.pewresearch.org/religion/2008/12/08/a-post-election-look-at-religious-voters-in-the-2008-election/; David P. Gushee, *The Future of Faith in American Politics: The Public Witness of the Evangelical Center* (Waco, TX: Baylor University Press, 2008).
61. Republican National Convention, "Growth and Opportunity Project," December 2012, https://www.wsj.com/public/resources/documents/RNCreport03182013.pdf.
62. Michael Suh, "Pew Research Center's Exit Poll Analysis on the 2012 Election," *Pew Research Center*, November 7, 2012, https://www.pewresearch.org/2012/11/07/pew-research-centers-exit-poll-analysis-on-the-2012-election/.

Chapter 8

1. Cooper Dowd, "Francesca Battistelli Stands Up for Her Children's Rights in *God's Not Dead: We the People*," September 7, 2021, https://www.movieguide.org/news-articles/francesca-battistelli-stands-up-for-her-childrens-rights-in-gods-not-dead-we-the-people.html.
2. Doug Van Pelt, "The Alternative Beauty of Christian Rock," *Electric Jesus Podcast*, May 17, 2021, https://www.youtube.com/watch?v=wX8plv9DFBw&t=376s.
3. Mark Wingfield, "Brentwood Benson Music Announces Sudden Closing and the End of an Era," *Baptist News Global*, December 8, 2021, https://baptistnews.com/article/brentwood-benson-music-announces-sudden-closing-and-the-end-of-an-era/#.Y3zSkuzMIV8.
4. Emma Wenner, "One Year After Unite, CBA Is Dead," *Publishers Weekly*, June 26, 2019, https://www.publishersweekly.com/pw/by-topic/industry-news/religion/article/80507-one-year-after-unite-cba-is-dead.html.
5. The Parable Group, "2022 State of Christian Retailing 8 Reasons Why Sales are Soaring," February 3, 2022, https://static1.squarespace.com/static/5c5b264ffd679327d34bd03f/t/61fc5065c2bb2b471a7e4554/1643925618756/2022-StateofChristianRetail.pdf.
6. Rebecca Berdar, "Creation Returns to County," *The Huntington Daily News*, June 29, 2022, https://www.huntingdondailynews.com/news/local/creation-returns-to-county/article_8204b0f1-985d-508a-9edf-e988ad5caa31.html.
7. K. C. McGinnis, "God and Metal: Scenes from a Hardcore Christian Music Festival," *The Guardian*, July 21, 2017, https://www.theguardian.com/world/2017/jul/21/audiofeed-christian-rock-music-festival-illinois.

8. Ryan Burge, "Mainline Protestants Are Still Declining, But That's Not Good News for Evangelicals," *Christianity Today*, July 13, 2021, https://www.christianitytoday.com/news/2021/july/mainline-protestant-evangelical-decline-survey-us-nones.html.
9. Mark Ostreicher, interview with author, January 25, 2022.
10. Murray Stassen, "We Have a Deep Sense of Who the Artist Is and How to Support Them," *Music Business Worldwide*, August 3, 2022, https://www.musicbusinessworldwide.com/we-have-a-deep-sense-of-who-the-artist-is-and-how-to-support-them/. The NRB reported that the Christian format has grown on the radio, even though radio's influence is in decline. See: "Religious Formats Dominate Radio's Top Ten Genres," February 16, 2023, https://nrb.org/religious-formats-dominate-radios-top-ten-genres/; Geoff Mayfield, "As Streaming Dominates the Music World, Is Radio's Signal Fading?," *Variety*, February 10, 2021, https://variety.com/2021/music/news/radio-signal-fading-streaming-1234904387/.
11. "Salem Media Group, Inc.'s (SALM) CEO David Santrella on Q2 2022 Results—Earnings Call Transcript," August 6, 2022, https://seekingalpha.com/article/4530981-salem-media-group-inc-s-salm-ceo-david-santrella-on-q2-2022-results-earnings-call-transcript; Daniel Silliman, "Largest Christian Radio Company Faces Financial Crisis Due to Coronavirus Downturn," *Christianity Today*, May 14, 2020, https:/christianitytoday.com/news/2020/may-salem-media-radio-economic-stock-crisis-coronavirus.html.
12. Dr. Nathan Myrick, email, 2023.
13. Caris Adel, "You're My Scum Sweetheart: Audio Adrenaline, Contemporary Christian Music, and White Jesus" (distinguished major thesis, University of Virginia, April 24, 2020).
14. Nicole Alcindor, "Newsboys' Michael Tait Talks Deconstruction, Being the 'Honorary Negro' and Division in the Church," *The Christian Post*, October 5, 2022, https://www.christianpost.com/news/newsboys-michael-tait-talks-deconstruction-racial-divisions.html.
15. Allison Theresa, "Sadie Robertson Huff Preaches Submissive Womanhood. Her Message Is Uncomfortably Compelling," *Cosmopolitan Magazine*, November 8, 2022, https://www.cosmopolitan.com/lifestyle/a41559535/sadie-robertson-huff/.
16. Rachel Seo, "Meet the TikTok Generation of Televangelists: These Young Influencers Want to #MakeJesusViral," *Christianity Today*, October 20, 2020, https://www.christianitytoday.com/ct/2020/november/meet-tik-tok-generation-z-televangelists-seo.html.
17. Butler, *White Evangelical Racism*; Du Mez, *Jesus and John Wayne*; Gerardo Martí, *American Blindspot: Race, Class, Religion, and the Trump Presidency* (Lanham, MD: Rowman & Littlefield Publishers, 2020).
18. Marisa Iati, "What Is Critical Race Theory, and Why Do Republicans Want to Ban It in Schools?," *The Washington Post*, May 29, 2021, https://www.washingtonpost.com/education/2021/05/29/critical-race-theory-bans-schools/#LRM3F7NVEZBNREQT2IV7RD3BGI.
19. Alex Rogers, "Trump's Response to Police Killing Threatens to Further Deepen Unrest in America, Democrats and Republicans Say," *CNN*, May 31, 2020, cnn.com/2020/05/31/politics/trump-george-floyd-protests/index.html.
20. Lecrae, "My Thoughts on the Term 'Black Lives Matter,'" *Facebook*, June 10, 2020, https://www.facebook.com/watch/?v=902756986874614; "About," *Black Lives Matter*, https://blacklivesmatter.com/about./.
21. Lecrae, "Lecrae Raps about Jesus and Christianity on His New Mixtape 'Church Clothes 4,'" *NPR*, December 27, 2022, https://www.npr.org/2022/12/27/1145579316/lecrae-raps-about-jesus-and-christianity-on-his-new-mixtape-church-clothes-4.

22. Sarah Pulliam Bailey, "Q&A: Rapper Lecrae on His Discomfort with Hearing Slavery Described as a 'White Blessing,'" *The Washington Post*, June 16, 2020, https://www.washingtonpost.com/religion/2020/06/16/qa-rapper-lecrae-his-discomfort-with-hearing-slavery-described-white-blessing/.
23. Michael Tedder, "Christian Music in Trump's America: Two Artists on the Pressure to Keep Quiet," *Billboard*, April 6, 2027, billboard.com/music/music-news/Christian-music-donald-trump-response-interview-7751669.
24. Christina Edmondson Lecrae and Ekemini Uwan, "Facts About Lecrae," *Truth's Table*, September 30, 2017, https://overcast.fm/+xYDI3Mme8.
25. John Piper, "Piper: My Hopeful Response to Lecrae Pulling Away from 'White Evangelicalism,'" *Christianity Today*, October 9, 2017, https://www.christianitytoday.com/ct/2017/october-web-only/john-piper-lecrae-white-evangelicalism-gives-me-hope.html.
26. Executive Order 13950, "Executive Order on Combating Race and Sex Stereotyping," https://trumpwhitehouse.archives.gov/presidential-actions/executive-order-combating-race-sex-stereotyping/.
27. Jennifer Knapp and Nancy VanReece, "Contemporary Christian Music Changed Nashville, but It's Not without Shortcomings," *The Tennessean*, July 25, 2019, https://www.tennessean.com/story/opinion/2019/07/25/contemporary-christian-music-koinonia-coffeehouse-belmont-church/1780081001/.
28. Rachel Seo, "Is the Future of Christian Music on TikTok?," *Christianity Today*, September 9, 2022, https://www.christianitytoday.com/ct/2022/september-web-only/montell-fish-future-of-christian-music-on-tiktok.html.
29. Emily A. Vogels, Risa Gelles-Watnick, and Navid Massarat, "Teens, Social Media and Technology 2022," *The Pew Forum*, August 10, 2022, https://www.pewresearch.org/internet/2022/08/10/teens-social-media-and-technology-2022/.
30. Ashley Capoot, "TikTok Is Upending the Music Industry and Spotify May Be Next," *CNBC*, September 5, 2022, https://www.cnbc.com/2022/09/05/tiktok-is-upending-the-music-industry-and-spotify-may-be-next.html; John Brandon, "One Reason TikTok Is the Most Popular Social Media App of the Year So Far," *Forbes*, April 28, 2022, https://www.forbes.com/sites/johnbbrandon/2022/04/28/one-reason-tiktok-is-the-most-popular-social-media-app-of-the-year-so-far/?sh=7bf1ada941ed.
31. Seo, "Is the Future of Christian Music on TikTok?"
32. Jim Harrington, "Big Changes for K-LOVE, Air1 Radio in San Francisco Bay Area," *Silicon Valley*, July 1, 2022, https://www.siliconvalley.com/2022/07/01/big-changes-for-k-love-air1-radio-in-san-francisco-bay-area/.
33. Kelsey Kramer McGinnis, "Our Worship Is Turning Praise into Secular Profit," *Christianity Today*, April 19, 2023, https://www.christianitytoday.com/ct/2023/mayjune/worship-music-industry-business-song-royalties-ccli-ccmg.html.
34. Gregory A. Smith, Alan Cooperman, Besheer Mohamed, Elizabeth Podrebarac Sciupac, Becka A. Alper, Kiana Cox, and Claire Gecewicz, "In U.S., Decline of Christianity Continues at Rapid Pace," *The Pew Forum*, October 17, 2019, https://www.pewresearch.org/religion/2019/10/17/in-u-s-decline-of-christianity-continues-at-rapid-pace/; Ryan P. Burge, *The Nones: Where They Came From, Who They Are, and Where They Are Going* (Minneapolis, MN: Fortress Press, 2021); Brad Christerson and Richard W. Flory, *The Rise of Network Christianity: How Independent Leaders are Changing the Religious Landscape*

(New York: Oxford University Press, 2017); Weaver, *The New Apostolic Reformation*; Marla Frederick, *Colored Television: American Religion Gone Global* (Stanford, CA: Stanford University Press, 2015); Maiden, *Age of the Spirit*.

35. Leah Payne, "The Rise and Fall of Hillsong's 'Hypepriests,'" *NBC*, April 10, 2022, https://www.nbcnews.com/think/opinion/justin-biebers-former-church-hillsong-usa-decline-hypepriests-will-end-rcna23685.
36. "Maverick City Music Collective Brings Diversity to Contemporary Christian Music," *WBUR Here and Now*, April 19, 2023, https://www.wbur.org/hereandnow/2023/04/19/maverick-city-christian-music.
37. Tyler Huckabee, "The Rise of Maverick City Music," *Relevant Magazine*, September 1, 2020, https://relevantmagazine.com/magazine/the-rise-of-maverick-city-music/; Chandler Moore, *Facebook*, April 23, 2022, https://www.facebook.com/kidcmoore/posts/pfbid0sg2zssDrt4Ti3kBbKwM3Nd3tZU2Y1HaHMxref51Udd6YH1KWbJnWCGJdh2FnK8xJl.
38. Chandler Moore, *Facebook*, April 23, 2022, https://www.facebook.com/kidcmoore/posts/pfbid0sg2zssDrt4Ti3kBbKwM3Nd3tZU2Y1HaHMxref51Udd6YH1KWbJnWCGJdh2FnK8xJl.
39. Lifeway Research, "Churches Are Open but Still Recovering From Pandemic Attendance Losses," November 8, 2022, https://research.lifeway.com/2022/11/08/churches-are-open-but-still-recovering-from-pandemic-attendance-losses/.
40. Andrew Rinard and Matt Dunn, "Is Praise and Worship Driving Guitar Sales?," *Ultimate Guitar*, April 26, 2021, https://www.ultimate-guitar.com/articles/features/is_praise_and_worship_music_driving_guitar_sales-118340.
41. Adam Perez et al, "(Almost) 100% of the Top 25 Worship Songs Are Associated with Just a Handful of Megachurches," April 11, 2023, Worship Leader Research, https://worshipleaderresearch.com/100-of-the-top-25-worship-songs-are-associated-with-just-a-handful-of-megachurches/.
42. Alejandra Molina, "Hate Watch Groups Voice Alarm about Sean Feucht's Portland Security Volunteers," *Religion News Service*, August 13, 2021, https://religionnews.com/2021/08/13/hate-watch-groups-look-into-worship-leader-sean-feuchts-security-team-for-extremist-ties/.
43. Adam Perez, "'It's Your Breath in Our Lungs': Sean Feucht's Praise and Worship Music Protests and the Theological Problem of Pandemic Response in the U.S.," *Religions* 13, no. 1, https://www.mdpi.com/2077-1444/13/1/47.
44. Leah Payne and Erica Ramirez, "The Christian Sect that Has Always Cheered on Donald Trump," *The Washington Post*, March 21, 2018, https://www.washingtonpost.com/news/made-by-history/wp/2018/03/21/the-christian-sect-that-has-always-cheered-on-donald-trump/.
45. Erica Ramirez and Leah Payne, "President Trump's Hidden Religious Base: Pentecostal-Charismatic Celebrities," *Religion News Service*, August 27, 2020, https://religionnews.com/2020/08/27/president-trumps-rnc-religious-base-pentecostal-charismatic-kari-jobe-paula-white/.
46. Payne and Ramirez, "The Christian Sect that Has Always Cheered on Donald Trump."
47. L. Bracewell, "Gender, Populism, and the QAnon Conspiracy Movement," *Frontiers in Sociology* 5, January 21, 2021; 2020:615727: https://www.ncbi.nlm.nih.gov/pmc/articles/PMC8022489/.

48. Bob Smietana, "Jericho March Plans DC Return in the New Year to Pray Pence Will Overturn Election," *Religion News Service*, December 31, 2020, religionnews.com/2020/12/31/Jericho-march-new-year-metaxas-trump-pray-pence-will-overturn-election-congress.
49. Jack Jenkins, Twitter post, January 5, 2021, https://twitter.com/jackmjenkins/status/1346511652695506945.

Epilogue

1. Emma Green, "A Christian Insurrection," *The Atlantic*, January 8, 2021, theatlantic.com/politics/archive/2021/01/evangelicals-catholics-jericho-march-capitol/617591; Leah Payne, "The Trump Shall Sound: Politics, Pentecostals, and the Shofar at the Capitol Riots," *Political Theology Network*, September 2021.
2. Paul A. Djupe, "How Many Americans Believe in Modern-Day Prophets? What Does that Entail?," *Religion in Public*, April 10, 2023, https://religioninpublic.blog/2023/04/10/how-many-americans-believe-in-modern-day-prophets-what-does-that-entail/. In 2006, the Pew Forum estimated that 23 percent of the US population could be categorized as "Renewalist" (Pentecostal or Charismatic), with much larger percentages in countries including Brazil, Guatemala, Chile, Kenya, Nigeria, South Africa, and the Philippines: Luis Lugo, "Spirit and Power—A 10-Country Survey of Pentecostals," *The Pew Forum*, October 5, 2006, https://www.pewresearch.org/religion/2006/10/05/spirit-and-power/; Fanhao Nie, Flavio Rogerio Hickel Jr., Leah Payne, and Tarah Williams, "The Future of 'Born-Again Evangelicalism' Is Charismatic and Pentecostal," *PRRI Spotlight Analysis*, June 29, 2023, https://www.prri.org/spotlight/the-future-of-born-again-evangelicalism-is-charismatic-and-pentecostal.
3. Even in postmillennial movements like the NAR, which embrace postmillennialism, Zionism remains strong. See: Irvin G. Chetty, *Journal for the Study of Religion* 27, no. 2 (2015): 297–312.
4. Warren Bird and Scott Thumma, *Megachurch 2020: The Changing Reality of America's Largest Churches*, Hartford Institute of Religion, 3; S. J. Hunt, ed., *Handbook of Megachurches* (Leiden, The Netherlands: Brill), 5. The COVID-19 pandemic may have changed this, but more recent data is not yet available.

Index

For the benefit of digital users, indexed terms that span two pages (e.g., 52–53) may, on occasion, appear on only one of those pages.